COVID
A Love Story

FROM TRAGEDY TO MIRACLE: ONE WOMAN'S BATTLE
TO SAVE HER HUSBAND AND THE COMMUNITY THAT
RALLIED BEHIND THEM

MARIA BROPHY

Copyright Page

COVID, a Love Story

First published in the USA in 2025 by Son of the Sea, Inc.

First Printing Date: July 1, 2025

(c) 2025, Maria Brophy. All rights reserved. No part of this publication may be reproduced, in whole or in part, stored in a retrieval system, or transmitted in any form or by any means, electronic, mechanical, photocopying, recording, scanning, or otherwise, without the prior written permission of the author, except by a reviewer who may quote brief passages in a review.

Cover Illustration Artwork © 2025, Drew Brophy.

Back cover photo by Vdon Farias.

Legal Disclaimer: This memoir is a personal account of the author's recollections of experiences. Many names and identities of the people involved and exact locations have been either changed or disguised. No reference is made regarding any specific hospital, facility, or medical professional. The people and places mentioned in this book have been changed for their privacy and protection. To the maximum extent permitted by law, the publisher and the author disclaim any and all liability in the event any information, commentary, analysis, opinions, advice, and/or any content contained in this book prove to be inaccurate, incomplete, or unreliable, or result in any losses in any way whatsoever.

Medical Disclaimer: Nothing contained herein should be construed as medical advice. The contents of this book are intended for entertainment purposes only and not for the purpose of rendering medical advice. The contents contained within this memoir are not intended to substitute professional medical advice, diagnosis, or treatment.

ISBN 978-0-9990115-4-6

Contact the author by mail: Maria Brophy, P.O. Box 836, San Clemente, CA 92674, USA.

Website: www.MariaBrophy.com

Email: consulting@mariabrophy.com

Instagram: @mariabrophy

YouTube https://www.youtube.com/@mariabrophy1

CONTENTS

Dedication   vii
Foreword   ix

PART I
DEATH

1. The Big Chill   3
2. The Lesson   9
3. When We Met   11
4. Hospital ER   15
5. Covid Dungeon   19
6. Trust the Doctors   23
7. If Things Get Worse   25
8. Nine Lives   27
9. Won't Make it Through the Night   29
10. Can't Breathe   35
11. Ventilated   39
12. Unwavering Faith   47
13. Guilty   53
14. Church   57
15. Every Day, Bad News   61
16. Text from Heaven   65
17. Prayer Circle   69
18. Thumbs Up   73
19. Pull the Plug   77
20. We Got Inside   81
21. Role Reversal   87
22. Lung Transplant   89
23. Vitamin C   93
24. Dylan   97
25. Reality vs. Faith   103
26. Pretty Lady Dead   105
27. The Choice   111
28. Accepted   117
29. Good to Bad   121
30. The Recovery Room   125

31. He is a Surfer — 127
32. The Portal — 131
33. Near Death — 135
34. Aviptadil — 139
35. Vax or Else — 145
36. Aviptadil Fight — 149
37. Broken Mirrors — 153
38. Burning Eyes — 157
39. Money Vs. Patient — 161
40. Beautifully Denied — 165
41. Believe — 171

PART II
REBIRTH

42. Sliding Door Moment — 177
43. So Many Angels — 183
44. Dreams — 189
45. Trached — 193
46. Christmas Miracle — 197
47. "I Love My Wife" — 201
48. Christmas Day — 205
49. The Other Side — 209
50. Falling in Love — 213
51. Fights — 217
52. Aviptadil Day 1 — 223
53. Aviptadil Day 2 — 227
54. Aviptadil Day 3 — 231
55. A New Year — 233
56. Let's Cry Together — 237
57. Food Wars — 243
58. Changes — 249
59. The Light — 255
60. Four Good Days — 259
61. Trust Danielle — 261
62. How I Feel — 265
63. New Hospital Rules — 267
64. Sweatpants — 271
65. ICU Psychosis — 275
66. Hope and Miracles — 279
67. Transferred — 283

31. He is a Surfer	127
32. The Portal	131
33. Near Death	135
34. Aviptadil	139
35. Vax or Else	145
36. Aviptadil Fight	149
37. Broken Mirrors	153
38. Burning Eyes	157
39. Money Vs. Patient	161
40. Beautifully Denied	165
41. Believe	171

PART II
REBIRTH

42. Sliding Door Moment	177
43. So Many Angels	183
44. Dreams	189
45. Trached	193
46. Christmas Miracle	197
47. "I Love My Wife"	201
48. Christmas Day	205
49. The Other Side	209
50. Falling in Love	213
51. Fights	217
52. Aviptadil Day 1	223
53. Aviptadil Day 2	227
54. Aviptadil Day 3	231
55. A New Year	233
56. Let's Cry Together	237
57. Food Wars	243
58. Changes	249
59. The Light	255
60. Four Good Days	259
61. Trust Danielle	261
62. How I Feel	265
63. New Hospital Rules	267
64. Sweatpants	271
65. ICU Psychosis	275
66. Hope and Miracles	279
67. Transferred	283

CONTENTS

Dedication — vii
Foreword — ix

PART I
DEATH

1. The Big Chill — 3
2. The Lesson — 9
3. When We Met — 11
4. Hospital ER — 15
5. Covid Dungeon — 19
6. Trust the Doctors — 23
7. If Things Get Worse — 25
8. Nine Lives — 27
9. Won't Make it Through the Night — 29
10. Can't Breathe — 35
11. Ventilated — 39
12. Unwavering Faith — 47
13. Guilty — 53
14. Church — 57
15. Every Day, Bad News — 61
16. Text from Heaven — 65
17. Prayer Circle — 69
18. Thumbs Up — 73
19. Pull the Plug — 77
20. We Got Inside — 81
21. Role Reversal — 87
22. Lung Transplant — 89
23. Vitamin C — 93
24. Dylan — 97
25. Reality vs. Faith — 103
26. Pretty Lady Dead — 105
27. The Choice — 111
28. Accepted — 117
29. Good to Bad — 121
30. The Recovery Room — 125

68. Santa Ana	291
69. Full Moon	295
70. Breaking Point	299
71. It's OK if I Die	303
72. Talking	305
73. Angel	309
74. Good is Coming	313
75. Out of ICU	317
76. The GOAT	319
77. The Test	323
78. 48 to Go	325
79. Milestones and Lies	329
80. Love Vs. Evil	331
81. Chess Moves	335
82. Dog Collar Gone	339
83. Hate Mail	343
84. Generosity	347
85. Valentine's Day	351

PART III
TRANSFORMATION

86. Restore	357
87. Belief	361
88. Fired Kamatow	365
89. Progress	369
90. 100 Days	371
91. The New Normal	373
92. Released	377
93. Happy Birthday	381
94. Going to be OK	385
95. Mountain To Climb	389
96. Nicole	391
97. Week 2	395
98. Routine	399
99. A Miracle is Not Enough	403
100. Reason to Live	407
101. Good Sign	411
102. Drugs	415
103. Back to ER	417
104. Inogen	421

105. Board Riders	423
106. Shimmer The Web	427
107. Ocean Medicine	431
108. June	435
109. July	439
110. Surfing	443
111. Bye Blue Monster	447
112. October	449
113. Costa Rica	453
114. The Journey	457
115. Trippy Trip	459
116. Transformation	463
Afterword	467
BIOGRAPHY	469
RESOURCES	471
Books by Maria Brophy	473

*"There are hidden angels among us.
They hold the world together."*
Charles Eisenstein

This book is dedicated to my sister-in-law Andrea, a living angel who dropped everything to be by my side and bring a bright light of hope and positivity during a dark time.

It's also dedicated to Paul, a dear friend and medical professional who saved Drew's life again and again with selfless devotion—and to his wife, Daylene, who never lost faith that a miracle was coming.

The three of you stand as avatars for every healer, friend, family member, and stranger who gave selflessly to save Drew. You represent all the earth angels who gave us love in the form of medicine, prayers, donations—and, most importantly, held a clear vision of his recovery.

Your good intentions, joined together, generated a life force so powerful that it made a miracle happen. You helped make this a love story to remember.

You are the love story.
And I'm forever grateful.

FOREWORD

Covid, A Love Story is a love story of epic proportions. It's not just about two people in love who refused to be pulled apart; it's about the love from a huge community that wouldn't let them fail. It's about death and life and the miraculous power of intention.

It takes place during a time of sheer brutality suffered by millions—the Covid pandemic—when too many people had to say goodbye to their dying loved ones through a window. It's my story, having stood outside one of those windows as my soul mate, Drew, was sentenced to death by ventilator. There we were: me, fighting on the outside, he on the inside.

I catch myself telling this epic story to anyone who will listen: the guy at the bar at Nick's, waiting for his Scotch whiskey; the mom in line at the grocery store; the nurse who walks into my gallery to look at art. The story is so unbelievable that every time I tell it, it feels like I was a spectator, not the person living it.

I wish I could have included all the incredible people and important events, but this book would be 1,000 pages long if I did. There were

Foreword

countless angels who came to our aid, and without them, this book would have had a very different ending.

I've spent the last three years trying to make sense of all that happened during that time when Drew was "terminal." I analyzed what worked, what didn't, and what brought about the miracle.

If I were to explain how I think the miracle occurred in words that most people would understand, it's this: Drew was going to die; that much was true. The evidence was that no one before him, with his condition, ever lived. Not one of his doctors saw anyone survive what he survived. And to this day, I have not found one other person in the world who did.

But despite the reality, I refused to let him go. My obstinance was backed by thousands of people worldwide—some who loved Drew, some who only knew of him—all of whom refused to accept his fate. They prayed, wished for, and demanded a miracle. Some took action, and others gave support. The intentions of all these people collided, expanded, and sparked a series of coincidences that led to the miracle.

It was as though a long, drawn-out game of chess was being played between Life and Death, and Death was winning, but in a few surprise last-minute moves, Life took the King and won.

I wish I could promise that this story will restore your faith in God or humankind, but I can't. I can only promise that it will make you question everything you thought you knew.

This story will make you sad and angry, and hopeful. It will show you the darkness and the raw beauty of life. It will show you how miracles happen and what "true faith" looks like. And it will show you a version of true love that you have never seen before.

I want to warn you, though, that you will find some things I wrote difficult to believe. And I wouldn't blame you; I still can't believe it myself. You might judge me on things I did. You'll hate me for how difficult I was at times. And you might even think that some of the fantastical things that happened were made up in my head.

I'm not here to convince you of anything. But I assure you, this story is written exactly as it unfolded. I was insistent on telling it with great accuracy. I wanted it to be not only my truth but *the* truth, and I did my best to recreate events and conversations as I remembered them.

My writing meticulously followed five journals I wrote during this one-year period. Two are "Dear Drew" journals, a recording of each day as it happened. Two were Drew's medical journals, where I recorded daily doctor's reports. The fifth journal was my personal diary, which I wrote just for myself. In rare instances, the date or time indicated isn't precise, but it is close.

I also referred to recordings I made and videos that I filmed; it was the best way for me to keep track of Drew's progress. These records were crucial to helping me keep the timeline accurate. Many of the names mentioned were changed to protect people's identities for various reasons.

This memoir is not meant to be a clinical account, and you may notice that I don't always use proper medical terms. I wrote it from my layman's point of view, and I did my best to describe the things I'm not trained in.

Regardless of how you feel about the stories within this story, there is one thing you will be sure of after reading it. A miracle did occur, and the love of many people helped make it happen. And you might even come to know that your mind is powerful enough to make the impossible possible.

If you only get one thing out of this, I would love for it to encourage you to trust the little voice in your head that goes against the grain, the one that believes what the eyes cannot see. And let this story give you trust in your powers and the powers of those you love.

1

THE BIG CHILL

Only two hours into the drive, and Drew had to pull the car over.

"Spunk, can you drive? I'm too sick." Drew had a nickname for everyone he liked, and mine was "Spunk" for the last twenty years, short for "Spunky," because he says I'm full of energy.

I was starting to feel sick, too. My head hurt, and my arms felt weak. But I didn't say no because I knew he must have felt really awful if he asked me to drive. I could barely hold the wheel. My eyes didn't want to stay open. It took every ounce of energy to pay attention to the road.

We spent the night in a Best Western in Flagstaff. We barely spoke that night, both of us miserable and stuck in our own worlds as we tried to sleep on a hard hotel mattress. The next day, it was another torturous eight-hour drive back home to California. It was the last leg of our road trip after visiting our son Dylan, who had just moved to North Carolina for a job. A feeling of dread filled me.

Something was very, very wrong. But was I overreacting? Dylan told me once, "Mom, you're afraid of everything," after I warned him not to walk the beach trail alone at night.

And he was right. I was afraid of dogs. I was afraid of dying and Drew not finding the passwords to the bank accounts. I was afraid of going blind. I was afraid every time Drew went off to surf giant waves.

My fears sometimes turned to unshakable anxiety. When Drew and I were traveling in Egypt, I had a panic attack on a bus ride to the Osirian Temple because he told me he had his favorite pocket knife with him. I imagined him being arrested, and there would be nothing I could do. The fear of being separated from him made me irrational. "You can go to an Egyptian prison for ten years if you get caught with that," I yelled as everyone on the bus turned their heads. I made him go into a restroom at our next stop and throw his knife in a trash can.

This time, though, my fear felt different. It was a foreboding that something terribly dark was about to happen.

~

I screwed up. If I could turn back time, I would have remembered to pack our Covid kit. I would have asked Joan for help. I would have taken Drew to a doctor sooner. There's so much I would have done differently.

It all started on our drive back home after visiting Dylan in North Carolina. At only 19 years old, our son had already been given a great opportunity to work as a software engineer, and we were so proud of him. Drew and I were now empty nesters, and it felt like we were starting our lives over again.

Before the trip, Drew had been working long hours nonstop. Still reeling from business lost through the Covid lockdowns, he had run himself down. This adventure was something he had been looking forward to, a way to wind down and take time off.

The Big Chill

Our new silver Subaru Outback was on its maiden voyage. It was only the second brand-new car we ever bought, and we loved how we could strap our surfboards on top and take it four-wheeling on off-road adventures.

We only had two more days of driving before we would be home. We took a longer route and stopped in Colorado to look at a twenty-acre property we wanted to buy. The day before, a guy at a deli in Texas had warned us, "Don't stop for gas near native lands. Covid is rampant there." We didn't listen and got gas somewhere between Cimarron, New Mexico, and the Colorado state line.

When we arrived in Pagosa Springs, Colorado, we stopped to walk our dream property—a beautiful place surrounded by miles and miles of forest. We wanted to buy land and build our next home on it. Drew envisioned riding horses in the mountains, and I dreamed of writing books from a room with a forest view. That evening, we drove downtown to the Nightingale Motel.

As Drew pulled into the motel parking lot, I noticed the temperature had dropped significantly. As soon as he stepped out of the car, he started to shake. His body trembled in an exaggerated way. I thought he was faking it, and I said, "Cut it out. It's not that cold!"

We checked into our suite and turned up the heat. Drew flopped onto the bed and rolled up in a ball, shivering uncontrollably. I put the back of my hand to his forehead like my mom used to do when I was little. He was burning up.

I only knew Drew to be this sick once before, after a surfing trip to Tahiti eighteen years earlier. He was bitten by a mosquito that infected him with a virus similar to malaria. He had night sweats that soaked the sheets so severely that I had to change them every morning. It took months for him to recover. Since then, he hasn't had more than a cold.

Was it Covid? I wondered. Eighteen months into the pandemic, and neither of us had caught it yet, though we knew that eventually, everyone would get their turn. The great pandemic of 2020 had died down, and people weren't talking about it much anymore.

Drew's aunt Mary was the one person we knew who died of Covid in June of 2020. That was when it became personal for us, and I made a kit with all the remedies that help you beat Covid if you catch it early enough: Vitamins C and D, Zinc, Quercetin, NAC, Ivermectin, Elderberry, and a nebulizer. We never traveled without it, but I forgot to pack it on this trip. My mistake would turn out to be one of a series of unfortunate incidents that led to Drew's near death.

I wet washcloths and put them in the freezer in the hotel fridge. Every thirty minutes, I would put the cold cloths on Drew's forehead, ears, and neck. He barely moved. It was strange to see him weak. I felt in my gut that something was terribly wrong. I suddenly felt a pang in my stomach, the flutter of guilt for all the times I wasn't nice to him.

I texted my friend Raz, "Drew is very sick. I'm worried about him."

Raz and I had become close friends a year earlier when we took Reiki energy training together. She and Drew had known each other from surfing for many years before that. She was fun and cute, young enough to be my daughter, but I loved hanging out with her. Two months earlier, Drew and I had hired her to run our art gallery. She had no experience in the art business, but she was a fast learner. She did a great job of running the gallery while we were gone.

The following morning, Drew was feeling better. Before the seven-hour drive to Flagstaff, we stopped at the Root House Coffee Shop near the river. A homeless guy was screaming maniacally at people passing by. Drew handed him a coffee and a croissant, looked him in the eyes and asked, "What's your name?"

Instantly, the man shifted from psychotic to clear-headed. "Matthew," he answered. Drew asked him where he grew up, and Matthew told him he was from Denver and he used to be a carpenter. They chatted until Matthew sat down and quietly drank his coffee.

The Big Chill

Drew and I walked down a trail to the river. "How did you get that guy to calm down so fast?" I asked.

"People just want to be seen. When you ask their name, they feel visible." He said. And this was one of the things I loved about Drew; he was the kindest man I knew. I wanted to be more like him.

We reached the river's edge. It was a new moon, and I thought it would be fun to do a manifestation exercise. He wasn't into my silly spiritual practices, so I was happy when he agreed to do it. I ripped a piece of paper out of my journal, tore it in two, and handed half to Drew.

"Okay, now write down one thing you want to let go of," I instructed. We sat down on a large rock and wrote on our papers. Then, I lit them on fire and dropped the ashes into the river as I declared out loud, "Let this river wash away those things that no longer serve us. So it is, and so it shall be."

"Find me a heart," I asked Drew. His eagle eye had been finding me heart-shaped rocks for years. And within minutes, Drew spotted a rock, slightly underwater and glistening in the sun. He handed it to me–an almost-perfect heart shape. I shoved it in my pocket and planned to add it to my heart-shaped rock collection when we got home.

We got on the road. We would arrive at Flagstaff by dinner and be home tomorrow. I was anxious to get back to work selling art. We had been gone too long and were entering our busiest season, the Christmas holiday.

Drew drove while I scrolled through my phone, posting photos of us by the river on Instagram. We rode in silence–Drew liked the peace, especially on a country road.

"I wrote on my paper that I wanted to let go of feeling insignificant." What did you write?" I asked. Drew replied, "I wrote that I want to stop working so hard."

Nov 6, 2021 Pagosa Springs, CO

2

THE LESSON

Sixteen grueling hours later, we pulled into the small beach town of San Clemente. The sight of palm trees lining the main street was always our welcome home after a long trip. But this time, all we cared about was getting into the house.

Drew parked the car in our driveway, and I rolled out, dying to lie my sick body in my bed, a growing feeling of uneasiness consuming me. I went straight to the bedroom closet and grabbed the Covid kit. I prepared two servings of the dosage and swallowed mine, then handed Drew his pills with a glass of water. He threw all of them in his mouth and gulped the water down. A minute later, he ran to the toilet and threw it up. His forehead was burning up. I got our thermometer out to check his temperature, but it was broken.

Next, I pulled the nebulizer out of the Covid kit and read the instructions. This illness made my brain fuzzy. I couldn't understand the words on the paper. Frustrated, I left it on the kitchen table and gave up.

This was the sickest Drew and I had ever felt. We had different symptoms; mine affected my brain, and I couldn't think, and I lost my sense of taste, smell, and hearing. He had a fever and a stomach ache and couldn't eat. For the next three days, Drew and I lay in bed. I continued to take the Covid remedies, and he continued to throw them up.

One night I gave him an energy healing as he lay in bed. I said a prayer and pulled energy from the heavens into my hands, just as I was taught in Reiki training. The energy flowed to me and through my palms. I directed the energy by scanning my hands slowly over his head, throat, heart, stomach, and legs.

At the end of every healing session, I always finish with a question for Spirit, "What is one thing we need to know right now?" The answer comes in words I hear in my mind, and it always is a positive message.

But this time was different. An ominous message was clearly spoken in my ear, "The lesson is not over yet."

I felt a chill run down my spine.

3

WHEN WE MET

They say that your rebound relationship never lasts, but sometimes, they are wrong. I met Drew at the worst possible time, in 1996, only months after I left my first husband, who had an affair. Brokenhearted, I left my home of Huntington Beach and started a new life in the quaint little town of San Clemente, California.

San Clemente is a Spanish-style beach town exactly 66 miles south of Los Angeles and 66 miles North of San Diego. I didn't know anyone there, but I loved the laid-back vibe. Surfers come for the world-class surf, and people who live there don't seem to age. You'll see forty-year-old men bombing the hills on skateboards and girls and their moms carrying surfboards into the waves.

I settled into a rental cottage uphill from the San Clemente Pier. The first person I met was a guy named Michael at a coffee shop across from the pier. He invited me to a party at his house. It was October 25th, 1996, a date that I will always remember.

As I got ready that night, I pulled on a pair of light blue jeans and turned to look at my ass in the mirror. I had lost a lot of weight -

down to 116 pounds. I liked being skinny: it suited my short, five- foot-three-and-a half-inch frame. Losing my appetite was one of the benefits of a broken heart, I thought. I put on a pink crop top with long, loose sleeves that showed off my silver belly ring.

Michael's party was a random sampling of three guys and three girls, all new to town. When I arrived, I was instantly intrigued by a guy in the living room standing tall and confident like a warrior. He held a wine glass in his hand, and he appeared to be deep in thought. I had never seen a young man stand in such a noble way. There was something incredibly powerful about him.

I remember the scene like it was yesterday: exactly what he was wearing, how tanned he was, and how a voice inside my head screamed that I needed to know him.

His long, sun streaked hair and strong shoulders told me he was a surfer. His bronze Doc Martens shoes said he was a non-conformist, and his blue jeans and plain white V-neck T-shirt told me he was a minimalist–all things I loved in a man. And the bonus: he had the physique of a Greek God. He was perfect.

A bolt of electricity ran through me. I knew him, though we had never met before. I felt a remembering mixed with elation. It was as though we had spent years together, in another life, on another land. I was instantly obsessed. I walked up to him confidently; I was used to getting attention from men. I put my hand out, "I'm Maria."

"I'm Drew," he said, with a hint of a Southern twang drawing out the "aaahm" part. He was kind but disinterested. That surprised me. And it made me want him even more.

We all drank wine late into the night and took silly photos of each other with disposable cameras. Drew warmed up to me, and at midnight, we left and walked to the beach. The waves were turbulent, and I fell into the ocean in my jeans. Drew waded in to pull me out. We were soaked when we walked back, and Michael gave us sweatpants to wear. In the last two hours of the night, the others disappeared, and it was just Drew and me at the kitchen table, deep in conversation.

He was mysterious and intelligent. He knew everything about ancient cultures. He was like a walking history book, and I loved that. I leaned my elbow on the table and put my chin in my hand as I listened to him go on about the origins of Christianity. Or was it the fall of Rome? I leaned in closer and closer until my lips touched his. Drew wrote his phone number on my hand before we said goodbye. After that, we were inseparable.

At the time, Drew was painting surfboards for a living, and I was working for an insurance firm. Four years later, we got married. We wrote lists of things we dreamed of doing and places we wanted to see, and we did all of it. I quit my job, and we built a business around Drew's talent. It was difficult, but we never gave up. I became skilled at making business deals for Drew's art. Drew had a strong work ethic and was a highly prolific artist. Together, we made a great team.

We opened an art gallery and built a business while traveling the world and raising a family. I started coaching other artists and published a best seller titled *Art Money Success*. I hiked many peaks, including Mount Whitney, and Drew rode giant waves. He set a world record by stand-up paddling the Colorado River through the Grand Canyon. We worked hard and played hard.

Over dinner, we would talk about how we had created a life full of great memories. Drew always said, "I could die today, and it would be okay because I've done all the things I dreamed of." And there was still so much more we wanted to do.

1996, the day we met

4

HOSPITAL ER

November 14, 2021
Hospital Day 1

Covid hits fast. It's an insidious disease that goes after your weaknesses. For me, it hit my brain and hearing. But for Drew, it went straight to his lungs, those beautiful organs that he had relied on for big wave surfing and holding his breath for long periods of time.

The first Covid strain went after sick and old people. But we caught the Delta Variant, the one that targeted strong, healthy men, the worst one you could get.

We were too sick to get out of bed. Raz left a pot of soup on our doorstep, but we could barely take a bite. My Covid brain fog wouldn't let me put coherent thoughts together. It was as if someone turned off my brain.

I ordered a pulse oximeter from Amazon. A friend said we were okay if it read over 90. Drew's read 88 most of the time, and we thought, *well, that's close enough.* We were wrong.

One day, Drew thought he was feeling better, so we went for a drive to check the waves at Lowers, his favorite surf spot. Halfway home, he had a coughing fit so bad he had to pull the car over.

Drew was getting worse, and I finally scheduled an online appointment with a doctor. She didn't ask about Drew's oxygen levels, but she did prescribe something. I don't remember driving to CVS to pick up the medicine. But months later, I found the bag of meds unopened in a kitchen cabinet. I have no memory of putting it there.

One day, I saw Drew lying on the bed, rolled up in a ball. His skin was grey. A vision flashed in my mind; tomorrow, I would find him dead. As a divine intervention, just then, Drew's sister Andrea called. I said, "Your brother isn't doing so well."

"What do you mean?" Andrea yelled. "Get him to a doctor right now!"

Andrea's screaming woke me out of my stupor enough to take Drew to Urgent Care. As I was getting dressed, my friend Joan knocked on the front door. She was wearing white linen pants and a red scarf that matched her bright red lipstick. Joan's long black hair whipped in the wind, and she flashed a big smile, her perfect teeth so white they almost glowed.

"Take these every two hours," Joan said, handing me a box full of Juice Plus vitamin supplements. "It will help." Joan was the most optimistic of all my friends. She stood there, waiting to be invited in.

"No, you don't understand," I told her. "He's really, really sick. This is bad."

Drew peeled himself out of the bed, put on his shoes, and mumbled, "I gotta get out of here." He could barely walk to the car.

Joan left, and I drove us to Urgent Care. A male nurse recognized Drew. "I've been a fan since I was a kid. I had your posters all over my walls." He put a pulse oximeter on Drew's finger. It read 76. They sent him for a chest X-ray.

Hospital ER

The X-ray was bad enough that the nurse said, "You need to take him to the hospital, right now." Drew and I looked at each other, afraid. We had heard of people going into the hospital and never coming home. She saw our hesitation. "Don't worry, they'll give him oxygen and fluids, and he'll be home in a few days," she assured us.

We didn't want to go but didn't know what else to do. It was a twenty-minute drive to Hospital One. The clinic had called ahead, and a nurse was waiting for Drew when I pulled up. She scooped him out of the passenger's side and into a wheelchair and whisked him inside.

I parked the car and walked up to the Emergency Room to wait with Drew. I was surprised to see a security guard at the entrance. He refused to let me in. I didn't even get to hug Drew goodbye.

I called Andrea, and she booked a flight from Atlanta for the next day. I stood outside the ER doors, begging the security guard to let me talk to the medical staff. He blocked my entry, and it felt like Drew had been put in prison.

I kept texting Drew, but there was no reply. "Why aren't you answering?" I yelled. "What's happening in there?!"

I sat in my car in the dark parking lot for hours. It was as though a part of my soul had been ripped away from me. I felt a physical pain, not knowing if Drew was okay. Finally, I drove home.

I lay awake all night, my heart beating out of my chest with fear of the unknown. The anguish I felt was indescribable.

5

COVID DUNGEON

November 15, 2021

The phone woke me up. It was the ringtone of a sweet old blues song, belted out by Etta James, "At last...my love has come along."

I assigned this ringtone to Drew's number many years ago as a joke because he rarely called when he was on a surfing trip. And when he did call, I'd jump at the sound of Etta James singing, "At last..."

Drew told me he had tested positive for Covid and was admitted into the Covid ICU. In the background, I could hear the constant sound of beeping from the EKG, IV pumps, and other equipment.

They put Covid patients in a makeshift ICU in an unused part of the hospital on the bottom level. It was like a basement, dark and eerie. He couldn't see the faces of the staff; they wore blue gowns and face shields over N95 masks. There were glass walls between the patient's rooms that allowed the staff to be in one room and see what was happening with the patient in the next.

The nurses told him to stay lying down in bed. IVs were hooked up to his arm, and he had oxygen cannulas in his nose. He wasn't supposed to talk because it used too much oxygen. Hearing his voice gave me comfort. But then I would say, "Stop talking. Save your breath."

Drew instructed the doctors, "My wife will make all my medical decisions." This went into the records, and from that point forward, I was the one the doctors had to get consent from. This would turn out to be the most crucial decision Drew made, as it enabled me to advocate for him. It probably saved his life.

Andrea flew into John Wayne Airport and picked up a rental car. When she arrived, I was walking in circles in the living room, confused. I took another round of vitamins, then forgot and took more. She stood in the doorway.

"Don't come in, I don't want you to catch this," I said.

"I'm vaccinated. It's okay," she said and walked to sit at the far end of the room. I lay down on the couch, feeling a sense of peace that she was there, and I fell asleep. Andrea called her husband, Jackie, and talked to her three kids as I lay lifeless.

I woke up to my phone buzzing. Texts were flooding in from my closest friends, asking how they could help and offering to drop off food.

A text came in from my friend Nikki, a health researcher who lives on a farm in Tennessee. "Have the hospital give him Ivermectin. It's saving lives. And don't let them give him Remdesivir." She texted me links to a medical study that showed Ivermectin was helping Covid patients.

"Why not Remdesivir?" I asked, vaguely remembering hearing something about it in the news. She texted back, "It's killing people."

My phone rang. The caller ID read "Hospital." I put it on speaker so Andrea could listen.

"Hello, Maria, this is Dr. Steady, the Infectious Disease doctor." He gave me a rundown of Drew's condition: Covid pneumonia and hypoxia.

"I want to throw the 'kitchen sink' at it," he said. "We have an antiviral called Remdesivir that will help."

Nikki's text was in my head. I said, "No Remdesivir. I've heard bad things about it. Let's give him Ivermectin." I read him the headline of the study Nikki sent.

He said flatly, "No, we are not going to do that."

I asked why, and he repeated, "We just can't."

"What about monoclonal antibodies?" I asked. I remembered that it saved Drew's cousin from a critical case of Covid.

"He's past the time limit for that," Dr. Steady said.

I knew you had ten days from the onset for it to work, and for Drew, it had only been eight days. "There's still time," I begged. He said no.

After we hung up, Andrea asked me why I didn't trust Dr. Steady.

"It's not that I don't trust him. It's just that what they're doing for Covid doesn't seem to work for most people."

That night in bed, Drew's absence brought an eerie feeling of dread and darkness. The fear of him dying was too much for me to bear. It brought a physical pain that shot through my heart. I put my hands together and prayed, "Dear God, please give me the strength to get through this."

6

TRUST THE DOCTORS

The Covid pandemic brought great chaos to the healthcare system. Doctors were handed a bomb that they had to diffuse while working long hours, with no days off, for years. They were exhausted, doing their best to save lives while following an imperfect protocol given to them. I started to see how the doctors were handcuffed by the Covid protocols and strongly discouraged from trying anything else, even if it worked.

Since Dr. Steady said no to the monoclonal antibodies, Andrea tried ordering them through a cousin who worked at the company that produced them. But there was too much red tape to overcome, and we couldn't make it happen.

Drew had two primary doctors: Dr. Steady and Dr. Q, a pulmonologist. They would call at random times, so I never turned my ringer off. If I missed a call, getting them back on the phone was impossible. And because I needed Andrea to listen in with me, we never left each other's side. I would put them on speaker, and Andrea would ask most of the questions.

The doctors talked fast and were always in a hurry, so I began recording the conversations in a medical journal. I documented everything because there was too much to remember. Drew's condition was constantly changing. Some days, he would say that he was feeling better and that he was going to come home, and then, on other days, he would get worse.

Every morning, I'd get an uplifting text from Joan, "Beautiful Maria, I'm praying for Drew. Can I bring you anything?" And she would drop food off on my doorstep, even if I didn't answer back.

At this point, I only told close friends and family how sick Drew was. Even so, the medical advice started flooding in, and it was overwhelming. I felt an enormous pressure to make the right decisions – and fast.

Nikki texted me the same thing every day: "Get him Ivermectin. It is saving lives!" She would include more links to clinical studies. And again, I would ask Dr. Q and Dr. Steady for Ivermectin, and the answer was always, "We can't do that." Andrea was getting annoyed about all the advice I was getting from friends. "You need to trust the doctors," she said.

Maybe she was right. My lack of faith in doctors started ten years earlier when I was told I needed to have my gallbladder removed or I would die. At the time, we didn't have insurance and couldn't afford it. I desperately researched a way to heal naturally and did a seven-day cleanse. Though I was skeptical that it would work, it actually did, and I didn't need to have my gallbladder cut out after all. That was when I realized that doctors are sometimes wrong.

Oh, how I wanted to just blindly trust. It would have been so much easier. Then I could relax and sleep and not fight so hard. But my logic told me that if millions of people died on the standard Covid protocol, then Drew would die on it, too.

Something inside me screamed that I had to do something different if I was going to see my Drew again.

7

IF THINGS GET WORSE

Dylan kept calling every day, asking, "Mom, should I book a flight home?" And I kept saying, "No, your Aunt Andrea is here and everything is going to be okay." The truth was, I didn't want to admit that it was that bad. I kept telling myself, *If things get worse, then I'll ask him to come.*

Dr. Steady called again today, and Andrea and I had him on speaker phone as he strongly encouraged Remdesivir. I said no—again—and he asked why.

"Because I heard it's killing people," I said.

He replied, "If Drew were my brother, I would have given it to him days ago."

I struggled against my Covid brain fog. I asked, "How many patients have you given it to, and what were the results?"

He said, "I've given it to four or five hundred patients, and only one had a problem with her kidneys. We can monitor him, and if he shows any sign of kidney or liver damage, we'll stop it."

My head hurt. I wanted more time to do my own research, but Dr. Steady pushed for a decision—right now, this minute. Andrea looked at me and mouthed, *Trust the doctor.*

I wanted so badly to believe this drug could help Drew. So I agreed, reluctantly. After all, only one of Dr. Steady's patients had a problem. Trusting him was so much easier than arguing.

But Drew's condition got worse. A few days later, he called me and said he overheard nurses talking outside his room. One said, "We need more beds."

The other answered, "Room 28 will be empty soon. He's not going to make it."

Drew thought, *But I'm in Room 28.*

8

NINE LIVES

Drew cared about three things in life: his family, surfing waves, and making art. The surfing inspired his paintings, and his work and life blended into one. He had a rare, photographic memory that made it easy to hold an image in his mind, and he could free-draw on the canvas, in perfect detail, just about anything.

Drew's life revolved around the surf. He was a strong athlete and kept his body in top condition. Sometimes, he'd hop on a plane with friends to chase a big swell to Hawaii, Tahiti, or Mexico—places where the waves get huge. It was what he lived for, and I would book his flights for him, though secretly, I wished he'd stop the big wave surfing. It was so dangerous. But I never said it out loud. I didn't want to take away what mattered most to him.

Like every athlete, most big wave surfers have their injuries. I've been through many with Drew. The worst was when a giant swell hit Tahiti, and Drew and his friends booked a last-minute flight. There was a surf break there called Teahupo'o, on the southwestern coast of the island, that Drew absolutely loved. He'd surfed it many times before, but this time, I had a bad feeling.

After he left, I felt a pain in my stomach. Was it a premonition? I was just learning to trust my intuition back then. Two days later, my phone rang, and a man with a French accent said, "There's been an accident."

The surf in Tahiti is powerful and shallow, breaking over a razor-sharp reef. Only the best surfers attempt to ride those waves. Drew and his friends took a boat to the break, and he was the first to paddle out—alone—while his friends stayed in the boat.

He paddled for a big wave, and it clipped him. It slammed him head-first into the reef, and the coral ripped the top of his scalp off, leaving it hanging by just a thin piece of skin. He had only seconds to decide what to do before the next giant wave hit. He grabbed his board with one hand and held his scalp to his head with the other. When the wave hit, he dove into it, came out the other side, got on his board, and paddled like hell toward the boat, blood gushing down his face.

His friends rushed him to the hospital, where a surgeon sewed his scalp back together like a jigsaw puzzle.

Drew came home from Tahiti with a bandaged head and the doctor's warning to watch for brain swelling and concussion. But to everyone's surprise, he recovered quickly, left with only scars on his scalp.

After all the close calls Drew had with death over the years, I was starting to believe he might actually be invincible.

That was, until now.

9

WON'T MAKE IT THROUGH THE NIGHT

November 24, 2021
Hospital Day 11

It was the day before Thanksgiving, and Drew had been in the ICU for eleven long days. The first thing I did when I opened my eyes was reach for my phone, hoping for a message from him. Nothing.

Andrea was on her laptop, having a business meeting at the kitchen table, as I made a cup of coffee. My mind was scattered. I didn't know what to do with myself. Everything felt surreal. Life had become a nightmare.

I wanted so badly to tell Drew how scared I was—how much it hurt not knowing if he'd ever come home. But I didn't want to make this harder for him, so I made sure that every conversation I had with him was upbeat and positive.

I needed an outlet for the feelings bottled up inside me. I rummaged through our tiny bedroom closet and grabbed an empty notebook. I decided I'd write in it every day and planned to let him read it later, after this ordeal was over. With a bright blue marker, I wrote on the front: "Dear Drew... from your Beloved. A healing journal."

Drew finally texted, "They gave me a greasy burger for dinner last night. I didn't eat it. Can you bring me something healthy?"

I blended up two fruit smoothies in the Vitamix, drove to the hospital, and dropped them at the front desk for delivery to Drew's room. They still wouldn't let me in to see him, so I drove back home.

Later, he texted, "I feel a little better today." It gave me relief to read it. *Soon, this will be all over*, I thought.

He was now sitting up, taking long, deep breaths in, expanding his lungs. As a waterman, Drew was able to hold his breath for nearly three minutes. His lungs were strong from a lifetime of surfing in harsh conditions. He took in deeper and deeper breaths, thinking that he was helping his lungs.

What Drew didn't know was that his damaged lungs were like wet paper, stuck together. They were too fragile for deep breaths. That afternoon, a nurse came into his room and looked at him, and her eyes widened. She walked over and pressed her fingers on his shoulders. There was a crunchy sound as she probed his skin. Drew didn't know anything was wrong because he didn't feel a thing. But he read the worry on her face. She called for Dr. Q and told Drew that air was collecting outside his lungs. This was very bad.

They took him for a CT scan, which showed that Drew had popped a hole in his right lung. Things quickly went from bad to worse. Drew's oxygen had to be turned up to 100%, but it still wasn't enough. They hooked him up to another source of oxygen delivered through a mask that covered most of his face called "a blower." It was loud, and the noise was unnerving. This was what Drew later described as his "Oh Shit" moment.

That evening, Dr. Q came into Drew's room and urged him to agree to the ventilator. "We need to put you in a medically induced coma," he said.

Drew said, "But most people who go on a vent die, doc."

Dr. Q said, "Look, if you don't, you're going to die. More than likely, you'll have a heart attack or stroke tonight, and we won't be able to save you. You don't want to go that way. If we put you on a ventilator, we will sedate you into a coma, and you won't suffer."

Drew asked, "What are my chances on the vent? Give me a number, doc."

Dr. Q took in a deep breath, "Less than twenty percent."

Drew said, "But once you put me under, I won't know. It could be the last time I see my family." Dr. Q nodded, "Yes."

Drew called me so I could be involved in the decision. I put my phone on speaker, and Andrea and I listened in horror as Dr. Q laid out the grim reality for us. He emphasized to all of us, "If Drew doesn't go on the ventilator today, he probably will not survive the night."

Dr. Q danced around the fact that no matter what we did, Drew would die. But I refused to believe it. Drew was the strongest man I knew. I couldn't imagine his life ending this way.

Going on the ventilator could kill him, but he would die if he didn't. It was an impossible decision to make.

This was one choice I was not willing to make for him. I told Drew, "Whatever you decide, I will support it."

Drew said, "No, doc, I'm not going on the ventilator. I'll fight this."

I felt relieved; I was terrified of the ventilator. But Dr. Q was disappointed. Knowing that this would probably be Drew's last night alive, he had the nurses move Drew into the only room in the Covid unit that has a window. It had just become vacant.

That evening, Andrea and I drove to the hospital, glad to be able to see Drew, even if only through a glass pane. We parked in the staff parking lot and found Drew's room, with a large window, on the corner of the building. The ground in front of his window was lined with juniper bushes, about knee high. A few feet from the window stood a large, strong Eucalyptus tree, its branches reaching up into the sky. The window blinds were wide open, and the moonlight shone into his room.

Andrea stood in the bushes, putting her face up to the window. Drew was inside, five feet away, lying on his bed. He mustered a weak smile and waved. I joined her in the bushes and called him on the phone. He snapped a photo of us looking into his window and texted it to me.

Drew's breath was labored, making it difficult for him to talk. We put him on speaker, Andrea and I taking turns holding the phone as we pressed our noses to the glass. We talked about the weather, about what mom was doing, about Andrea's job. A few hours passed. Every time Drew tried to speak, we told him, "Don't talk. Save your breath!"

It got late, and we hadn't eaten all day. We said our goodbyes, and Andrea promised him, "I'm not leaving California until I get to hold your hand."

We drove to P.F. Chang's restaurant near the hospital. We pushed our food around on our plates, barely eating. We were shell-shocked.

Around midnight, as I was getting under the covers in bed, my phone rang with Etta James, "At last." My heart jumped. It was Drew, FaceTiming me.

"I'm scared, Spunk," Drew whispered. My stomach knotted up. This was the first time I had ever heard him say he was afraid.

I lay down, facing Drew's side of the bed. "I'm taking you to bed," I said. "Let's pretend you are here with me."

Won't Make it Through the Night

We stared at each other on the screens, me doing all the talking. He would try to talk, his breath labored. I would say, "Don't talk. Just listen."

Dr. Q's warning echoed in our thoughts. "He could have a heart attack tonight, and we won't be able to save him."

I was desperate for Drew's touch. It was a terrible feeling—needing something so badly and not being able to have it. It reminded me of when my sister Donna died, and I wanted her back so deeply it physically hurt.

Tears welled in my eyes, but I couldn't let him see me sad. So I talked to him about my belief in angels—something Drew had never shared. I admitted I'd been praying to Archangel Michael and Jesus to be in the room with him. He seemed more open to it now. I remembered something my mother used to say: "There are no atheists in foxholes." Now, I finally understood what she meant—when you're facing death, even non-believers pray.

We looked into each other's eyes. "I love you so much, Drew."

"I will come home to you. I promise." He said. For a moment, I believed him.

He said, "You give me strength." That made me feel so good because he was always the strong one.

It was three in the morning when Drew said, "I have to hang up. I'm going to try to sleep."

"Call me the second you wake up so I know you're alive," I pleaded.

He promised. Hanging up the phone felt like cutting a cord. I didn't know if I would ever hear his voice again.

I wrote in the journal:

Dear Drew, today Dr. Q said you may not make it through the night. He urged you to go on the vent, but you said no. You said you were scared. You said you would come home.

I think I believe you.

Somehow, I fell asleep, and four hours later, I woke up. It was Thanksgiving Day. Andrea looked up Drew's horoscope for the day. She read it out loud, "You will be tested. You will have the opportunity to show your mettle."

We looked at each other with wide eyes. It frightened us both.

10

CAN'T BREATHE

November 25, 2021, Thanksgiving Day
Hospital Day 12, Ventilator Day 1

At 7:00 a.m., I got a text from Drew. "I'm alive."

Relief poured over me. I could stop worrying, at least for the moment. I texted back, "I'm bringing you fresh juice. Andrea and I will be at your window in a couple of hours."

Covid had left my body, and my energy was coming back. But my brain fog remained, and I still couldn't hear out of one ear. I made a cup of coffee and added coconut cream, maple syrup, and three dashes of Ceylon cinnamon.

I got the juicer going, using all organic fruits and veggies. I added just a little carrot, cucumber, green apples, and a lot of ginger, because he liked it spicy. I poured it into a mason jar with a tight lid and stored it in the refrigerator until we left.

Andrea was at a work Zoom meeting in Dylan's old bedroom, which was now her temporary room, and I was at my laptop on the kitchen table. I had hardly worked in weeks and had over a hundred unread emails. I was feeling the stress; customers I needed to respond to, sales to make, and bills that were past due to pay because I just hadn't had time or energy to do anything.

I got a frantic text from Drew. "Something's wrong. I can't breathe."

Dr. Q's prediction was coming true. *So, this is how it's going to happen.* A feeling of panic tied up my insides. *Move fast, Maria, move fast.*

I frantically dialed the hospital and texted Drew. "I'm calling the nurses' station. Stay calm. It's going to be okay."

The wait on hold for the Covid Unit felt like forever. I continued to text Drew, "You are okay. Focus on the breath. This will pass. Help is coming. Hang on for me, Honey."

Nurse Ally answered and checked on Drew immediately. Andrea and I rushed to get dressed, hopped in the car, and raced to Hospital One.

Andrea drove. I was shaking, my jaw clenched tight, and my stomach flip-flopping. Another text came in from Drew's phone. It read: "Hi, this is Ally, the nurse you talked to. I'm here with him."

Andrea and I found our places back in the bushes at the window. I was on speaker phone with a new doctor, Dr. Black, who was by Drew's bedside. He was filling in for Dr. Q, who was off for the holiday.

Drew said, "I can't do another night of struggling to breathe like last night."

Dr. Black strongly suggested the ventilator, and this time, Drew agreed.

The ventilator would provide life support because Drew's body couldn't breathe on its own. But, they would have to put Drew into a coma, and there was a very good chance he would never wake up from it.

I stood in those bushes thinking, *Oh my God, I'm going to be one of those people I read about, saying goodbye to my husband through a window.*

11

VENTILATED

A ventilator is essentially life support—without it, you die. But many Covid patients die just days after being put on one, and of those who survive, some are never the same afterward.

There are things they don't warn you about being on a ventilator, but they should. Your chances of dying increase significantly the moment you're put in a medically induced coma. They pump you full of paralytic drugs, and those drugs can cause brain injury and respiratory distress. They stick a catheter in you so you can urinate, and you wear diapers. The ventilator gets shoved down your throat and damages your vocal cords.

Dr. Black didn't tell us any of this. He explained the procedure in two sentences. I couldn't think clearly enough to ask the right questions. My energy had left my body, and I felt faint. All I knew was that this was the worst moment in my life.

"If Drew were your brother, Dr. Black, what would you do?" I asked, reaching for anything to make me feel better.

"I would have put him on the ventilator days ago." Dr. Black said.

Dr. Black didn't warn us how the sedatives would destroy Drew's body, that he would lose half his body weight and suffer things that most people never recover from: muscle atrophy, mental trauma, the torture of feeling pain while in a coma, and the worst part–if he survived, Drew would wake up paralyzed.

If I knew then what I know now, I would have asked more questions. I might have demanded things be done differently to prevent the destruction of his body. Or maybe I would have done nothing differently. I don't know. When you find yourself in this situation, it's like you're blinded in a blizzard with a polar bear chasing you. No matter what you do, the outcome isn't good.

Drew and I stared at each other through the window. *I can't believe this nightmare is happening.* I remembered when I was eleven years old, and my sister Donna died, and I thought, *these things happen to other people.*

My hands were shaking, and I felt dizzy. "It's going to be okay," I heard myself say feebly into the phone. Drew broke down and cried. I had never seen him so vulnerable. I wanted to hold him so badly, but a pane of glass separated us.

This was the moment when part of my soul left me. My vision darkened, and I couldn't breathe. My body went numb. Tears welled up from deep inside, and I stopped them. I didn't want his last memory to be of me crying. I stuffed the feelings deep until my stomach hurt.

Nurse Ally stood beside Drew, rubbing his back like a loving mother. I felt grateful for her giving him the comfort I wanted so badly to do myself.

At that moment, my love for Drew deepened. I saw a side of him I didn't know: a curious mix of vulnerability and sadness, yet he was surrendering to his fate with the inner strength of a warrior. A tape of memories ran through my mind of all our adventures together and how I would be alone now. All I could think was, *How will I learn to live without you?*

Ventilated

Nurse Ally told us we had an hour before the procedure. "You have time to make some phone calls, Drew," she said.

Drew asked to talk to his mom and Dylan. This required just one phone call because Dylan was at Mom's house for Thanksgiving. We got them on a three-way call and told them of Drew's decision to go on the ventilator.

Mom sobbed, "Drew, I will pray for you, my son."

Dylan's voice was strong, but I knew that the easy life we gave him hadn't offered training to deal with something this terrible.

Drew told Dylan, "Don't worry, son. I got this."

I instructed all of them, "Don't say goodbye. Say 'see you later'."

Dylan said bravely, "I love you, Dad. See you later."

Andrea forced a smile and waved through the window, and told Drew she loved him. I took the phone off speaker; it was just the two of us.

This was the last time I would ever talk to him, and I didn't know what to say. Drew was my best friend, the most incredible, loving person I knew, and his life was about to end. How could I possibly find the words to tell him just how much he meant to me?

I wanted to tell him how badly I needed him. How I physically hurt, knowing he was suffering. I wanted to show him my soul, my deepest feelings, how I worshipped him as a man. How there were not enough words to describe the connection I felt to him.

But all I could say was, "I love you," over and over again. "I love you so much, Drew. I will be at this window every day until you wake up."

His voice became strong and deliberate. "I'm going to beat this," Drew declared.

"I am not afraid," he said, louder, with confidence. That was the Drew I knew–strong and defiant. I thought of something I read once: *Your mind will decide whether you live or die.*

Nurse Ally interrupted, "It's time. I'll come out and let you know when it's finished."

Drew said, "I got this. I love you—now hang up."

"No, you hang up."

"No, you hang up."

I said, "Sleep well, my love. I'll see you soon." I felt the other half of my soul separate from me as I hung up. My knees gave out, and I fell down in the grass in slow motion. The pain in my heart was unbearable.

Nurse Ally closed the curtains. Andrea sat on the ground. Me under the big tree, she on the curb next to the driveway.

I closed my eyes, "Dear God, please let this go smoothly. Please let it heal his lungs. Please keep him safe." Then I visualized calling in Jesus, the master healer, Archangel Michael, Archangel Metatron, and Archangel Raphael to be in the hospital room with Drew, to guide the hands of his medical team.

As I prayed, Andrea was on the phone with someone, tears streaming down her face.

A flock of crows flew above us. One landed in the tree by the window and called out. As it perched on the tree limb, it called out again and again, getting louder and louder with each howl. The crow taunted us, screeching over and over towards Drew's window. It clearly spoke to us: me, Andrea, and Drew.

Andrea Googled the meaning of a crow and read it out loud, "Crows show up to let you know that there are spiritual shifts happening and to pay attention to the messages that are sent to guide you. Crows represent transformation and insight into unseen realms."

Is there a spiritual shift happening for Drew, or me, or all of us?

Ventilated

As we waited, I called my sisters, Brenda, Christine, and Caroline. I called a few of Drew's closest friends. Then I called my "prayer warriors," Nikki, Joan, and Denise. Denise offered to bring us Thanksgiving dinner that night.

I called the people who worked for us: Raz and then Cory, our website manager, who lived in Denver, Colorado. "I'm booking my flight. I'll be there tomorrow," he said, offering to help with the business.

I paced the parking lot, making more calls to friends and family and sharing the bad news. I looked down at the pavement, and something caught my eye. It was a piece of plastic that had melted into the asphalt into a perfect heart shape. I looked over at Drew's window. A message of love.

A cloud floated in front of the sun, and it was getting chilly. Andrea and I moved to a cement seating area outside the hospital's back door. Two more hours passed before Nurse Ally came outside. This was the first time we had met any of the medical staff in person. She said the procedure went well, and when they reopen the curtains, we can see him. She brought us water, crackers, cheese, and yogurt. We hadn't eaten all day.

Then she handed me a large bag. I looked inside and saw the clothes and shoes he was wearing when I dropped him off two weeks earlier. My heart skipped a beat when I saw his cell phone and wedding ring in the bag. *Why would she give me these?*

Nurse Ally read my mind. "The road is long and bumpy, but the sun is always shining," she said, and she hugged me.

"I don't want him to be alone in there," I said.

Since no one was allowed to visit the Covid unit, Nurse Ally said there is an iPad for families to call and let their loved one hear their voices. She said that I could call the nurses' station anytime, and they would set up FaceTime in Drew's room for me. "I'm going to call that iPad every day," I told her.

My phone lit up with text after text, and while my attention was diverted, Andrea pulled Nurse Ally aside and asked, "Tell me the truth. How bad is this?" Nurse Ally hugged her and whispered, "Prepare for the worst."

Just then, a man came out of the back door and sat on a bench near us. He was wearing a mask and blue scrubs, and he was mumbling as he fiddled with his phone. I didn't realize at first that he was talking to me. "I tried to get to him before the procedure," he said, his eyes looking sad.

He pulled his mask down, and I recognized him. Paul and his wife Daylene had commissioned Drew to paint a surfboard years ago, and I was friends with his sister. Paul was a Respiratory Therapist in the NICU, where the babies are.

Paul was wracked with sorrow. A short time earlier, a nurse told him, "We are about to intubate your friend Drew." He ran down the halls to reach Drew before the procedure, but he was five minutes too late. He was devastated. As a respiratory therapist, Paul understood how bad it was.

"Will you check on him every day?" I asked. Paul promised that he would.

They finally opened the curtains to Drew's room, and Andrea and I found our spot back in the bushes, faces against the glass.

Drew was in what seemed like a peaceful state. The ventilator was down his throat, and he was lifeless. The sun went down, and the glass on the window felt cold. Nothing seemed real. *This can't be happening.* The reality of my Drew being plugged into a machine was too terrible to face.

We stood outside that window for a long time. Seven hours had passed since we arrived. I didn't want to leave him, but we couldn't sleep there. Andrea and I drove home in silence.

When we got home, food containers with Thanksgiving dinner were on the doorstep: turkey, mashed potatoes, green beans, and a lovely note from Denise. I put the food in the refrigerator. We didn't have an appetite.

As I settled into bed, I called the nurses' station to arrange for the iPad to be set up in Drew's room. A nurse explained she would have to suit up in the gown, gloves, shoe covers, face mask, and headgear and then set it up on a table next to his bed. Once she got it set up, she would call me back on the iPad.

Fifteen minutes later, Hospital One's iPad called my phone. I saved the number under "Drew" in my iPhone so that the next time we did this, it would be the same Etta James ringtone as Drew's. The nurse set the iPad up on a table next to Drew's bed so I could see him.

I spoke to him for three hours on FaceTime, promising never to leave him alone. I made up a healing mantra and repeated it over and over: "Your lungs are healing. Your body knows how to repair itself. It is getting stronger every day."

After I hung up, I wrote in my Dear Drew Journal:

> *My love for you is so deep. I cannot live without you. You have to come home to me.*

12

UNWAVERING FAITH

November 26th, 2021
Hospital Day 13, Ventilator Day 2

*W**hat if he dies?*
I woke up to a feeling of uneasiness gnawing at my stomach. It felt hollow, empty. I disassociated my consciousness from my body to shield myself from this terrible reality. I wanted to be blind to the truth. It would be easier that way.

Maybe I should bring him home to die. His last breath should be taken as I hold his hand and stare into his green eyes, telling him how grateful I am for the adventures he's taken me on. And when his spirit leaves his body, his last view of this life should be of me, loving him.

I started to imagine what would happen after he died. The surfing community would hold a "paddle out" for him, a memorial ritual for surfers after they pass away. It's like a funeral, but at the beach, and everyone brings their surfboard. Together, they paddle out into the ocean, form a human circle, and join hands. Someone leads with a prayer, and then everyone splashes the water at the end. Drew's paddle-out would have hundreds of people; there were so many who loved him.

I grabbed the journal off my bedside table and wrote sadly, "Dear Drew, this is the first day I cannot call you. I have your phone, and you are asleep."

I wanted to hold him so badly. But I wouldn't be allowed in until after he tests negative and is moved out of the Covid unit. The hospital required visitors to give proof of a Covid vaccine or a negative test, and I wanted to be ready when he was moved, so I went to CVS for a Covid test. Two hours later, I got my results, and was happy to see that it was negative.

Andrea and I drove to Drew's window again. I brought a few symbols of faith to place under the tree: a large black stone with the word "hope" etched on it, a heart-shaped beach stone that Drew had found for me, and an assortment of clear quartz crystals. It was a makeshift tribute facing the road, and as the staff drove by to park their cars, they could see it.

We straddled the bushes, watching Drew "breathe" with the machine. We had the hospital iPad on speaker, and we took turns talking to his comatose body. We spent hours outside that window. Nurses would walk past and wave hello.

There was no new information on Drew's condition from the day before. On the drive home, I thought, *I'm not doing enough. Someone out there has to know how to save him.*

That night, I researched everything I could find on Covid ventilated patients. I joined a Facebook group called "Ventilator Survivors," with members who were either a survivor of being vented or a family member, like me, who was trying to save their loved one. I scrolled through the posts, looking for clues, anything that would tell me what to do next. But they were all people like me, desperately trying to understand their situation.

Dr. Steady called. I asked him again for Ivermectin, high dose Vitamin C, anything, please, other than what was given to all the other people who died. He refused it all but admitted, "Some family members sneak Ivermectin to the patient." It made me wonder. *Was I doing everything I could to save him?*

I texted Alicia, a shamanic practitioner with whom I had completed my Reiki training a year earlier. She was a gifted healer who had studied under indigenous healers in Central America. I asked if she could show me how to send healing energy to Drew.

We scheduled a session at Alicia's home. I invited Andrea, even though I knew she wasn't into the spiritual stuff. "Do you want to join me for a session with a shaman?" I asked her.

"What's a charman?" Andrea asked.

"Not a char-man, it's a sha-man," I laughed. I explained that a shaman is a wise mystic who practices ancient rituals to connect with Spirit guides for energy healing. To my surprise, Andrea said yes.

When we arrived at Alicia's home, we took our shoes off at the door, and she greeted us with warm, loving hugs. Then she led us into a small room with cushions on the ground, formed in a circle. Sage was burning in an abalone shell. She had prepared an altar on the floor with candles and a photo of Drew in the center. Around the photo were neatly arranged crystals of selenite, rose, and clear quartz.

She motioned for us to sit on the floor facing the altar. Then she set her phone on a tripod and placed it next to Andrea, where Raz was joining us on FaceTime from her vacation in Florida.

Alicia guided us in meditation. She had us visualize Drew's body healing and his lungs releasing the sickness. She channeled information from Spirit and explained that my role was to bring in light and that Raz and I could bring him healing energy together.

Next, the wisdom from Spirit spoke through Alicia directly to Drew: "We are anchoring a frequency in your lungs, one which settles with a higher calling as your armor has increased tenfold. It is a freeing, a liberation of energy."

I looked over at Andrea, wondering if she thought this channeling was fake. Her eyes were closed, and she was allowing herself to settle into this new experience.

Spirit's words continued to flow through Alicia for Drew. "Since you are purging the heaviness, you have to experience letting go, knowing that you are freeing yourself from more than a condition known as Covid. It is a condition that has echoed through many lifetimes, and it has held you in this pattern. This pattern is about being strong; it has to do with providing. It's been a pressure for you. We want you to release all of that along with it."

I tried to understand this message from Spirit. It was true, Drew always felt pressure to take care of everyone. He would give the shirt off his back to someone in need, and he would give his life to save the life of someone he loved. He gave and gave and gave, to his detriment. And now, he couldn't give anymore. He was being freed from that.

Spirit finished by saying, "You are strong enough to fight this. You are strong enough to hold the spirit of your life and light force again."

Alicia taught me a healing prayer that I could recite to Drew. She handed me an index-sized card with the prayer typed on one side and a picture of the Angel Helerion on the other.

"How much do I owe you?" I asked after we were finished.

"This was a gift," she said as she hugged both of us goodbye.

Andrea and I got into the car. "I really enjoyed the char-man," she teased. She had a way of making everything fun. I was proud of Andrea; she went along with the meditation and the ceremony, and she seemed to like it.

Unwavering Faith

Driving home along Pacific Coast Highway, I started daydreaming about Drew's imminent death. I imagined all the friends who would do a paddle-out ceremony for him. Then, I started planning Drew's funeral. *Should we do it here, or should we do it in Myrtle Beach, where the family is?* I was mentally making a checklist of things to do when he dies.

And then, suddenly, my thoughts were interrupted by what felt like a bolt of lightning. It struck the top of my head, and I heard a very loud voice in my ear say, "If you want him to live, you must plan for him to come home."

It shocked me. I looked around–did Andrea hear that? And then a powerful knowing washed over me. Suddenly, I understood that if I wanted Drew to live, I needed to believe that he was coming home and that every thought I had, every action I took, and every decision I made had to follow that belief.

I turned to Andrea abruptly and said, "I just made a decision. I am going to have unwavering faith that Drew is coming home. No matter what."

Andrea nodded in agreement.

"I don't know how to have faith," I told her. "But I'm going to figure it out."

Just then, Andrea shared a true story about a boy who had fallen through the ice and drowned. When his mother came into the hospital, it was filled with people mourning his death. She yelled at them to stop, then ran into his room and prayed over his lifeless body, demanding that he come back to life. And he did.

This story was exactly what I needed to hear to show me who I needed to be, if I was going to have any influence over Drew's fate. I felt an unstoppable determination well up inside me, a fierce intention to do whatever it takes.

In that moment, I decided I wouldn't waver in my faith—not even when a doctor called with bad news, not when the data said he was going to die, not when everyone else on a ventilator with holes in their lungs died. I was not going to lose my faith, no matter how bad it got.

And I wasn't going to allow anyone to mourn him because everyone else needed to believe, also.

I will not give up until after he takes his last breath.

It was clear now what I had to do. It was up to me to direct the thoughts of everyone who loved Drew, so that when they thought of him, they saw him coming home alive.

Never again did I make plans for Drew to die. From that moment on, I planned for him to come home.

Andrea and I pulled into the driveway and walked up the steps to the front porch. I glanced down and saw a heart-shaped leaf lying on the patio, right at the front door.

13

GUILTY

November 27, 2021
Hospital Day 14, Ventilator Day 3

My heart pounded so hard, it felt like it was jumping out of my chest. It woke me in the middle of the night. Anxiety hit as my mind flooded with all the things I had done wrong. It was all my fault—the broken thermometer, waiting too long to get medical help for Drew, forgetting to pack our Covid kit.

The guilt was overwhelming. I should have done a better job of getting him the remedies. I should have taken him to a doctor sooner. I should have asked for help. I prayed, "God, please forgive me. Please help me forgive myself."

Andrea was up early, working. It was comforting to hear her in the next room. She could have blamed me. She could have complained about all the things I did wrong. But she never did, not out loud, anyway.

I called the nurses' station to set up the iPad. Five minutes later, Etta James' "At Last" ringtone sounded, and the iPad was carefully set up on Drew's side table. In the background, I could hear the rhythmic sound of the ventilator.

I felt so helpless. The man I loved was dying in a coma, and I was at the mercy of a medical system that was hard to reach. The only thing that I had control over was my connection to Spirit. I closed my eyes and called all of my Spirit guides. I visualized clearly in my mind Jesus kneeling by Drew's side and the angels in the room with him. I felt a hint of peace, knowing that Drew was protected.

"Your body knows how to heal. You are deeply loved. Your lungs are getting stronger." I continuously repeated my healing mantras, hoping that Drew's consciousness would have enough awareness that his body would actually respond to them.

I paced around the house as I talked to Drew, then handed the phone to Andrea. She told Drew, "Today is Jackie's and my seventeen-year wedding anniversary," and shared stories about their wedding day.

When she handed the phone back to me, I played the Norah Jones album *Come Away With Me*. Drew and I would always listen to Norah Jones' music as we cooked dinner. I wanted him to feel good memories of being at home.

Next, I called Dylan from Drew's cell phone and let him talk to Drew through the iPad.

This became my daily routine. I would call Drew early in the morning, ask our Spirit guides to be in the room to protect him, repeat healing mantras, play music, and let Dylan and Andrea talk to him. I would end the day the same way. Most days, I would FaceTime him for six to eight hours. The nurses must have thought I was crazy. I didn't really care what anyone thought, though, because I knew that Drew could hear us through the coma and that our voices comforted him.

Saturday after Thanksgiving was always our biggest money maker at the gallery, but I was in no shape to work. Raz was still in Florida, so I closed the gallery. We were losing money, but I needed to stay focused.

Later in the morning, Dr. Steady called with good news: They had lowered Drew's oxygen to 70%. I didn't get too excited, though. I had already learned that his condition was either up or down every day, and most of the time, it was down. Andrea texted the family to recap what the doctor had said, and that became her daily job: to decipher the doctor's words, put a positive spin on them, and then share them in the family group text.

That afternoon, Andrea and I drove to Drew's window. I promised him I would be there every day, and I was keeping that promise. His hair was becoming greasy. It was hard to see him with all the tubes and things sticking out of so many body parts. It struck me how barbaric this was.

We stayed until we got hungry, and I took Andrea to one of Drew's favorite restaurants, Rocco's, to celebrate her wedding anniversary. It had been two weeks since she arrived, and now she's missed Thanksgiving and her anniversary. But she never complained. Andrea was smart, confident, and always positive, even when things got tough. Without her by my side, I would have crumbled.

Our website manager, Cory, had just flown into town, and he met us at the restaurant. We ordered a bottle of my favorite wine, J Lohr Cabernet, and an escargot appetizer. It was Andrea's first time trying escargot, and she loved it. All night, we talked about Drew. Andrea joked about how Drew was always the center of attention growing up. As we ordered our second bottle of wine, we laughed about the waiter, who we were convinced was drunk. We cracked a lot of stupid jokes, and it was the most I had laughed in a long time.

As soon as we got home, Drew, being an inch from death, crept back into my awareness. *I need to do something more*, I thought. I sat quietly on the edge of my bed, asking out loud, "How can I turn this thing around?"

Then, a divine strike of inspiration gave me an answer. "Encourage everyone in the family to visualize Drew surviving," that little voice in my head said. I put my phone on a tripod and made a video, urging, "Please believe, with unwavering faith, that Drew will come home. As a collective, we can create the energy needed to help him heal." I sent the video to the family group text.

As I got under the covers, I called the Covid Unit, and a night nurse patched me into Drew. For the next hour, I talked to him. "I'll never let you be alone," I promised.

14

CHURCH

November 28th, 2021
Hospital Day 15, Ventilator Day 4

Andrea and I went to meet my friend Denise and her husband at Shoreline Church. Founded by surfers, this church was called "a sandy feet friendly church" because people attend service straight from their morning surf, still wearing flip flops.

Drew and I weren't churchgoers. As a kid, Drew had questions about how things worked in the Universe, and the Catholic school he attended didn't allow questions. When I was in my twenties, after I realized that there were thousands of religions in the world, all claiming to be the only way to salvation, I decided to create my own belief system. But you could call me a "spiritual chameleon" because I can assimilate into any religious ceremony and find the beauty in it.

As Andrea and I drove, my phone rang. The caller ID read, "Hospital." My heart sped up as I pulled over and put the phone on speaker. I took a deep breath and grabbed my medical journal. Dr. Black had bad news. Drew's right lung had collapsed, and they were doing a procedure to put a chest tube in. Andrea asked all the smart questions as I sat there, frozen. Things were getting worse.

Andrea tried to put a positive spin on it, "This isn't that bad. They put a chest tube in, and Dr. Black said that it would repair it."

I felt dizzy; the bad news was too much to bear. I wanted to go home now, but the church was only a block away.

The sun was hot, and the church patio was packed with people laughing over coffee and donuts. The men were dressed in their best Hawaiian shirts, and the women wore cute beachy dresses. There was a choice of joining the service inside, where the stage was or outside, where people brought beach chairs to sit in.

As we navigated our way around the crowd, I tried to smile. I knew many of the people there from the surfing community. There were a lot of tanned, sun-bleached blonde heads.

Someone brought us chairs to sit in. Denise and Andrea chatted as I stared into space. During the service, I had trouble hearing the pastor. I couldn't focus on anything but images of Drew in his hospital bed, suffering with a collapsed lung.

After the service, I bumped into a guy named Dave Talbot. A year earlier, Drew had painted a big beautiful cross on his son's surfboard. I told Dave how sick Drew was. Dave got the pastor and gathered twelve other people who knew us. They formed a circle around me as they prayed for Drew's recovery and for me to remain strong. I felt a powerful wave of love that gave me a bump in my energy.

Later, at home, a car pulled in the driveway. It was the respiratory therapist, Paul, and his wife, Daylene. Somehow, she knew that cupcakes were my weakness, and she brought me a homemade batch. Paul told me he had been checking on Drew every day he was at work at the hospital. Then he confessed he had been going in to see Drew on his days off, too. I hugged Paul with gratitude. I knew as long as Paul was there, Drew would be okay.

We were receiving kindness from so many people. It brought me a little peace, just enough to keep going. I wrote in the journal, "Dear Drew, all of your good deeds are coming back to you in great abundance!"

Until now, I had kept the news of Drew's illness in our tight circle of family and friends. I decided that it was time to let the rest of the world know. Drew has fans all over the world, and our lives are normally very public. But when it came to his health, Drew was very private. Every time he ended up in the Emergency Room with a surfing injury, he would tell me, "Don't put this on social media."

But now word was getting out, and I had to make sure that every person who thought about Drew did not think of him as dying. I had to direct their thoughts and visions towards his healing. Maybe, if everyone believed, then it would become true.

It took two hours for me to draft a simple public message as I agonized over every word. It had to tell the grim reality yet inspire the reader to believe that Drew would survive.

I posted a photo of Drew holding a paintbrush on Drew's Facebook and Instagram pages, and added the words "Pray for Drew" across the front of it.

The caption read, "I am deeply saddened to bring news that two weeks ago, Drew admitted himself into the hospital with Covid Pneumonia. His condition has worsened, and we are working to get him healed. The last thing Drew told me before he was put into heavy sedation on Thanksgiving day was this: 'I know I'm going to beat this. I'm not afraid.' And I believe him. Please take a moment to visualize Drew dropping in on a big wave or painting one. See him in your mind as healthy and vibrant. Send Drew your positivity and love. Pray for his health to be restored, as I believe miracles are possible. Thank you all for your love and support! Maria Brophy."

At 11:30 p.m., I called the Covid unit, and a new nurse answered. "I'm a fan of Drew's art. I was just showing his work to the other nurses." Good, I thought to myself. *It will make them care about Drew even more.*

The iPad was positioned so I could see Drew's face. I asked him, "Where are you? Do you know I'm here?" My devotion to him felt different now; it was deeper, stronger. It was as though seeing him this vulnerable made me love him even more.

I repeated his healing affirmations again and again. "You are healing every minute of every day. Your body knows how to repair itself. You are deeply loved." Two hours later, the iPad ran out of battery, and we disconnected.

15

EVERY DAY, BAD NEWS

November 29th, 2021
Hospital Day 16, Ventilator Day 5

Drew's brother Jamie called and said, "I'm going to set up a GoFundMe for you."

"Oh, we aren't going to need that. We have good insurance," I said. Besides, I knew that Drew would be angry if I asked anyone for money.

Jamie insisted, "You have no idea how high the medical bills are going to be." Despite my hesitation, he set up the page and shared it on his Facebook. Later, I was grateful he did. It ended up being a lifesaver for us.

Today was Day 5 on the vent, and I thought Drew would have been taken off of it by now. But Dr. Q said, "Let's wait a few more days and see how he's doing." And then he offered to have a priest visit Drew.

"Absolutely not," I said. Having a priest come meant that Drew was dying, and I wasn't going to allow the spiritual energy of death to enter our world.

I tried to have a peaceful morning. I sat in the backyard with my feet in the grass. A family of birds made a nest in the plum tree, and they were singing. Raz was back from Florida, and she and I talked on the phone, planning a prayer circle for Drew. The gathering would be held on the evening of December 1st in the art gallery.

I called the Covid unit to set up the iPad. An hour passed, and no callback. What could be taking so long? My feeling of peace turned to a flutter of panic. I called again. The nurse said there was a situation, and they had to sedate Drew more. My heart pounded, and I felt a sharp pain in my chest.

She finally set up the iPad, and Dr. Q was in the room with Drew. Andrea and I listened as Dr. Q told us that Drew's left lung now had a small hole forming. His right lung had already collapsed, and now the same thing was happening on the other side.

You can live without one lung, but you can't live without both. My hands started shaking, and my throat got tight. *Things just keep getting worse.*

Andrea asked a few questions to clarify what they could do about it. As Dr. Q answered, I couldn't focus on his words; I just kept hearing "two collapsed lungs" in my head.

Dr. Q ended the call with, "You have to fight for him, and I'm going to fight for him."

Every day, there was bad news. I kept saying to myself, *I am not afraid. I am not afraid. I am not afraid.*

But I was. I was afraid that Drew was slipping away, and I couldn't stop it. I was afraid every time the phone rang. I felt powerless. I had to take my faith another step further. I had to get my mind to where I had unwavering belief in his recovery and also accept whatever happens. This was a paradox that I had trouble wrapping my head around. How do you have faith and simultaneously surrender?

I prayed, "Dear God, no matter what, I will keep my faith that Drew will live. But, if you decide to take him, I will surrender to that."

Saying the words out loud helped me get my heart into the feeling of it. I started to understand what true faith is. *Faith is having an unshakable belief that Drew will survive and, at the same time, accepting that he may not make it.* It was a mind-bender.

It was three p.m. when Andrea and I made our daily drive to the window. Drew looked smaller in that bed today. He no longer resembled the strong athlete that he was; he looked like a weak, old man. Today's visit was shorter than usual. We came home to more food left in a crock pot on the front porch by a friend.

That night, I lay in bed thinking about the reality of the situation. I felt a dark, deep dread creep over me, knowing that he could die at any moment. I wondered where I would end up after he died. *I won't be able to live in this house without him.* I imagined moving to Costa Rica and starting my life over, lonely and sad.

And then, I stopped those thoughts and said out loud, "NO! Drew is coming home!"

I wrote in the Dear Drew Journal:

> Drew, you are the first thing I think of when I wake up and the last thing I think of before sleep. I miss you calling me your "little honey." I miss your naked body on mine. I miss your kisses.

That night, I dreamed that a nurse called with more bad news: "His other lung has collapsed." In my dream, instead of crumbling, I stood tall. I didn't flinch. I said to the nurse, "I am so strong now."

Though it was just a dream, it was a sign that I was gaining armor. I was going to fight through this. And I wasn't going to give up on Drew.

16

TEXT FROM HEAVEN

November 30, 2021
Hospital Day 17, Ventilator Day 6

It had been almost a week since Drew was put on the ventilator, and I was getting weary. My body was worn down from the lack of sleep and food, and my heart was always racing in panic. My spirit was dimming. The happy, spunky Maria I used to be was gone.

But, my friends refused to let me lose faith. They held me up with encouragement and kindness. Every morning, Nikki would check in and ask how Drew's vitals were. She'd always add a friendly, "Call me if you need to talk."

And every day, someone offered to bring food. Today it was Joan. She texted, "Praying for Drew. Dropping a chicken dinner on your porch tonight."

In an effort to uplift me, Raz brought over a bunch of cut-out slips of paper, each printed with words of encouragement. "These are things

Drew would want to say to you right now," she said as she taped them all over the house.

She taped "I trust" to the kitchen mirrored doors. Then, on the wall in my bedroom, she taped "Spunk, I am coming home. Keep the faith." On the bathroom mirror, it read: "Thank you for all you're doing to keep me strong. I love you. —Drew."

Those messages stayed up for months—a constant reminder to hold on to my faith.

I had been neglecting our business, and I was worried about money. But today, the Universe threw us a safety line. Our good friend, Greg, bought two of Drew's tiki paintings. I was grateful because the money bought me time.

Greg is a champion black belt in the martial art of jiu-jitsu, and when he picked up the paintings, he shared a vivid dream he'd had. In it, Drew was being held in a deadly jiu-jitsu hold with an opponent. Greg explained that in jiu-jitsu, white belts tend to panic and get hurt. But black belts, he said, learn to master their minds. They stay calm, breathe through the pressure, and slowly find their way out of a deadly situation.

Greg's dream about Drew was violent and felt so real that it shook him up. But then, like a master black belt, Drew breathed into the situation and completely relaxed. In the dream, Drew said, "I got this," and masterfully released himself from the deadly hold.

"I got this," were the exact words Drew said to me right before he was put on the vent. *Was he sending a message through Greg's dream?*

That afternoon, Andrea bought a gift basket with goodies for the nurses. She added a box of chamomile tea, pretzels, caramel candies, a dozen Burt's Bees lip balms, and a wooden sign that read "Nurses make a difference to lives." We wrote a thank you card to go with it.

We dropped the gift basket to the nurses at the hospital when we did our daily window visit. Andrea and I stood in the bushes, talking to Drew through the iPad, when Drew's mom called.

"I got a text from Drew last night," Mom said.

Andrea and I looked at each other, startled. "Mom, that's impossible. Drew's in a coma, and I have his phone," I answered.

But mom insisted. She said that at 12:30 in the morning, she received a text from Drew's phone. She was afraid to look at it; she thought it was bad news. She waited until morning to read the text.

She said Drew's text read, "Mom, I'm going to beat this."

Andrea started to cry, and I felt a strong emotion well up from my heart. We both felt a mix of renewed hope and an understanding that something powerful was happening.

Mom said, "He must have been sending me messages on the phone, in thought, and they got through to me."

Andrea and I had tears streaming down our faces. It was another message from Drew, sent through the quantum field and delivered to us in a way that cannot be explained.

17

PRAYER CIRCLE

December 1, 2021
Hospital Day 18, Ventilator Day 7

One week on the ventilator, I thought. I made a cup of coffee and took Drew on FaceTime back into the bedroom. Andrea was working on her laptop. She teased me, "You just want to have Drew in your room all night and day!"

Drew's fever had been consistently high for weeks. But last night, the fever broke. Dr. Steady said that if Drew went 24 hours without a fever, they would move him out of the Covid unit. Then we would be able to go in and be with him, and I couldn't wait for that to happen.

That night, Raz, Andrea, and I prepared the gallery for the prayer circle. We put candles on the window sills, and Raz set up a beautiful altar with a photo of Drew in the center, surrounded by rose buds. We had our crystal sound bowls set up, and our friend Beebs, a professional musician, offered to play a song on her guitar after the prayer.

I felt nervous, knowing that the people coming were from various religious backgrounds. The prayer we were about to lead leaned toward the New Age side, and I worried it might offend some of the Christians with its talk of energy and Spirit. But I had to shake that off—because in the end, we all wanted the same thing: a miracle.

Before the event, I set the intention to be an example of trust in Drew's healing. I prayed that I could influence all of our friends to have unwavering faith along with me.

Old friends, new friends, and surfing friends showed up. One by one, as Andrea and I greeted them at the door, nearly every person had a sad expression on their face. There were many tears. I resolved to stand strong, never cry, only smile, and tell every single person, "He is going to make it."

We didn't have enough chairs for the large crowd, so most people sat on the floor. Raz, Andrea, and I sat at the front of the room, cross-legged, on floor cushions. For the first time since Drew had been in the hospital, I turned my phone ringer off. The odds of a doctor calling in the next thirty minutes were slim.

I began the session by thanking everyone for being there and setting the intention and belief for Drew's complete healing. "I know everyone here is from different religious backgrounds. I ask all of you to do this work with an open heart and the absolute knowing that Drew will be healed."

It was 6:30 p.m. when I gave control of the room over to Raz. She guided a meditation prayer and had everyone in the room send Drew energy of love and light.

Next was Andrea's turn. She told stories of how Drew had been sending us messages from beyond. She told them about the crows and about the text Drew sent Mom.

Then, we called Beebs up to the front with her acoustic guitar. Beebs sang one of her songs, "Wake Up, Wake Up." She added the chorus lyrics, "Wake up, Drew Brophy. Wake up, Drew Brophy."

While Beebs was singing, I looked at my phone and saw a missed call from the hospital at exactly 6:35—the same time we were saying our prayer. I panicked and ran into the back room to call them back. I realized it was the hospital iPad that had called. Until now, the iPad had only contacted me when a nurse was setting it up in Drew's room after I'd asked them to.

I called back on FaceTime, and the iPad answered. I saw two nurses at the station, looking up at the screen with bewildered expressions. The iPad was sitting on a shelf above them.

I asked, "Why did you call me?"

One of the nurses replied, "We didn't call you. And we didn't even answer the iPad just now—it answered itself." They glanced at each other, confused.

I apologized and hung up.

Another message from Drew. He was with us during the prayer.

Raz closed the prayer circle by handing rose petals to everyone present. She instructed them to say a prayer into their petals and place them into a crystal bowl filled with water.

One by one, each person whispered a prayer into their petal and placed it in the bowl. I hugged everyone as they left, and this time, instead of tears, I saw smiles. The mood had shifted—everyone felt lighter, lifted to a higher vibration than when they arrived. The prayer, the music, and the belief that Drew would come home were already working. The entire group had been touched by a little seed of hope.

That night, I wrote in the journal:

Thank you for calling me, my love. You are so powerful.

18

THUMBS UP

December 2, 2021
Hospital Day 19, Ventilator Day 8

This morning I read Drew a passage from Abraham Hicks' book *Ask and It Is Given*.

"Your survival has everything to do with your thoughts. And so, if some are dying from it, say to yourself, 'that may be true for others, but it is not so for me, for I am the creator of my experience, and I choose recovery, not death.'"

Not long after, Dylan texted, "I bought my plane ticket. I'll be there Saturday." I was so happy. I didn't want to be alone, and Andrea had to return to her life in Atlanta. We both hoped we'd be allowed to see Drew before she left—after all, she promised she wouldn't go until she held his hand.

I got dressed and slipped on a pair of skinny jeans. In the mirror, I saw how loose they were—jeans that once clung so tightly I could barely pull them up now hung off my hips. I had lost so much weight, and part of me was glad. I'm small-boned, and being thin suits me.

But then I looked at my face. New wrinkles had formed around my eyes and mouth, my skin looked tired, and my jowls were beginning to sag. I had aged five years in just three weeks. "Ugh," I said to my new, old face staring back at me in the mirror.

The phone rang, and it was Dr. Q. He said that he expected Drew to remain on the ventilator for another week. My heart dropped. Another week! *Now, his chance of survival fell another ten percent.* Dr. Q said they couldn't move Drew out of the Covid Unit because his fever came back, he had a low blood cell count, and medical jargon that my mind heard as, "blah blah blah."

Later, Andrea, Raz, and I drove to Drew's window. A big note was taped to it: "Hi, thank you for your positive conversation! Have a lovely day. :) Nurse Lori."

Now, the nurses were leaving us love notes. We pressed our foreheads to the glass and spoke to Drew. Nurse Ally was on duty, and I was glad because it meant that Drew was getting the best care and a little love. I brought her a gift bag full of Drew's art prints, keychains, and stickers.

Raz brought the crystal bowl of water and rose petals full of everyone's prayers from the night before. The three of us stood in the bushes as Raz led us in prayer, then poured the blessed water onto the ground beneath Drew's window.

Andrea was sad. She knew she had to go home soon, and she did not want to leave her brother. The three of us hugged each other under the tree, Raz and Andrea crying and me fighting the tears back like I always did.

On our drive home, I received a text from Paul: "I'm in Drew's room. He heard me talking. He just gave me a thumbs up."

I read it to the girls. "That means he can hear us!" We were all excited. This was proof that Drew had awareness, and despite the drug-induced stupor, he was listening.

For dinner, I made spaghetti, Raz tossed a salad, and Andrea made garlic bread. Andrea started to cry again. She didn't want to leave California without seeing Drew. We poured three glasses of wine, and I turned on an episode of Sex and the City. It was the only thing that could make me laugh. The girls laughed, too. For a little while, we forgot how terrible everything was.

Raz went home, and Andrea went to bed. I was brushing my teeth just before midnight when I received a text from a woman named Debi, a crystal energy healer. I had gone to her many times for healing sessions. Debi had psychic abilities, a gift of knowing things, and a big heart. I hadn't talked to her in months, and her late-night text surprised me.

She wrote, "We've got a solar eclipse tomorrow. Maybe we can flip Drew's situation with the blackening and lighting of the sun."

What she texted next blew my mind:

"Thoughts came to me from Drew's stream of consciousness. He is swimming in Tahiti. He says: 'Teahupo'o, Teahupo'o, the rocks are smoother now! Like long ago. Hey, I can breathe underwater and swim really far. My shoulder doesn't hurt. I feel like a superhero.' He's reaching out further from himself to swim harder, faster, and having so much fun. He stops and looks back for you. He says, 'C'mon Maria! It's great down here. You can do it too! Promise me you will come swimming with me."

I pictured Drew's spirit swimming deep in Tahiti. I felt a tinge of sadness that he was calling for me to join him, and there was no way I could.

Then Debi's final message from Drew: "And ya know I can hear you without the iPad. I can hear and feel everything you feel real easy...don't stress on that."

I knew Debi had channeling abilities. I'd seen them before, though the skeptic in me still questioned them. Debi and I rarely spoke, and there was no way she knew about his shoulder injury from his last surfing accident. Maybe Debi was one more way Drew was getting through to me.

Her message gave me comfort, knowing the possibility that Drew was outside of his painful body, swimming in one of his favorite places on Earth. And, if he could hear me without the iPad, then I would have to be even more careful with my words and thoughts.

I called for my nightly FaceTime. The nurse on duty said that they had to raise Drew's oxygen back up to 92%, and they had to change his medications. He sounded nervous, and I worried if he knew what he was doing.

During our FaceTime, alarms started going off in the room. It was frightening. I called the nurses' station and asked the nurse to run in and check on Drew. The alarms were so loud through my phone that it woke Andrea up all the way down the hall. She ran into my bedroom, and we watched on FaceTime as the nurse anxiously fiddled with the machines to get it under control. We were watching Drew die right before our eyes.

My chest hurt, a sharp pain with every breath. *This could be it. This could be Drew leaving this earthly realm to swim in Tahiti until the end of time.* I prayed and asked Jesus to protect him.

Finally, the nurse got it under control, and the beeping stopped.

I wrote in the journal:

> Drew, don't leave me, not yet. We belong here a little longer together. Swim back to me, honey.

19

PULL THE PLUG

December 3rd, 2021
Hospital Day 20, Ventilator Day 9

I woke up to my heart racing with anxiety. I had been carrying so much stress in my body that I was clenching my jaw and grinding my teeth. And that was pulling on a muscle in my throat, which throbbed 24-7. Every time I swallowed, I felt like I was being stabbed in the neck. I tried to relax my jaw, but it had a mind of its own.

As usual, I made my morning call to Drew. The nurses must have thought it was ridiculous that I called three times a day and stood in the bushes every afternoon to talk to a man who was in a coma. But I didn't care what they thought. I hoped it made them care more about the man lying in the bed, knowing he was important to someone.

Nurse Ally poked her head into the iPad. "Dr. Q wants to meet with you in person at 10 a.m.," she said. In three weeks, the doctors had never met with me in person. A bolt of fear struck my heart. I had to breathe slowly and deliberately, so that I couldn't feel the stabbing pain in my chest. *This must be really, really bad.*

Andrea tried to calm me down, "This could be good news, Maria."

But I had a bad feeling about it. Nurse Ally left the room, and it was just me and Drew on the iPad. This could be Drew's last day on Earth, so I did something absolutely ridiculous: I took him on FaceTime into the car and drove him around to talk to friends.

First, I took him to the gallery, where our longtime friend and healer, Kim, was giving a Yamuna body rolling class to a group of students. Kim rented the gallery every Friday to do her classes.

I brought my phone in before class began and said, "Say hello to Drew." Kim was surprised as I showed up unannounced, and her students were bewildered that I had my comatose husband on FaceTime.

Kim had been Drew's healer for two decades. After every surfing injury, Kim would get her monkey fingers deep into the hurt muscle and fix it for him. She was a miracle worker; we would see Kim before going to a doctor for most things.

Kim talked into the iPad, "Drew, brother, I love you. You're going to be okay." Then her students took turns saying encouraging words, like, "Get strong, Drew," and "We love you."

Next, I drove over to Raz's house. When she answered the door, she was still in her nightgown. She said some loving words to Drew, and then I drove back home to pick up Andrea and drive to the hospital.

We kept Drew on FaceTime the entire drive, and when we arrived, we stared in his window until Dr. Q came out the back door to greet us. I was glad to see Nurse Ally walk out with him. Her warm smile took the edge off my anxiety.

Dr. Q motioned for us to sit on the concrete chairs near the back door. He pulled his mask down for a moment so that we could see his smile. He was a young, slender Italian man with perfectly tanned olive skin. I told him, "Wow, you're handsome *and* smart!" My weak attempt to keep the mood light.

Drew was still on the iPad, and I put us on "mute." I didn't know what Dr. Q had to say, and I didn't want Drew to hear it if it was bad. Even though he was in a coma, I knew that he could hear everything.

Dr. Q said in an ominous tone, "We're at a crossroads." He leaned in and delivered the bad news: Drew needed a lung transplant. It was his only chance.

I felt my coffee rise from my stomach and burn my throat. Plot twist. This was one of the worst possibilities I couldn't have guessed.

I took in a breath, and surprisingly, I felt strong. The armor around my energy body was thickening. I don't know if I was fooling myself or if I was getting used to hearing bad news every day. As we listened to Dr. Q, I kept reminding myself to trust. *No matter what bad news you hear. Keep the faith.*

Dr. Q felt very strongly that if Drew did not improve in a few days, he would die without a lung transplant. But, he explained, the hospitals that do lung transplants were maxed out and putting a priority on younger people. There was a good chance that Drew would not be accepted, and if that happened, we should pull him off life support and let him go.

Andrea's eyes got red. Tears flowed from the corners. No positive spin could be put on this one. As Dr. Q's words sank in, Andrea's phone rang, and she walked away to answer it privately.

Now that we were alone, Dr. Q leaned in closer to me and said, "This is a terrible way for Drew to die. He is suffering. If nothing changes in a few days, we should remove life support. Will you give us permission to relieve his suffering?" He held out a piece of paper and a pen for me to sign. My signature would stop Drew's pain.

Time slowed down, and my vision blurred. A sudden wave of weakness washed over me, but I pushed it away and sat up straight. A million thoughts raced in my head as he waited for my answer. I saw the image that Dr. Q had planted in my head: my beloved Drew suffering, tortured by the ventilator, only to die anyway. And I, his wife, was the only one who could stop his pain by giving consent to pulling life support. It was a terrible choice to make.

I don't want to be the reason he's suffering.

As my mind wrestled over this decision, I saw a vision of Drew floating away from me as my hand reached out to pull him back. I thought, *How can you ask me to let go of the only thing I've ever truly loved?*

And then I remembered my promise. *Have faith that he will come home, no matter what.* A surge of strength shot up my spine. An absolute knowing came over me that pulling the plug was the wrong choice. *I will not give up, not until after he takes his last breath.*

I looked Dr. Q in the eyes, mustered the strongest voice I could, and said with great conviction, "I will never agree to that. Please, don't ever ask me again."

He nodded. It was the last time he ever asked.

20

WE GOT INSIDE

People in my ventilator survivor group say that when a doctor asks to remove life support, it means they've lost all hope that the patient will survive. Drew was dying, and Dr. Q didn't want to drag it out. I never told anyone he asked me to turn off the machines and let Drew go. I kept that secret to myself—because I wasn't ready to give up on him, and I didn't want anyone else to, either.

When Andrea walked back to the concrete seating area to rejoin us, Dr. Q surprised us both by standing up and abruptly saying, "Let's get you inside!"

In a display of compassion, Dr. Q wanted to give us a chance to say goodbye, even though it was against the rules.

This was the moment Andrea and I had been waiting for. He led us into the back door of the hospital, no Covid test, no vaccine check. Nurse Ally's eyes smiled as she handed each of us a mask and ushered us down the hallway and to the double doors of the Covid Unit.

It was like entering a high-security prison. The entry doors were locked and Ally had to enter a code to get in. The doors opened into a station where two nurses worked on computers. Huge sheets of plastic were taped to the doorways; I guessed it was to prevent the germs from migrating. The stench of stool and blood mixed with rubbing alcohol filled my nose. The halls of the unit were dimly lit, and I could feel the heaviness of death in the air.

There were ten rooms in the Covid Unit. From the nurses' station, you could see all of the patients' rooms. Each room had large glass windows, and straight ahead, I saw a man in his hospital bed, sitting up, looking at his cell phone. He was big, with a huge beard that needed trimming. He had oxygen being delivered through a nasal cannula, the same thing Drew had before things got worse.

In the next room over was a pretty Hispanic woman lying in her bed, a ventilator tube shoved in her open mouth. She was younger than me, maybe forty. It reminded me of alien scenes I saw in old movies, where victims of abduction were placed on machines for medical experiments. Her body was limp as the machine pumped her with oxygen. Drew was in the room next to hers at the end of the hall.

Nurse Ally instructed Andrea and me on how to suit up. We each put on a disposable blue isolation gown, which had long sleeves and was floor length. Mine was huge for my 5'3" height and dragged on the floor. She pointed to blue latex gloves to put on. And, for the final layer of Covid protection, she gave us plastic face shields to wear over our masks.

Ally led us into Drew's room, where we finally got to see it from the inside. There were machines and beeping noises and the constant hum of the ventilator. Next to Drew's bed was a large monitor that displayed his vitals. All patients in the ICU have this monitor, which tells you at a glance their heart rate, blood pressure, oxygen saturation, and other details. The monitor will beep if one of the vitals goes outside of the normal level, or if there's a malfunction of the machine. It seemed to always be beeping.

We Got Inside

The air felt heavy, crowded with the ghosts of all the other patients who suffered in here. *How many have died in this very room?* I could feel their presence, the curse of being an empath.

I looked around for somewhere to sit, but there were no chairs.

To the right of his room was the large window that I was usually on the other side of. To the left was a large, thick windowpane looking into the room of the woman on the ventilator. I could see her pretty face through the glass. I wondered if she had children or a husband and if they were going to get to see her, too.

I cautiously approached Drew's bed. What do you do when you see your beloved in a coma, lifeless? I followed Andrea's lead as she walked over and held his hand. I was glad she was with me; she always knew what to do in every situation.

It was the first time I touched my Drew in three weeks. His big, muscular body was small now. There were tubes and IVs plugged into his flesh. The ventilator tube was intrusively stuck down his throat. His eyes were closed. All I could think was that this was so barbaric. *This can't be right.*

His beard was grown out and showed gray that I hadn't seen before. But his face looked peaceful and smooth. I touched his cheek. His forehead wrinkles were gone. Andrea and I looked at each other, and she read my mind and joked, "Are they giving him Botox in here?"

She had a way of making me laugh, even in the most dire of situations.

Andrea stepped to the side to give me time with him alone. I stared at his face. *Where are you right now? Do you know I'm here?* He was stuck somewhere between life and death. His heart was beating, but he was gone.

I closed my eyes and tried to tap into his energy. I wanted so badly to connect with him. I wanted to know that he was still there, inside that lifeless body. I focused my energy on his, begging him to send me a sign to let me know that he was aware. But I felt nothing. Just a limp hand in mine.

I placed my hands on the crown of his head. Breathing in deeply, I visualized a white light beaming down from heaven, bringing him life-force energy. I touched his heart. It was beating abnormally fast for someone who was resting. His feet were freezing cold, and I warmed them with my hands. It occurred to me that this body had not moved in weeks. I rotated his feet and ankles in a circular motion to get blood flow and circulation.

Even though the sunlight was pouring in through the window, it felt dark and ugly inside. Tears welled up, but I shoved them down to that secret place deep in my stomach. *There's plenty of time to cry later.* I didn't want him to sense my sorrow. I knew in my heart that there was still a part of his consciousness right there in the room.

Andrea reached for my hand, and together we stood on the side of his bed and prayed over him. We held his hands. I played music on my phone for him. We took a photo of us smiling at the foot of his bed, his lifeless body in the center. It was all so surreal.

Time flew by—five hours had passed, and our feet were aching. I didn't want to leave him, but we finally said goodbye. Our stomachs were growling. It was another day without food.

We thanked the nurses for letting us stay so long. We felt so much appreciation for this gift. Ally unlocked the prison doors to the Covid unit and let us out.

Raz called as we were leaving the hospital. She made our biggest sale in the gallery ever of some of Drew's older artworks. Word was out that Drew might die, and this was the start of a run on his art by collectors who saw value in buying up the few paintings we had left. I was grateful for the money. It bought me time to keep the gallery for a couple of months longer.

We Got Inside

On our drive home, new waves of emotions hit. Touching Drew and seeing him unresponsive made this nightmare feel more real. I had to work harder to hang onto my faith because the reality was that he was on the edge of death, and it could happen at any moment. *Keep the faith, keep the faith,* I said to myself, over and over again.

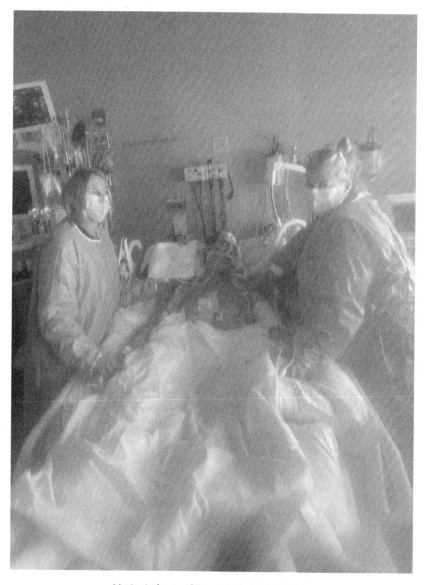

Maria, Andrea, and Drew inside the Covid Unit.

21

ROLE REVERSAL

Seeing Drew like that, so vulnerable and helpless, was shocking. He was no longer the strong, capable athlete I had leaned on for everything. He now lay silent, a vegetable, hooked up to machines and dependent on others just to keep breathing.

I had always relied on him, probably too much. But he naturally just did everything. If something broke, he fixed it. If we had friends over for dinner, he cooked. His ears would perk up at night, listening for danger, ready to protect me and our home. I slept well, knowing I was safe with him there.

Being married to Drew was one great adventure. He planned most of our travels— long road trips to the mountains in Idaho or Montana or all the way to Maine and back. Dylan grew up paddleboarding on lakes all over the country and surfing on beaches around the world.

Drew was stronger than most men. Like the Incredible Hulk, he would easily lift three big, heavy paddleboards over his head and put them up on top of our tall van. And he had saved many lives over the years: a young surfer drowning at the pier, a woman who was nearly dead after her boat capsized in the Colorado River, and one time in

Hawaii, when he stopped the attack of a woman by her abuser and was nearly killed for it.

He was also incredibly brilliant, though he hid it behind sandy feet and wild, edgy artwork. He was an expert on history and ancient cultures, highly skilled at mathematics, and studied theoretical physics for fun. Our dinner conversations as a family were always centered around the meaning of life. It was never boring with Drew around.

To me, Drew was Superman. He could do anything. Now, everything was backward. I had to do everything on my own, and I was now his protector. And I couldn't even ask him what he wanted.

Our roles had drastically reversed. *I don't know if I can do this*, I thought.

22

LUNG TRANSPLANT

December 4, 2021
Hospital Day 21, Ventilator Day 10

Tonight, Dylan was flying in from North Carolina, and Dr. Q had promised that Dylan would be able to see Drew. He also gave Andrea and me permission to visit again today. But from now on, we would have to follow the official rules: enter through the front entrance, show proof of vaccination or a negative Covid test to the security guards, and take turns—only one of us would be allowed in at a time.

Dr. Q asked for another meeting today. *What now?* Andrea frowned—this time, she couldn't hide her worry. We met with him in the same spot as before. It struck me as odd that our meetings never took place in a professional office—always outside, on cold concrete benches.

Dr. Q emphasized, "The only chance Drew has is to get a lung transplant." He applied to eight different hospitals that specialize in transplants. But, he warned, none of them are obligated to take Drew, and there's a chance that none will.

Andrea asked, "What can we do to get a hospital to accept him?"

Dr. Q suggested we make phone calls to all of the hospitals and try to influence the decision. *If I can't get a doctor on the phone here, how in the world will I get anyone on the phone in a hospital that Drew hasn't been admitted to yet? This is impossible,* I thought.

Dr. Q's phone vibrated, he looked at it, then hurriedly slipped into the back door of the hospital.

Andrea and I took turns visiting Drew. She went first, and as I waited outside the window, I started to feel the enormous stress of figuring out how to get Drew accepted into a hospital that would do a lung transplant. I put my arms around the big tree trunk and let it absorb my angst. Nurses were coming and going, staring at me, hugging the tree. The staff was getting used to this now.

Andrea came out ninety minutes later and then it was my turn. I went through the security guards, showed proof of my negative Covid test, and then walked the long hallway to the Covid Unit. Once there, suited up in a mask, blue gown, and blue gloves.

I held Drew's hand, "Do you know I'm here?" No squeeze. No movement. He was limp from head to toe. I hovered my hands above his head and closed my eyes. I visualized a white light above Drew's head, beaming from Jesus' hands through mine. I moved the light energy with my intention, flowing it into Drew's head.

I whispered, "Your lungs are getting stronger. Your body knows how to heal. Every cell in your body is filled with a healing, life force energy." I recited the mantras over and over again.

Two hours flew by and I finally had to leave, as Andrea was waiting outside. On the drive home, we mapped out a plan to get Drew accepted by one of the hospitals.

I felt frenzied as we were up against the clock; he could die any day now. We needed to inspire the hospital decision-makers to care about Drew, and we needed to do it fast. We had to show that Drew was worth saving, that he was important to the community, that he mentored kids, and that he lived a healthy lifestyle. They needed to know that he inspired people in a positive way.

We came up with the idea of creating a full-color flyer featuring photos of Drew painting with kids and surfing. The flyer would show that "he is a pillar of positive light around the world, connecting people with art and encouraging them to follow their passions."

But how do I make a flyer like that? I didn't have graphic design skills.

Literally, moments later, my phone rang. It was Drew's longtime friend Matt. "How are you holding up, Maria?"

Matt and Drew had been friends for 25 years. When they were younger, they made history together in the surf industry back when Drew painted for Matt's company, Lost Surfboards.

"It's critical, Matt. I need help." I filled him in on the urgency of getting a hospital to accept Drew. Matt offered to have his graphic design team create a flyer for the hospitals. This took a huge burden off of me.

Andrea and I went to work on what to write on the flyer. I put a message on my Facebook page: "Please share a story about how Drew positively impacted you. Your stories will help us get him into a hospital for a lung transplant. Thank you."

Hundreds of comments poured in from all over the world. People shared stories of how Drew had helped them in times of trouble, done favors for their kids, and inspired them.

One person wrote, "There aren't words to express how Drew has had a positive impact on my life. He was there when I really needed him for some tricky parts of life and helped point me in the right direction."

And another, "Drew is a generous soul. One automatically becomes a better person just by knowing him."

All of Drew's good deeds were coming back in the form of loving memories from many people. I read through hundreds of comments, trying to figure out how to use their words to convince the hospitals that Drew's life was worth saving.

23

VITAMIN C

The Universe works in magical ways. When I look back now, I see how the solutions came to me in the most unexpected forms.

I had been praying and praying for guidance on how to save Drew. I knew we had to do something—I just didn't know what. And then, the answer came. A woman I'd never met, named Kayla, texted me out of the blue. She said she'd heard about Drew from a mutual friend. Her brother had been dying from Covid, just like Drew, and she told me she saved him—with high-dose Vitamin C IV treatments.

Kayla sent me links to medical studies where megadoses of ascorbic acid had been used to help critical ICU patients. She even gave me clear instructions: "Have them administer it through an IV—twenty grams—for seven days.

Next, she told me something I didn't know—something that changed everything. Kayla explained that, by law, doctors were required to consider alternative treatments if I requested them. It was part of a law called the Right to Try, which says that if your loved one is dying, you have the right to try anything.

If high-dose intravenous Vitamin C saved her brother from dying, it might save Drew, too.

Kayla coached me on how to make the demand, "Be calm, assertive, and direct. Remind the doctor you have the 'right to try.' Tell him you understand that there are risks and you have researched and believe this treatment could help."

Her last text was encouraging. "You are the advocate. Don't give up until they do what you ask."

Kayla texted me nonstop for days which annoyed Andrea because we didn't know Kayla, and who the hell was she to text me medical advice? I agreed that her constant texting was odd, but I believed that my prayers were being answered through other people. And I wasn't going to say "no" to that.

After all, we had been begging for a miracle. And anyone who has seen a miracle will tell you it shows up in ways you least expect. I was starting to do a lot of things I normally wouldn't do. I was learning to trust in the unknown and to follow my intuition.

When Dr. Steady called, I asked him for the high-dose Vitamin C. "We don't do that for Covid patients," he said.

I pushed, "Well, I legally have the right to try anything, so this is what I want to try. And besides, you wanted to 'throw the kitchen sink at it," I said, using his own phrase to motivate him.

He rebutted, "Our pharmacy doesn't have that dosage. It will take time."

I texted Kayla back and told her what he said.

"Not true," she replied. "My cousin is a pharmacist at the hospital. They can get it very quickly. Keep fighting," she encouraged.

She emailed me a sample letter with clinical trial evidence that I could use, demanding the Vitamin C and an explanation for why I was requesting it. The letter included quotes from the National Institute of Health on how Vitamin C alleviates complications from Covid-19.

I wrote letters to Drew's doctors and scrambled to get them delivered. I found an email address for Dr. Steady, but Dr. Q did not have one. I called the hospital for a fax number for the doctors and was told there was none. Then I asked for a mailing address, and they didn't have that, either! There was no way to mail or fax a letter to a doctor at Hospital One. I emailed the letter to Dr. Steady and made copies to hand-deliver to the hospital.

I went to the Hospital's reception desk and asked to deliver the letters to the doctors. "Ma'am, there is no way to get a letter to a doctor here." The woman at the desk said.

I argued for a few minutes, then gave up, and walked the letters to the ICU and asked a nurse. She said, "Just leave them in the room, and the doctors will see it."

I put the letters in Drew's room, taped them to the wall, and then took a photo to prove they had been delivered.

24

DYLAN

December 5, 2021
Hospital Day 22, Ventilator Day 11

Dylan flew in from North Carolina late at night. He had to sleep with me in my king-sized bed because Andrea was in his old room. I didn't mind; when he was little, Drew and I did the "attachment parenting" thing and let him sleep with us because Dylan would cry when left in his crib. We never wanted him to feel lonely. Now, I was the one who didn't want to feel alone.

An early call with Dr. Steady revealed more bad news; they had to hold off on Drew's CT scan because when they tried to move him, his heart rate spiked and his oxygen levels dropped. I sighed heavily. More fear shot through my stomach.

I asked Dr. Steady if he had read my email. He said Drew was currently being given 1.5 grams of Vitamin C. I knew that was not enough to stamp out the infection. I remembered what Kayla told me, and I stayed firm: "A high dose is ten grams or more. That's what I'm requesting."

He said, "We will try for a higher dose tomorrow when the Head Pharmacist returns to work. " This delay was slowing Drew's chances of recovery. I resolved to fight for it until they gave in.

Dylan was going to see Drew today. "Dad's going to look real bad," I warned. I worried it would traumatize him, seeing his father lifeless. The only time Dylan experienced critical illness was when he was twelve and Drew's dad, Poppi, was dying.

Dylan said, "Mom, I can handle it." He kissed me goodbye and drove to the hospital.

But at 9 a.m., Dylan called and said they wouldn't let him in. I rang the nurses' station. The nurse on duty was Jovan, and his voice was angry. He told me they had an emergency and couldn't have visitors.

Dylan waited in the hospital parking lot while I tried to sort it out. I called the nurses' station a few more times, but no one answered or called me back. I started to panic. What if that emergency was about Drew?

Desperate, I texted Paul. "Are you at work?"

He responded, "It's my day off."

I told him what was going on.

He wrote, "I'll go see what's happening." Ah, relief. I was so grateful to have an inside man.

Paul drove to the hospital and found Dylan in the parking lot. He escorted him into the front doors, down the hall, and, despite Jovan the Terrible's attempts to stop them, right into Drew's room. There was no emergency.

Paul showed Dylan how the machines worked and what the monitor numbers meant. Dylan held Drew's hand and told him about a big tech project he was working on and couldn't wait to show him. And for a brief moment, Drew's eyes opened, and he stared at Dylan!

When Dylan left, it was my turn. Paul was still there and escorted me past a furious Nurse Jovan, who clearly didn't want us there.

I held Drew's hand, and he opened his eyes and looked at me. I pulled my mask below my chin and smiled big for him. He gave my hand a weak squeeze. I was so excited to get a response from him. I FaceTimed Andrea and let her talk to Drew.

Drew made a movement with his right hand. "What's he asking?" I asked Paul.

"He wants to write." Paul put a marker and a piece of paper in Drew's hand. But his hand was too weak to hold the pen.

I asked, "Drew, are you trying to say something hurts?" He shook his head no. "Are you trying to say you need something?" He shook his head no.

"Are you trying to say you want to come home?" He nodded yes.

Communicating with him brought a flood of new emotions. I stayed with him as long as possible, soaking in the connection to the Drew I knew.

At 6:30 p.m., Jovan the Terrible told me I had to leave, and he was not friendly about it.

I kissed Drew on the forehead and told him ten more times how much I loved him. Now that he was awake, it was harder to leave.

As I ripped off my gown and gloves in the nurses' station, Jovan snorted, "You know, the vaccine would have prevented this." *Ah, now I know why he was so mean.* This was a time in the world, at the tail end of the pandemic, when some people held hatred for those who did not get the Covid 19 vaccine. It was an ugly, polarized issue, and I hated how people fought over it.

Now, I was afraid to leave Drew with him. *I need divine intervention. This is getting scary.* Driving home, I prayed for an answer when inspiration hit me. *What I need to do is generate a powerful energy from a large number of people all at once–from the collective.*

I wrote a Facebook post asking for help. I was careful not to let on how bad things were because I didn't want anyone to visualize Drew on his deathbed; everyone must see him recovered in their minds.

It read:

"To all who love Drew,

I need your help.

You CAN help because YOUR positive intentions are very powerful.

Take a moment right now, in your mind, to see Drew charging on the biggest wave of the day or painting his next masterpiece. Close your eyes, feel his joy, and then say, 'Drew is healed and in good health.' Do this as often as you can every day.

This positive intention multiplied by thousands of those who love him will supercharge Drew's healing!"

It was as though I were a conductor orchestrating the thoughts of thousands of people who were the instruments. The orchestra was a symphony of faith and expectation, and the audience was the Universe. Maybe, together, we could shift the spell of death into a rebirth.

At home, Dylan and Andrea were heating up a sausage pasta dish for dinner. Raz came over with a check for me. She had sold another big painting. Andrea, Raz, and I watched an episode of *Sex and the City* with a glass of red wine. Raz made cookies in the oven. It was my evening routine now: cookies, wine, and *Sex and the City*.

When I made my nightly call to Drew, the nurse told me that his temperature had gone back up and that she had to increase his oxygen to 75%. A familiar seed of worry took space in my belly.

Dylan

One step forward, two steps back. *Can't we get a break?*

As I lay down to go to sleep, I thought about how I was living in a horror movie. I wondered, *How is this going to end?*

25

REALITY VS. FAITH

December 6, 2021
Hospital Day 23, Ventilator Day 12

Drew's situation was as critical as it gets. One lung had collapsed, and there was so much escaped air around Drew's neck and shoulders that he looked like a blown-up balloon. One little misstep and Drew's other lung would collapse, and then he'd die. Dr. Q didn't want to take any risks, so he ordered his staff to do nothing except keep Drew stable until another hospital would take him.

The reality was that no one with his condition, as bad as it was right now, had ever left the hospital alive. Literally no one.

I found an article online that said that after one week on a ventilator, a Covid patient's chance of survival drops below 10%. We were running out of time. *I have to move faster*, I thought.

I frantically wrote letters to all eight lung transplant hospitals that Dr. Q applied to. If I could help them see Drew as the amazing person he was, rather than just a number, maybe they wouldn't deny him. I wrote about how Drew was an athlete who took great care of his body and how much he gave to the community. I included quotes from people who posted on Facebook about how Drew had made a positive difference in their lives.

When Paul visited Drew, a friend who worked in the Covid ICU said casually, "Oh, you know that guy? He's not going to make it." It infuriated Paul. That night, he went home feeling very depressed. He never took work home with him, but watching Drew die was becoming too much to bear.

Paul's wife Daylene tried to comfort him, "Drew is going to be okay. I know it in my heart."

But, as a respiratory therapist, Paul knew things she didn't. He saw the reality. It was impossible for Drew to come back from this.

Daylene dismissed all of Paul's proof and repeated, with absolute confidence, "He's going to live through this." She had the faith of a fairy. They don't see the evidence; they only see the possibility. The beautiful thing about fairies is that they have no doubt—they just know.

It felt like there was an invisible war, a clash of expectations, between those who saw reality and those with a strong belief in miracles. All we needed was a few more people to believe blindly, so we could generate enough energy in the quantum field to tip the scales.

Because blind faith leads to action, and action can change everything.

26

PRETTY LADY DEAD

Jamie's GoFundMe for Drew had donations pouring in from all over the country. I was grateful, but I couldn't shake the guilt of accepting money from people. At that point, I still naively thought we wouldn't need it.

My body was feeling stressed, so I took a walk to the beach to relieve some of it. As I approached the pier, I took in the beauty of the skyline, speckled with tall Mexican fan palm trees. The sight of palm trees always filled me with a feeling of adventure, freedom, and joy.

Putting my bare feet in the sand felt good. A local surfer was waxing up his surfboard and asked, "How's Drew doing?"

"He's doing great," I lied. "Can I ask you a favor? When you're out there surfing, will you imagine him out there with you?"

He thought for a moment and nodded his head, "Sure."

Over the next hour, I ran into more people who asked about Drew. A local news reporter, the town Mayor, and a man Drew and I helped get on his feet when he was homeless. I asked each person to help Drew by visualizing him out there surfing again.

When I headed back, the walk up the hill had me winded. I still didn't feel normal after having Covid. But my spirit felt refueled by the love from the community.

My good mood was ruined when I got back to the house. Something terrible had happened. This day would end up being one of the most traumatic.

Dylan came home from the hospital visibly distressed. He told Andrea and me that when he got to the hospital, Nurse Jovan left him waiting outside for an hour, and when he finally let him in, he angrily muttered that Dylan shouldn't be there. It was evident that he didn't like our family at all. But that wasn't what traumatized Dylan. It was what he saw from inside.

When he arrived, Drew was completely unresponsive, so heavily medicated that he didn't move a muscle. Dylan played music from the band Tool and held Drew's hand. Suddenly, his visit was interrupted by the loud emergency beeping of the ICU monitor of the pretty woman in the next room. Dylan watched in horror as the numbers on the monitor dropped and her oxygen levels plunged. "Oh, this isn't good," he thought.

He watched as her vitals destabilized and the beeping got louder. He could see, through the thick glass separating her room from Drew's, Jovan leading three other nurses into the woman's room. A nurse locked eyes with Dylan through the glass as she pulled a curtain closed, blocking his view.

Dylan closed his eyes and whispered, "Please let her be okay."

As Dylan recounted what happened, I watched Andrea's face change with the realization that Drew would be next. She started to cry, and I suddenly had a stomachache. We both were deeply disturbed. This woman dying with the same condition as Drew was a grim reminder of how close we were to losing Drew.

I drove to the Hospital to visit Drew next. When I arrived, Jovan was extra grumpy and muttered something angry under his breath to me.

As I walked past the dead woman's empty room, I felt an eerie energy. I entered Drew's room and noticed right away that he was oversedated. I was starting to notice a pattern: when Jovan was on duty, Drew was lifeless. I was very afraid that Drew was not safe with him, so I stayed as late as I could. My only solace was knowing that the nurses switched out every twelve hours and Jovan would be gone soon.

Drew's face was different. His peaceful look had transformed into a grimace. The wrinkles on his forehead had returned and were deeper. His hair was falling out. He had aged significantly overnight.

I prayed over him, "Dear God, please protect Drew from harm and guide the actions of others to help him heal. And please give me the strength to endure another day."

As I drove home, I grieved the woman who died. I felt a deep sorrow for what the doctors and nurses saw day after day for the past two years of this horrible pandemic. It was a revolving door of death. I hurt for all the Covid widows who felt helpless and locked out of their loved ones' hospital rooms. And I couldn't get the picture of that pretty woman's face out of my head; how sad it was that she died alone, without family.

My heart was breaking. I reached a level of despair that I didn't know how to process. This tragedy was so much bigger than Drew and me. It was everyone. And all I could think was, Drew could be next. I pushed that terrible thought away. *Unwavering faith, Maria.*

I couldn't allow my thoughts to go to death. I needed someone to cheer me up. I thought of an old friend, Kathy. And I realized that I hadn't heard from her since Drew got sick. *Oh my God, she doesn't know about Drew! I need to tell her.*

Kathy and I had been close friends for twenty-five years. She always had something positive to say, and I needed to hear her uplifting voice. I put my phone on Bluetooth and called. She answered on the second ring, sniffling like she had been crying.

"Are you okay?" I asked.

"Yes, I'm just sick. I got a booster today, and I'm not feeling well."

"Oh, I'm sorry. Well, I hope you feel better." I paused, not knowing how to break the news to her. "Kathy, I have bad news about Drew."

"Yeah, I know." She said, her voice suddenly flat and cold.

I was confused by her lack of compassion. It was not like her. "Oh, well, I hadn't heard from you, and I thought you didn't know," I said awkwardly.

"You know," she said coldly, "this was totally preventable. If he had gotten the vaccine, he wouldn't have Covid."

Her tone cut like a knife. Drew was like a brother to her. He helped her move from place to place. He was there for her when her husband left her, and was always there for her through her challenges, but now she was disconnected. I wondered how she knew he wasn't vaccinated. Was there a secret list of people who didn't get the vaccine?

"Are you saying he deserves to die, Kathy?" I asked.

Silence. After a long pause, she asked sharply, "What do you want me to say, Maria?"

"Just say, 'I wish you well.' Pretend you care," I said.

I found myself defending Drew. He was dying, and she didn't care. Where did my Kathy go? She was the girl who never judged anyone. I always tried to be more like her in that way.

I remembered how hard it was for Kathy, watching her father suffer when he died from cancer. He was a heavy smoker, and it was totally preventable. And yet, I would have never pointed that out as she grieved him.

Kathy was not the same person I knew. I had read about people changing through the pandemic. For some, the fear of death was so intense that their entire personality changed.

She remained cold and distant. I didn't know how to reach the girl I had known so long ago. There were no more words. I told her, "I love you," and hung up. I pulled the car over and sobbed, grieving the loss of a friendship that meant so much to me. I knew it would be the last time I ever spoke to her.

That night, Andrea, Dylan, and I were shell-shocked. So many bad things happened in one day. "She's lucky I wasn't there when you were on the phone with her; I'd have let her have it," Andrea said.

I put my head down in defeat, "I feel like I'm living in a bad movie."

Just then, I received a text from a strange number: "Hi Maria, I surf with Drew. I work at the hospital. Would you like me to help?"

I remembered Dr. Stan from last summer when Drew painted his son's surfboard. "Yes, we need all the help we can get. Thank you!"

Dr. Stan's offer to help was a beam of light on a very dark day. The Universe threw me one act of kindness to remind me of what humans are capable of: love and compassion.

I set my alarm for 6:00 a.m. so I could get Drew on FaceTime before Jovan the Terrible came in at shift change.

I tossed and turned all night. Kathy's words kept me awake, running like a bad loop through my mind. My heart was broken. I loved her dearly. And now, I had to let her go. I couldn't allow any dark forces in our lives right now. I finally fell asleep, and two hours later, my alarm went off.

27

THE CHOICE

December 7th, 2021
Hospital Day 24, Ventilator Day 13

I beat Jovan the Terrible to the iPad before the shift change. When the night nurse answered, she gave me great news: Dr. Q had ordered the high-dose Vitamin C IV. I was so happy it was finally happening! Drew would be given ten grams every twelve hours for the next five days. This gave me so much hope. I wondered why they finally gave in, and I figured it was to keep me quiet since I had been so demanding.

Raz came over to borrow one of Drew's paddleboards, the Rasta one with colors of red, green, and yellow. "I'm taking Drew's spirit in the water with me," she said. As she paddled out, she thought of all the things he taught her about life. He was like a father to her. She sang and prayed, and as she glided across the ocean, two dolphins emerged, playfully swimming beside her. Raz took that as a sign that

God was listening to her prayers. When she got out of the water, she filled a glass container with ocean water to take to Drew later.

I had just emailed the final hospital flyer edits to Matt for his graphic team when there was a knock at the door. It was a delivery of a beautiful arrangement of flowers in a glass vase. The card read, "I wish you well, Kathy." I felt a surge of anger flash through my veins. I picked up the vase, carried it into the backyard where the dumpsters are, and threw the entire thing into the trash. I couldn't afford to be reminded of her harsh words every time I looked at those flowers. I needed to keep my thoughts pure.

I shook the dark feeling off my shoulders and went back to my laptop, researching lung transplants. Everything I read said that Drew's condition was too critical to move him to another hospital. The risk of death during transfer was extremely high. I was also wary of the hospitals on the lung transplant list. None of them were allowing visitors, and I knew Drew wouldn't survive being locked away from his family.

Dr. Q called and told me he had great news. One of the hospitals he applied to, UHC, was considering taking Drew. They were one of the best lung transplant hospitals in the state and were doing their fifth transplant for a Covid patient today.

Then he sternly warned me, "If Drew is accepted for a lung transplant, you are required to give up all rights."

"What does that mean?" I asked, my stomach knotting up.

"It means that you will have no say in any of his care and that you can no longer question any treatment that he is given," he answered.

I took a deep breath. So, he would be their guinea pig—or worse, a prisoner. Giving up all his rights was not something Drew would ever agree to. I knew that.

Now my choice was this: let him die, or literally hand Drew over as property, without having any say over what happens to him.

The Choice

On the outside, I went along with what Dr. Q wanted–the lung transplant. If it was true that it was Drew's only chance to survive, I wanted it for my own selfish reasons.

But, on the inside, I was conflicted. The stipulations were a huge red flag. Something felt terribly wrong, but I couldn't put words to what it was. I had a bad feeling about it, and I needed more time to sort it out.

The decisions were getting too big for me to handle. I needed more help. Drew and I had trusted friends who worked in the medical field, so I started making more phone calls. The first was to Dr. Sue, a surgeon who worked with Covid patients in a large hospital in Seattle. We met her five years prior in Egypt and remained friends.

"Maria, I've been following your story on Facebook. I'm heartbroken over Drew," she said.

Dr. Sue sounded weary as she told me how painful it was for her to watch so many Covid patients die. She worked seven days a week, sometimes eighteen hours a day, during the pandemic. She wanted to save lives so badly. We talked about the lung transplant, and she agreed that he may not survive the transfer. I was hoping she would have a magic answer to save him; but she didn't. She promised to check in with me every couple of days.

Next, I called a Physicist friend who works with a team of doctors in France. Then, I had another friend connect me with an internist at the famous Mayo Clinic. And I reached out to a Covid patient advocacy group. I was building a team of advisors that I trusted. No one had the one magic answer I was looking for to save Drew, but they all offered me their medical expertise, and it gave me comfort. Over the next few months, every one of these people stayed in touch and supported me behind the scenes.

Later that day, I got a text from Dr. Stan. He was helping us with the hospital transfer. His text read, "UHC has promised to take him in the next couple of days."

Andrea and I broke down with relief. It felt like twenty pounds of worry was taken off our shoulders. Though, in the back of my mind, something nagged at me. For now, I pushed it aside. *Worry later, Maria. Let it evolve.*

And then, that night, the Universe smacked me in the face again. A friend texted me a link to an article written on a popular surfer's blog called *Beach Grit*. The headline read, "Iconic Surf Artist Drew Brophy on Ventilator After Being Hit by Covid, Family Turns to Crowdfunding." The subtitle read, "Surfboard artist to the stars is real sick, and it'd be nice to see him back in the water."

The article was written tongue-in-cheek, and one line read, "Was Drew vaxxed? He can't say." That one sentence brought out the trolls in droves. I read through the comments one by one, all by anonymous posters who wrote hateful comments about Drew being an artist "who probably doesn't have health insurance" and "being unvaccinated, he deserves to die."

The level of hate cut me like a knife. How could people be so cruel? This was not the collective energy I was trying to generate to save Drew. And if Drew ever saw this, it would kill him.

The Choice

Brophy and classic spray.

ICONIC SURF ARTIST DREW BROPHY ON VENTILATOR IN ICU AFTER BEING HIT BY COVID; FAMILY TURNS TO CROWDFUNDING TO PAY EXPECTED "SIX-FIGURE MEDICAL BILLS", "DREW IS FACING THE BIGGEST CHALLENGE OF HIS LIFE!"

By Steve Rees

San Clemente surfboard artist to the stars is real sick and it'd be nice to see him back in the water…

28

ACCEPTED

December 8, 2021
Hospital Day 25, Ventilator Day 14

I had trouble sleeping again last night. Between the hate comments in the *Beach Grit* article and Drew's transfer, I had a lot to fret about. I knew I should have been happy about Drew being accepted for the transfer, but now that it was happening, it didn't feel right to me.

The day started with a positive text from Dr. Stan, "Drew's numbers look better today."

"Oh, thank you for letting me know!" I texted back. "Can you go in and talk to Drew? Tell him that you're looking out for him. I know he can hear."

"If you'd like me to, I will." Dr. Stan's presence gave me comfort, knowing that Drew had one more friend looking out for him from inside the hospital.

Andrea, Dylan, and I celebrated the good news that Drew's numbers were up. Andrea joked, "It must be the high-dose Vitamin C!" She didn't really believe it would help, and she often teased me about it. The three of us snuggled with blankets on the couch while we had Drew on FaceTime, telling funny stories about Poppi. It felt good, all of us together.

I got permission from the hospital for Raz to visit Drew by saying she was family. In a way, she was. Raz wore her usual cute, funky style to the hospital: tight leopard-print pants, chunky-heeled shoes, and a movie-star white fluffy coat. I giggled, thinking about what the nurses must have thought when they saw her.

Today's Nurse, Lindy, had shaved Drew's craggy beard and washed his hair. On the iPad, I could see his face grimacing in pain; I found out that a few days prior, Drew had tested positive for a bacterial infection. This is one of the dangers of the ventilator. It can cause deadly infections.

Nurse Lindy had lowered Drew's sedation, and he was alert when Raz came in. "It's not your time, you know," Raz told him. Drew nodded. Raz pulled out the container of salty ocean water and dabbed it on his forehead, his hands, and his feet. "I know you've been dying to get in the ocean. This is the best we can do right now," she said tearfully. When she put the salty water on his skin, Drew's eyes teared up as if he remembered how much he missed the ocean.

Meanwhile, I was working at the gallery when a reporter from the OC Daily, a prominent newspaper, stopped in.

"I'd like to do a story on Drew since he's a well-known artist, and we can promote his GoFundMe," she said.

Being in the art business, I learned a long time ago that any press is good press, even if it wasn't about the art. "Yes, let's do it," I said happily.

Accepted

She pulled out a pen and a notepad and started asking questions, like, "When did he catch it?" and, "How long has he been in the coma?" and then she asked, "Was he vaccinated?"

"Let's not mention the vaccine," I said, thinking back to the *Beach Grit* blog and all the hateful comments.

"I have to," she insisted.

"No, you don't," I countered.

"My editor won't let me tell the story without it. If you want, we can write that you said, 'No comment,'" she said.

I closed my eyes for a moment and imagined the public response to just the mention of a vaccine. It was such a polarized topic that no matter what, it would spark hate.

I knew that any negative energy around Drew would harm him, that it could even kill him. I didn't want to risk any chance we had of making a miracle. It was up to me to make sure that everyone who thought of Drew wished for his recovery.

I stood up and said firmly, "Then, no, I'm not going to do the article."

She was surprised and tried to change my mind. "But it would get a lot of people to your GoFundMe."

"The way you want to write the article will create hate," I said. "I'm not going to let you do that."

I walked her to the door, and that was the end of that.

29

GOOD TO BAD

December 9, 2021
Hospital Day 26, Ventilator Day 15

For most of my life, I needed an alarm clock to wake up early. But now, I was automatically waking up at the crack of dawn, and Drew was the first thing I thought of.

I can't believe it's been two weeks since Drew was ventilated. I lay in bed thinking about all I've witnessed and why people are afraid of the hospital. Once you're sedated, you lose control over everything, and if they lock your family out, there's no one to fight for you. The Covid rules turned patients into prisoners.

That was the dark side. There was also a lighter side being revealed. Behind the scenes, Dr. Q was pushing to get Drew moved out of the Covid ICU and up to the CICU. In CICU, Drew would have normal visitor hours and a better standard of care. And best of all, it would get him out of the dark energy of the dank dungeon where everyone dies.

I looked at my "Pray for Drew" post on Instagram. There were now 2,500 positive comments from people who loved us. A large Instagram account, @Kookoftheday, reposted it, along with the professional surfers who were friends with Drew. Word was spreading out like wildfire now, and love was pouring into the comments.

This was precisely what I had been trying to do: inspire a large number of people to generate feelings of love and healing for Drew, so that those emotions would enter the quantum field—the part of the Universe that guides all matter through frequency and vibration.

It was as if I were a conductor of thought, orchestrating everyone to imagine Drew healed and healthy again. This was what it would take to make a miracle.

I called the hospital early in the morning. Today's nurse said that Drew had his third good night in a row. He is absorbing the oxygen better, and his nitrous has been lowered from 40 to 10, which is good. *Maybe it is the high-dose Vitamin C.*

I recited my healing mantras to Drew and played Jack Johnson songs. Then Andrea took over and talked to him, and then Dylan. Three hours went by, and we were still on the iPad with Drew.

A friend connected me with a surfer who had a lung transplant a few years ago. The guy told me that the transplant ruined his life. He was no longer able to surf, and he was dependent on invasive medical treatments for the rest of his life. He said that he would almost be better off dead and that he regretted it. I was surprised because it saved his life. This conversation was sobering; I knew that Drew would be very unhappy if he couldn't surf again and if he was reliant on the medical system for his very existence.

I spent more time researching bacterial infections, Vitamin C, and the next possible step, a tracheotomy. In layman's terms, this is when they extubate a patient, move the ventilator tube out of the patient's mouth, and poke it through the throat. This will eventually enable Drew to eat and talk, and they can discontinue the harmful sedation.

Now that I was armed with more information, I wanted to push for the tracheotomy, maybe before Drew was transferred. When Dr. Q called, I asked, "When can we get him a tracheotomy?"

He pooh-poohed the idea of it. He said that before we can consider a trach, Drew's lung collapse must be healed, and his blood oxygen numbers must improve.

Then, he told us we were not allowed to visit Drew today. So, Andrea, Dylan, and I drove to Drew's window and stood in the bushes. When we arrived, Drew's window blinds were open, but they had moved his body so that now he faced away from the window. I called the nurses' station and asked to turn him around so we could see him. They set up the iPad for us on the table next to Drew so we could talk to him.

The Respiratory Therapist moved Drew around a little roughly. The movement created a crash; Drew's heart rate spiked, and his oxygen plummeted. The three of us watched helplessly through the window as the monitor went into emergency mode and Drew's vitals plunged. We were watching Drew die right before our eyes. The alarms were screeching in the background. I kept saying over and over again, in a very soft voice, "Drew, you're okay. Relax. You are safe."

Nurses ran into the room, and we couldn't see what they were doing, but they stabilized him. It was so incredibly traumatic that the three of us were shaking. After the nurses got Drew settled, the sun had set, and it was dark. We drove home in silence.

I knew how close we came to losing Drew tonight. I desperately needed good energy sent to him. Before going to sleep, I wrote an update on the GoFundMe page to all the donors. I kept it as positive as possible.

"We appreciate donations, but please know that more important than that is your LOVE and GOOD ENERGY to be directed to Drew. I believe it is helping him. Let's get him home."

30

THE RECOVERY ROOM

December 10, 2021
Hospital Day 27, Ventilator Day 16

On the heels of last night's horrific crash, the roller coaster ride took a better turn. Today, we got what we had been asking for. Dr. Q had Drew moved out of the Covid Unit and up to the sixth floor of the CICU. Now we could visit him daily and never have to see Jovan the Terrible again.

Drew upgraded from a dank dungeon to a luxury hotel room. It was big and bright, and it happened to be the largest room on the floor. There was a huge window looking out over trees and a peek-a-boo ocean view. The equipment was shiny and new. This room felt good.

Andrea went to a printer and had large photos of Drew's life printed out. We plastered the walls with pictures of Drew surfing Pipeline, paddleboarding the Grand Canyon, family gatherings, and the most recent one taken of the two of us in Pagosa Springs. Every space on the wall of his room was filled with images of Drew's amazing life.

The photos would serve two purposes: when Drew came out of the coma, they would remind him of what he had to live for, and the medical staff would see that the patient in the bed had a life worth living.

This new floor of the CICU didn't have an iPad for us to use, so I went over to the Apple Store in the mall and bought one. Now, we had our own device, which always stayed in Drew's room.

It was Andrea's last day, and she was in tears, knowing she was leaving her brother. But the timing of the move into this new room was divine. She announced, "I'm naming this 'The Recovery Room.'"

When we got home from the hospital, a heart-shaped leaf lay on the front porch, another message from Drew.

For Andrea's last night, we had a slumber party. Raz came over, and the three of us watched *Sex and the City*, ate cookies, and drank wine. Dylan hid in the kitchen to avoid the show's dirty jokes, and we laughed at that. It felt good having everyone with me.

I wrote in the Dear Drew Journal:

> *You are now in The Recovery Room and it is filled with hope. Andrea leaves tomorrow, and I will be okay without her now. I have passed Covid Boot Camp.*

31

HE IS A SURFER

December 11, 2021
Hospital Day 28, Ventilator Day 17

We drove Andrea to the airport at the crack of dawn. At the terminal, I hugged her tightly. We had been inseparable for weeks, and now I didn't want to let her go. Andrea couldn't wait to see her family in Atlanta, but didn't want to leave us. She was torn between two different worlds, and both needed her.

In the afternoon, art collectors arrived at the gallery with a U-Haul truck to pick up two of Drew's big paintings. I was at the hospital with Drew, so I left Raz in charge. They bought a seven-foot painted surfboard titled *Tribute to Rick Griffin*, and an eight-foot by six-foot canvas painting titled *The Trip IV*. It was a big job getting the art safely packed, and Raz had to get help from two artist friends to build custom boxes. Normally, Drew and I would be the ones to handle a big project like this; I was getting better at relying on other people now.

While Raz was handling things at the gallery, I was at the hospital, focused on Drew. His bloating was more noticeable today. The air escaping his lungs filled up around his shoulders and neck, and now he looked blown up like a balloon. I was becoming familiar with new, scary words like *subcutaneous emphysema* and *pneumothorax*, a label on what was happening to his body.

Today's nurse was cute and friendly. She looked at the photos of Drew on the walls and pointed to a picture of him surfing Pipeline, the giant wave in Hawaii.

"Oh, he was a surfer?" she asked. I didn't like how she said, "*was* a surfer," as if he were dead already.

"No," I corrected her. "He IS a surfer. He will surf again." She gave me a surprised look, as if I were delusional.

Today's nurse lowered Drew's sedation just enough for him to be slightly awake. But he choked violently every time he needed to cough. I felt his pain as though it were my own. It hurt me, physically, and I thought about how unfair that was. I could feel it in my own throat, like acid dripping down to my stomach. It was torturous, and the only way I could turn it off was to look away.

Drew was the most alert I'd seen yet. His eyes were open, and he weakly moved his right hand, motioning to write. He wanted to tell me something. I handed him a pen and held the paper for him. I asked, "Are you in pain?" His fingers were weak, and the pen fell to the floor. He shook his head.

I kept trying to guess, but every guess was wrong. I said, "I suck at guessing, don't I?" He nodded.

"Do you want to get off the ventilator? Is that what you're trying to say?" He surprised me by shaking his head no. I realized then that my optimism about his getting off the ventilator was bothering him. He knew that he wasn't ready yet.

He is a Surfer

Visiting hours were over at nine, but I didn't want to leave now that he was semi-conscious. Finally, at ten p.m., a security guard came into the room. "You can't be here, ma'am," he said in an irritated voice. He motioned for me to walk out and escorted me down the hall, into the elevator, and all the way out of the hospital doors.

TODOS SANTOS
photo-LonnieRyan surfer-DrewBrophy

32

THE PORTAL

December 12, 2021
Hospital Day 29 Ventilator Day 18

It was December 12th—a date some of my friends refer to as "The 12/12 Portal." They believe it's a day when a spiritual doorway opens, allowing for transformation. Maybe that would explain why it ended with such an unusual and mystical experience.

The morning began like always: me on FaceTime with Drew, using my voice to keep him tethered to this reality. I repeated my mantras again and again, commanding his body to heal: *"You are healing. Your lungs are clearing. Every day, you are getting better and better."*

The house felt empty without Andrea. I had grown so used to having her constantly by my side. Dylan had moved back into his own room, and I had my bed to myself again. Now, it was just the two of us—Dylan and me—making all the decisions.

Still no update about the transfer to UHC, so I went to the hospital early to catch Dr. Q. When I arrived, he was just leaving Drew's room.

"Good morning, Doctor," I greeted him. "Hey, where are we on the transfer to UHC?"

Dr. Q looked sideways at me and answered with a question: "They want to make sure Drew isn't a Covid denier?"

I asked, confused, "What does that mean–'Covid denier'?"

"Someone who doesn't believe that Covid is real."

"Well, obviously, he believes in Covid. Look at him," I said, pointing to Drew's comatose body.

Until this moment, I had never heard of someone not believing in Covid. And, it surprised me that UHC asked the doctor to assess Drew's personal beliefs before agreeing to save his life. This wasn't just a red flag. It felt sinister. *Would Drew be safe in a place like that?*

I should have expressed to Dr. Q just how disturbed I was over this, but I kept it to myself. I wondered, *Am I crazy, or are things getting weirder and weirder?*

When I came home, I was cheered up by a giant gift bag left on my doorstep by one of Drew's art collectors. It contained a loaf of sourdough bread, lentil soup, crackers, cheese, and chocolates.

That night, I ate the chocolates and watched *Sex and the City* on the couch. And that's when something profound happened to Joan. To this day, its meaning haunts me.

Here I was, praying for guidance every day. Yet the most powerful, spiritual messages around Drew bypassed me and went to my friends instead. I suppose it's because I was so focused on the 3D world of decision-making that I wasn't as open to the messages as my friends were. Or, maybe it was because I was too stressed to receive them. I don't know.

The Portal

All I know is this: what happened to Joan that night was no coincidence. I believe it was directly connected to an otherworldly experience Drew told me about later—something he experienced while he lay in a coma.

Joan explained what she encountered like this: She was driving home from the grocery store, listening to happy music, singing along, when out of nowhere, she felt a crushing weight on her chest—like an elephant was sitting on her. She started gasping for air; it was hard to breathe.

Then she saw, in a vision in her mind, Drew leaving his body. It was as real as the steering wheel in her hands. He was floating away—leaving this earthly plane. It was happening. He was dying.

Joan gripped the wheel and tried to stay focused on the road as she screamed, "No, Drew, you're not finished yet!" She felt him slipping away.

She began to cry hysterically. Desperate, she shouted, "Drew, come back to your body! We need you. Come back. Come back now!"

Shaking as she pulled into her driveway, Joan turned off the car, bowed her head, and pleaded for help. "Archangel Michael, please protect him and bring him back."

She sat in her car for an hour, waiting until she felt the darkness lift. She knew something big had just happened, even if she didn't quite understand it. Was he gone? Joan wanted to call me right then and there, just to make sure Drew hadn't died—but she didn't want to scare me.

She waited until morning. "What's the update on Drew today?" she asked, trying to hide the worry in her voice.

"He's stable. No new news," I answered. She was relieved to know that he was still with us.

When Joan described it to me later, I was in awe of her mystical experience. But, it would take over a year for me to truly understand how this event fit perfectly into what Drew told me later was his "near-death experience."

33

NEAR DEATH

We don't know the exact moment that it happened, but Drew's consciousness popped right out of his body. He had a near-death experience, and this would change everything Drew thought he knew. He never feared death again.

Later, Drew described his experience like this:

"I floated out and immediately realized I was not the body. I was expanding exponentially and being sucked into a river of light. It was a huge release, like I had been set free. I was surrounded by billions of lights, and they felt like children tickling me, welcoming me back home. It was beautiful. It was like a remembering. All I could think was, *How did I ever forget?*

The experience I had on Earth felt like microdust. Whoever I thought I was seemed to be vanishing. But it wasn't. I was just remembering who I really was—a part of everything and everyone.

A larger light came and picked me up, and I had to totally surrender to it. It felt like my father, the way he picked me up when I was a child, and all I could think was, *Thank God, he's got me.*

The river started flowing faster, and it seemed to be spiraling. We were all moving in it together, faster and faster. Then, out of nowhere, a huge light came up behind us. It was intimidating, powerful, like a guardian. It hit us with a burst of energy, and everything went flying, spiraling out of control. It was swinging what was like a flaming sword or a lightning bolt, knocking all the little lights off of me. The powerful light pushed us faster and faster. The other lights couldn't keep up.

It felt like I was about to disappear, and right when I thought I couldn't hang on any longer, it pushed us out of the river of light, and everything stopped. We were in a dark, peaceful void of nothingness.

I was given a message: 'You have to go back. There's no time to start over.'

It jolted my awareness back to the small part of me that was Drew. I suddenly had a nagging memory, like I had forgotten a very important appointment. And then I remembered, 'Oh no, Maria and Dylan are waiting for me. I promised.'

Yes, I'll go back. I thought. But I didn't know where that place was.

Then I was told, "We're sorry we had to do this, but we needed you to understand. You're going to have to fight to live, and it's going to be brutal. You must build yourself up so that you can help the others."

Then, with the swoosh of a tremendous burst of energy, the giant light sent me adrift, floating into nothing. It was so peaceful. After what felt like forever, suddenly it was as though I was being sucked down a drain, and my energy was painfully squeezed back into a dead body.

Coming back to my body was like being imprisoned within a broken machine. Nothing made sense. I thought they sent me to the wrong place.

Later, when I came out of the coma, this experience reminded me that I was much more powerful than my body. It helped me fight to live.

I would lie paralyzed in bed, and say over and over in my mind, 'I am the light. I am the light. You can't kill me. I can keep this body alive forever."

34

AVIPTADIL

December 13, 2021
Hospital Day 30, Ventilator Day 19

No one had any idea that Drew had a profound out-of-body experience that would permanently change his perspective on life. To the observer, he was just another critically ill patient lying in a hospital bed in a coma.

They say that when you're in an induced coma, you're "peacefully sleeping." But that's a myth. Drew floated in and out of painful awareness. He felt the poking and prodding being done to him, and he couldn't cry out to let anyone know. He had terrible nightmares—so vivid, it felt like he was being tortured. He heard the conversations around him and remembers nurses saying he was going to die. I regret that I didn't know any of this until much later.

Drew had now been in the coma for nineteen days, and today they increased his sedatives yet again. Had I known better at the time, I would've asked them to lower the dose.

A new nurse was there, and as she positioned the iPad for me, she said, "Oh, you're the one everyone's talking about."

"What do you mean?" I asked.

"The wife who talks to her husband all day. I think it's sweet," she said as she left the room.

I wondered—*am I the only one talking to my loved one who's in a coma?*

I played music for Drew as I prepared a list of questions for Dr. Q. My doubts about transferring Drew were getting stronger. I didn't trust the plan for a lung transplant. I had a nagging feeling of dread about it. There were a lot of things that concerned me - UHC's question about Drew being a "Covid denier," and then the fact that he was too critical to be moved. A little voice in my head kept warning me that it would kill him. But then I didn't know if it was just fear taking over my mind.

A text came in from a friend, "There's an Infectious Disease specialist named Dr. Gibbons, who has a reputation for saving critical Covid patients. You should call him."

This was the third time Dr. Gibbons' name had been mentioned to me. I was getting so many suggestions, I couldn't follow through on all of them. But when something is said to me three times, I pay attention. I've found it's the Universe's way of giving me what I'm asking for.

I looked up Dr. Gibbons and saw that he had a busy practice, which made me doubt I'd be able to reach him on the phone. After all, Drew's doctors were nearly impossible to get ahold of. But I called his clinic and left a message anyway.

At the hospital, I spent the day staring at Drew's lifeless body. The nurse came in and out, checking the machines and refilling the drug dispensers. His skin was pale gray, and his hair—what was left of it—had changed from brown to silver. There was absolutely no movement, not even when I gently opened his eyelids, searching for

Aviptadil

a sign of life. The sedatives were too high again. He just lay there, like a rag doll. I was in disbelief that our lives had come to this. I held his limp hand in mine and talked to him, hoping he could hear me.

I missed Dr. Q today—he'd come in much earlier, before I arrived. My questions would have to wait.

Dylan and I switched at 2 p.m., and I drove to the gallery to get a few hours of work in. While I was there, I was happily surprised to get a call back from Dr. Gibbons. Although he didn't work at Drew's hospital, he was part of the same hospital system, and with my permission, he could access Drew's medical records.

He pulled up the records and then took a long, silent pause, as if reaching for the right words. "Your husband is a very sick man," he said.

I read between the lines. "I know, Doctor, everyone thinks he's going to die. But I am not accepting that. I'm hoping you have advice for me."

Dr. Gibbons told me about an experimental drug called Aviptadil that was being used on ventilated patients and was in Phase 3 trials. The drug had been approved for critical patients at the well-respected St. Joseph's Hospital and it had a huge success rate: over half of the patients on Aviptadil survived. This was incredible! As he spoke, I felt hope spring up inside me. It was like sunshine entered the room bringing new solutions into focus. If I could get this drug for Drew, he would have a chance.

Suddenly, I saw a light at the end of this deadly tunnel. This was the first significant piece of hope anyone had given me, and it was coming from a well-respected doctor.

But, the doctor said, there was a caveat. The trials only tested patients who had been on the ventilator for less than seven days. Drew was past that time period. But, I thought to myself, that only meant that they didn't have the data. It didn't mean it wouldn't work. I decided right then and there that this would save Drew.

Dr. Gibbons stressed that we needed to get it to him fast. Then he warned me, "There's a difficult process to get this approved."

This is where the Covid protocols got sticky. At that point in the pandemic, doctors who saved critical patients by going outside the protocol were heavily criticized for it. That's why most of them stuck to the rules—even when they didn't work. Despite the battle I had ahead of me, I knew that doing something different could save Drew, and I felt a new ambition take hold.

I thanked Dr. Gibbons and told him I was going to move forward on this. He gave me the name of a patient's advocate, Chris, who was experienced with Aviptadil. A patient's advocate helps people navigate the very confusing healthcare system. Surprisingly, some of the best advocates are not medical personnel; they are people who learned the hard way dealing with their own loved one's illness.

When I got Chris on the phone, he was incredibly helpful. He was passionate about saving lives because, just six months earlier, he had been his friend's legal advocate and fought to get him Aviptadil. But by the time it was approved through the lengthy process, his friend had died on a ventilator. He didn't want to see anyone else go through what he did.

Chris emailed me documents and a legal letter I could use to request the drug. While I saw hope in having a new approach, I felt a flicker of fear—I was still wary of all drugs. I needed to research it first.

Dylan understood complex chemistry and was a huge help. We sat at the kitchen table with my laptop and pored over the studies on Aviptadil. They showed that 60% of ventilated patients were alive and free of respiratory failure at 60 days, and that there were only two possible side effects: diarrhea and lowered blood pressure. Both were easily monitored. This was excellent news.

Aviptadil

Next, I texted our friend Nassim, who is a theoretical physicist and researcher. He forwarded the studies on Aviptadil to the doctors he worked with. Later, Nassim texted me: *I talked to my colleague who works with Covid patients in France. She said this looks very promising.*

Then I texted Dr. Sue and forwarded her the research on Aviptadil. She agreed: *This is worth trying.*

And suddenly, my hyperfocus kicked in, and I had one goal: get Aviptadil approved, get it administered, and save Drew's life.

35

VAX OR ELSE

That night, Raz came over and we heated a pot of lentil soup. It was nearly 9:00 p.m. and Dylan was at the kitchen table playing a computer game. Raz and I had just turned on *Sex and the City*, when my phone rang. The caller ID read HOSPITAL. My heart raced. There was only one reason the hospital would call this late—and it couldn't be good.

Raz followed me as I took my phone into the kitchen and stood beside Dylan. The three of us surrounded my phone, as I put it on speaker and answered meekly, "Hello?"

It was Dr. Q. His voice was hopped up, like he'd drunk one too many Red Bulls. He sounded anxious and talked fast—like someone was holding a gun to his head. He spoke loudly, almost shouting:

"UHC Hospital is making a decision right now, Maria. They're deciding if they'll take Drew. And they have just one question for you, Maria. It's a simple 'yes' or 'no' answer, and I need it from you right now."

He was talking so fast, it was hard to follow.

I took a breath in. This should have been good news, but it didn't feel good. Dr. Q's shrill voice rattled me. I felt my heart beat faster, picking up on his frenetic energy. Raz, Dylan, and I looked at each other, confused and frightened by his tone.

And then he blurted out, "Will you get vaccinated tomorrow? If not, they will not take him."

Raz let out an uncontrolled gasp. I gave her a stern look and put my finger to my lips for her to be quiet.

Dylan's face changed from worry to shock and then anger.

My heart raced and my mind went crazy, thinking that in order to save my husband, I would have to risk my own life by getting a medicine that my doctors advised against. I saw myself in the hospital, sick, not able to care for Drew.

I tried to keep my voice calm, though my body was shaking.

Dr. Q added, "Not just you, but everyone living in your house needs to be vaccinated. Tomorrow. And we need written proof that you did it."

He pushed hard for an answer, right this very second. "It's yes or no, Maria. What's it going to be?"

I felt dizzy. This was like a scene out of a bad movie. I tried to slow my heart rate down by taking in a few deep breaths in my nose, blowing slowly out of my mouth.

I spoke soft and slow, trying to calm him down and buy me time to think this through.

"Dr. Q, the reason I didn't get the vaccine is because three of my doctors advised against it. I've suffered from Hashimoto's Autoimmune for many years." I paused.

"What doctors?" he demanded.

"My Endocrinologist, my General Practitioner, and my Holistic Doctor. All three of which are in totally separate practices." I hoped that was enough for him to know it was too risky for me to take the vaccine. After all, my doctors were intimately aware of my health issues. He wasn't.

He pushed, "I want you to go to your GP and get approval for the vaccine tomorrow. Will you do that?"

It was odd that he wanted me to go against my doctors' orders. He wasn't worried that I could have a reaction that would land me in the hospital, either. Something creepy was happening here. Someone was making him do this. But who and why?

He needed to hear me say yes. He had to go back and tell whoever was forcing this that I had complied. I knew I had to tell him what he wanted to hear: "Yes, of course, I'll do that. But don't they want Drew to be vaccinated, too?"

"Drew has to wait 90 days until after his negative test before he can get vaccinated," he answered.

"Well, don't I have to wait 90 days also?" I asked.

"No, you didn't have Covid."

I said, "Yes, I did. I caught it from Drew. We were sick together."

There was a long silence on the other end of the phone. I wondered if Dr. Q was kicking himself for letting me into the Covid Unit without a test. Or if he was trying to decide how to deliver this information to the person holding the gun to his head. And I wondered how he didn't know I had Covid when Drew did. They seemed to know everything else about me.

Finally, Dr. Q said, "Go to your GP and let me know when it's done." And he abruptly hung up.

All three of us were shaking. Our shock turned to anger and then melted back into fear. It was absolutely terrifying that Dr. Q had pushed me to take this risk.

Raz said, "Oh my God, that was pure evil," as she reached for a big bundle of sage resting in an abalone shell on the table. She lit the end of it, and the smoke billowed thickly, floating high up to the ceiling. She opened the kitchen windows and waved the smoke into all corners of the room, releasing Dr. Q's crazy energy out of the house.

Shaking, I opened the kitchen cabinet for a bottle of red wine and opened it. I poured a glass for Raz and myself. Dylan put hot water in the teakettle for his camomile. The three of us sat, quietly stunned, reaching for words, but nothing came.

I was in deep, way over my head. I tried to sleep but couldn't shake off the phone call. I felt a black energy surrounding me. I was battling so much more than I could understand. I tried focusing on my breath to slow down my rapid heart rate.

Still tossing and turning at 3 a.m. I sat up straight in bed, put my hands over my heart, and said, "Dear God, please guide me to make the best choices for Drew. Show me what to do."

I heard a clear message, "Keep doing what you are doing. Keep loving Drew."

36

AVIPTADIL FIGHT

December 14, 2021
Hospital Day 31, Ventilator Day 20

I woke up feeling sick, still trying to shake off the darkness from the night before. Something bad was happening behind the scenes, and I was growing more afraid of UHC by the minute. I made a bold decision: I wasn't going to see my doctor today. I couldn't risk ending up in the hospital and leaving Drew without anyone to fight for him. So, I chose to do nothing—and leave it up to fate. Strangely enough, Dr. Q never brought it up again.

Then Dr. Stan brightened my morning with good news. Drew still had a temperature, but his oxygen had been reduced to 60%. And the doctors were now considering extubating him and performing a tracheotomy.

My hyperfocus immediately shifted to getting Drew Aviptadil. The sooner we got it, the better our chances of it working. Chris, the patient advocate, guided me through the steps. First, we had to get the medical studies into the hands of Drew's doctors. This had to happen today, since it could take days to get the drug after it was ordered.

The second step, Chris said, was to stroke their egos. "Many doctors are resistant to things they aren't educated on," he explained. "Help them get to where *they* think it's a good idea."

The third step was to use the Right to Try law to push them to administer it.

And lastly, never take no for an answer. Chris gave me a quick pep talk: "You will have to be strong. They will try to make this go away. You have to fight for it."

The process was tricky. Drew's doctors had to approve it, but the head of the hospital's Institutional Review Board—the IRB Chairman—had to sign off above them.

I spent the morning compiling the Aviptadil medical studies and writing a cover letter to the doctors. I printed everything out, made multiple packets, and sealed them in envelopes: one for the IRB Chairman, one for Dr. Steady, and one for Dr. Q.

I drove to the hospital and handed the packets to the receptionist. She didn't know who the IRB Chairman was or how to get a letter to him. I already knew she wouldn't be able to get anything to the doctors, so I walked the packets up to Drew's room, taped them to the wall, and asked the nurse to make sure the doctors read them right away.

Next, I did some serious detective work to find out how to reach the IRB Chairman. Google told me his name was Dr. Yamagata, and after several phone calls, I finally tracked down the address of his office and drove over. Luckily, it was just down the road from the hospital, on the fifth floor of a tall building. I walked into his suite, where a long desk stretched across the room with five receptionists behind it.

I approached the friendliest-looking woman and handed her a packet.

"Please, give this to Dr. Yamagata immediately—it's a matter of life and death," I said.

She smiled and promised to get it to him.

I took the elevator down, and my phone rang just as I was getting in the car. It was Dr. Yamagata. "I had an envelope slid under my door with a note that says it's a matter of life or death. How can I help you?"

I was surprised to hear from him so quickly. I told him everything I could about Drew's condition and about the drug that had promised to save him.

As I spoke, he listened, asked questions, and read through the medical studies I'd included in the packet. Then he said—much to my happy amazement—"This looks like it's appropriate for critical Covid. It looks promising."

My stressed body relaxed for a moment. He was the main person who needed to approve this, and he had just given his blessing.

I asked, "Will you approve this when the paperwork comes across your desk?"

He said, "This falls under the Right to Try law, so there's no need to go through the IRB. Drew's doctors just need to talk with the company and order the drug."

And finally, he added, "Tell Dr. Q to call me with any questions."

What a relief. Now I just had to get Drew's doctors to complete the paperwork and order the drug. How hard could that be?

I thanked him. I felt a surge of hope—one big win. YES.

As I was driving back to the hospital, I got a text from Dr. Stan: "Great news. They are preparing to accept Drew at UHC."

This was the news everyone had been hoping for. So why did it feel like I'd just been kicked in the stomach? A wave of darkness filled the space around me. I suddenly had a strong, gut-level knowing: if they transferred Drew to UHC, he would die.

Helplessness consumed me. I didn't know how to move forward, knowing that Aviptadil might save Drew—and the lung transplant might kill him. Drew's doctors were some of the best in their field, so why was my intuition screaming for me to go against them?

A Harley motorcycle blew past me, loud and obnoxious. I started to cry hysterically, holding tight to the steering wheel. I couldn't fight this battle anymore. My body heaved uncontrollably as I let go of weeks of pent-up tears, sobbing out of control.

What if UHC wouldn't let me see Drew? Los Angeles was too far away. Drew always hated Los Angeles, anyway.

I can't do this anymore. I was on the verge of a nervous breakdown.

I parked in the hospital lot and tried to pull myself together. I wiped my eyes and went in and sat with Drew. He was overly sedated again. A lump of flesh, just lying there. His cheekbones protruded from his face. He didn't look like my Drew anymore. He looked like an old man about to die.

Still taped to the wall was the Aviptadil packet, unopened.

37

BROKEN MIRRORS

That night, my friends Christina, Kim, and Raz came over with food to cheer me up. Dylan got up from the kitchen table and said he was going to bed early. I followed him out to say goodnight.

He walked into the bedroom toward a Mexican-tiled mirror that had been hanging on the wall for ten years. I poked my head in to tell him I loved him, and just as Dylan walked past, the mirror jumped off the wall and, in slow motion, crashed to the floor at his feet.

The girls came running in to see what the loud noise was. The mirror had a fist mark, dead in the center of it—like someone had punched it from behind. I carried it out to the side of the house by the trash cans, placed it on the ground, and sat in front of it. This mirror had been hanging in the same spot for a decade, and for it to jump off the wall like that was baffling. It was clearly a supernatural event I couldn't explain.

Another message from Drew. But what was he trying to say?

There was only one person who might have an answer. I texted Debi a photo of the broken mirror. "What does this mean?"

Debi replied: "Drew's pissed off. He can't surf anymore. He's stuck in his body and trying to get to you and Dylan. He says, 'I don't want to go to Los Angeles, I hate it there. I'm frustrated, and no one can hear me. I just want to hug my Maria and smell my ocean. I burst through the mirror, trying to give Dylan some of my essence. I don't know if I can make it, Maria. I'm so tired. I want to get out of this body, and I'm trying to move my legs, but they don't work. I love you, honey. Don't worry, that boy of ours will take care of you."

I felt such sadness, knowing that Drew was on the verge of giving up. I no longer doubted Debi - there were things she couldn't have known, like how Drew always called Dylan "that boy" and how much he hated Los Angeles.

Then she texted again: "Drew says, "My eyes hurt. They are so hot and dry. I feel heavy and full of metal."

I didn't understand the part about his eyes burning. But I understood the despair that Drew was feeling. I felt a pain in my heart, my stomach, my neck - all the places in my body that stored grief and sadness. I didn't sleep well that night.

The next morning, I woke up to a message from our friend Rich, sent from his home in Costa Rica. It was just what I needed to uplift me. He sent a photo of his nine-year-old son at their dinner table, his head bowed over a drawing he had made inspired by Drew's art. "We pray for Drew at dinner every night," the text read.

This was one of hundreds of messages I received from families who dedicated time every day to pray for us. For *us*.

Praying like that, for others, was something I had never done myself. *Why pray for us?* In all my life, I hadn't been given so much love. Maybe I didn't need it until now. Or maybe, now was my time to learn about the enormous capacity people have to love. And it was time for me to learn how to receive it.

Broken Mirrors

38

BURNING EYES

December 15, 2021
Hospital Day 32, Ventilator Day 21

Debi's message from Drew weighed on me. He was giving up hope, and that meant that I had to take more action. But what? I set up a consultation with another patient advocate, a nurse named Heidi, who was referred to me by a friend.

Heidi explained that common practice in the ICU was to limit paralytic drugs and do early ambulation of patients to avoid death and paralysis. But, she said, most hospitals tossed "common practice" out the window for Covid patients. She asked, "How much physical therapy is he getting?"

"None," I said. "It's just me and Dylan moving his wrists and feet. Should there be physical therapy?"

Heidi explained that because he was immobile for this long, his muscles would atrophy, and he would be paralyzed when he came out of the coma. I was shocked.

Drew will be paralyzed?

No one told me that. Now, I felt even greater pressure to push for the Aviptadil. *Be the squeaky wheel*, I thought. I called the IRB Chairman, notifying him that the letters had been delivered to Dr. Q and Dr. Steady. Next, I called the company that makes Aviptadil.

I was running out of time. If we didn't get this drug quickly, we would miss the small window of opportunity to heal Drew's lungs. It was the battle of my life, and no one at Hospital One cared. It was all up to me to push, push, push. Exhaustion began to take over my spirit.

Raz came over. "I'm taking you out to clear your head," she said. She drove me to a cliff overlooking the beach. A storm had just passed, and the ocean was chocolate brown from the rain; the waves were huge and full of surfers. The sky was blue, and the clouds were fluffy white.

The sun shone as we bowed our heads. Raz led a prayer for Drew. Then she grabbed a stick from the ground and wrote in the dirt, "We love you, Drew," in huge letters, with the word LOVE as a giant heart.

Later, when I went to visit Drew, his eyes were eerily wide open and not blinking. They were blood red, dry, and painful-looking. I placed my hand gently on his eyelids and pushed them closed like you see people do in movies when someone dies. But they popped right back open again. I remembered Debi's text, where Drew said, "My eyes hurt. They are so hot and dry."

Dr. Q walked in. I held a list of items to discuss with him. I read the first line, "It's important that you order the Aviptadil right away," I said. "The papers need to be signed so we can get the drug as quickly as possible." I gave him the hard sell on Aviptadil, telling him how more than half of vented patients who get it survive.

He didn't look impressed. Instead, he replied, "It will be tough getting approval for it."

I responded, "Oh, but I already met with the IRB Chairman, and he said it falls under the Right to Try law, and I don't need approval. You just have to sign the papers and order the drug."

Dr. Q's eyes widened. He was surprised that I had gone over his head and talked to Dr. Yamagata. And then he agreed to read the paperwork. He pointed to my checklist, "What else?"

"Can we do another round of high-dose Vitamin C and increase it to twelve grams? It's already helped so much—maybe more would be even better?"

He replied, "No, we can't get anything over ten grams approved."

But he did agree to order a second round of the high-dose Vitamin C, which felt like a win.

When I left the hospital, I called Chris. "It looks like Dr. Q is going to order the drug," I said.

"You have to stay on it. Don't let a day go by without that paperwork being signed. They will drag it out. I've been through this," he warned. And then he threw me some encouragement, "You're doing a great job, Maria. Stay strong."

That night, Raz visited Drew at sunset. She brought him a seashell and a rock from the beach and placed them in his hands. His eyes were still wide open, not blinking. On her drive home, Raz called me to say she was looking at the sunset sky and saw a beautiful symbol in the clouds. It was a pink and purple image of half wings, like a Phoenix, similar to one of Drew's paintings.

"This is a sign, Maria. He is going through a huge transformation," she said.

39

MONEY VS. PATIENT

December 16, 2021
Hospital Day 33, Ventilator Day 22

I stumbled across a podcast called *Walking Home From the ICU*, where medical experts talked about best practices for ventilated patients. In one episode, they explained a concept I'd never heard of before: the "sedation vacation." A daily break from coma-inducing drugs, it's designed to reduce long-term damage and side effects. I listened, frozen. They hadn't been doing this for Drew. Until that moment, I hadn't questioned the sedation. But now I could see how badly it was damaging his body. Still, I thought—surely the doctors knew what they were doing. Right?"

Later that day, after three straight days of Drew's eyes being wide open, they finally closed. Kim visited Drew and did a therapy treatment on him, as much as you could do to someone in a coma.

She called me afterward with a warning. "He's starting to show signs of drop foot."

"What's that?" I asked.

She explained that drop foot happens when the muscles that lift the foot begin to atrophy. It can be prevented by wearing special boots that keep the feet in a neutral position while lying in bed. If left untreated, she warned, it could become permanent—and Drew would never walk normally again. I remembered seeing the nurses put those boots on him sometimes, but not always.

"Don't worry, sister," Kim assured me. "It's not going to happen on my watch." She promised to come work on him three times a week. I felt incredibly fortunate to have a friend with that kind of knowledge, and who was so willing to help.

I spent hours again today trying to get the hospital to order the Aviptadil. I called the Human Research Department and was told a special form was required from California hospitals to request the drug.

"How do we get that form?" I asked.

"The doctor has to request it." More red tape.

I nagged Dr. Q to move it along. Chris reminded me, "Don't let a day go by without demanding action."

I was so tired of battling everyone. I was worn down and had lost so much weight. Food made me sick. My chest pain was getting worse, and my body was falling apart—my throat and stomach constantly hurt. But I had to keep going. If I slowed down, Drew would die.

I made more calls to make sure the paperwork was being processed. I called the IRB Chairman's office again and left a message. He was the only person at the hospital who believed in the drug, and I needed to stay connected with him.

Then I called the company that makes Aviptadil to let them know that the order was coming. Their receptionist referred me to Clinigen, the company that distributes the drug and works with the pharmacist to mix it. They told me that before the drug could be sent, they needed the signed paperwork from Dr. Q.

There is so much bureaucracy in the healthcare system. It was confusing, and I didn't know how all this worked, but I figured if I kept making phone calls, someone would help.

Next, I left a message for Dr. Gibbons. He always returned my calls eventually. But Dylan was suspicious of how helpful Dr. Gibbons was.

"Mom, let's research this doctor and see if we can trust him."

Dylan Googled his name and brought up newspaper articles about Dr. Gibbons being a whistleblower at a hospital that had stolen funds from patients. He was ostracized by some, paying the price for speaking up for what was right. In the end, though, the truth prevailed, and Dr. Gibbons won a lawsuit against them.

"It looks like Dr. Gibbons cares more about patients than money," I concluded. Dylan and I decided that he was someone we could trust.

Dr. Gibbons returned my call that night after a long shift with patients. He had been working seven days a week as an infectious disease specialist since the pandemic began. I put the call on speaker with Dylan, and the doctor answered our questions about Aviptadil, ventilators, and Drew's slim chance of surviving.

After an hour, I said, "We appreciate being able to ask all these questions. Will you send me a bill for your consultations?"

But Dr. Gibbons refused to charge me.

"Dr. Gibbons, you have been so generous with your time, and you don't even know us. Why are you helping us?"

He replied, his voice heavy with sadness, "Because I'm tired of seeing people die from Covid."

40

BEAUTIFULLY DENIED

December 17, 2021
Hospital Day 34, Ventilator Day 23

This morning, my sister Christine texted: "Been sending Drew positive vibes. I scream, 'Come on, Drew!' out loud at least a hundred times a day."

People were doing what I asked—believing in Drew's recovery. And their belief was helping me hold onto mine.

My inbox was flooded with messages from all over the world, each one sending healing intentions into the Universe for Drew. During my FaceTime with him this morning, I read a few aloud.

From our friend Nia: "Every blessed healing breath I take, I take with Drew."

And from Lexi in Australia, whom we met in Egypt: "I'm doing a distance healing session for Drew every day until he's better. You are both so loved."

As I read the messages, I was overwhelmed by how many people were actively participating in this fight. It didn't matter that they came from all different walks of life—Atheist, Christian, Catholic, Jewish. Drew's life force was nearly extinguished, the light inside him growing dim. But every prayer, every thought, and every intention sent out was like a tiny ball of light traveling through the quantum field, slowly refilling his life force.

I was witnessing a beautiful side to this terrible event—true love, not just between two people, but between all people, operating as one, even if unknowingly. I saw the enormous capacity people have for love by simply setting intentions for Drew to heal. I joked to myself that I was outsourcing my prayers and my tears! I had no time for tears myself. I had to stay focused on problem-solving, and there were still big challenges on my mind.

I got dressed and left for the hospital earlier than usual. Today, I was hell-bent on catching Dr. Q to get that paperwork signed.

As I drove, hundreds of thoughts swirled in my mind. All my life, my Attention Deficit Hyperactivity Disorder had made it hard to fit in with most of the world. It made me late for appointments, take on too many hobbies, and forget people's names. But now, it gave me the gift of being able to hyperfocus on one thing only: saving Drew's life.

I was beginning to appreciate my ADHD because it allowed me to think of multiple, complicated things simultaneously. While my mind appeared chaotic, my ability to juggle many thoughts at once enabled me to accomplish difficult things.

I thought about the lung transplant. Dr. Q wanted the transfer to UHC to happen as soon as possible, and I knew we were getting close.

I asked myself, *Will the move to UHC be best for him?*

As I tapped into Spirit for answers, I felt a pain in my gut. Every time

I thought about moving Drew to UHC, I felt kicked in the stomach. In my mind, I reviewed all the reasons it was a bad idea.

Moving him was risky, and he could die in transit. The new doctors at UHC didn't love Drew like Dr. Q, Dr. Stan, and Paul did. They had a bias towards unvaccinated people. They could hold that against him. I was warned that UHC would not approve the Aviptadil, which could save Drew's lungs.

And the worst thing was that once I handed him over for a lung transplant, my Federal "Right to Try" would be rebuked. Drew would become their prisoner, and I wouldn't be able to be with him if they didn't want me to. The thought of not being able to see Drew was terrifying. There were so many things wrong with this move.

When I arrived in Drew's room, he was heavily sedated again, looking even thinner than the day before. I asked the nurse, "Can we weigh him?" She told me the scale on the bed was broken. I guessed he'd lost sixty pounds. Later, I would find out he'd lost far more than that.

Dr. Q came in and said, "UHC is very close to taking Drew." Then he paused and firmly emphasized, "We shouldn't do anything to complicate the move."

He pointed to my medical journal and asked, "What questions do you have for me today?"

Ignoring his suggestion to avoid complicating things, I asked, "Did the paperwork get submitted to order the Aviptadil?"

He sighed heavily. "I submitted it, and we are waiting for the drug company. All the paperwork is done."

"Thank you!" I said. Then, hesitantly, I raised my concerns about Drew's transfer to UHC. "Dr. Q, I'm not sure about this move. It's risky."

Dr. Q's friendly manner shifted to one of agitation. He saw where I was going with this and knew that I had the power to stop the transfer if I wanted to.

He became very angry. His eyes got huge, and he said in a loud voice, "If we don't move him, he will die."

He repeated himself, yelling this time, "If we don't move him, he will die."

I put my fingers to my lips and said, "Shhhh, he can hear you." I pointed to Drew in the bed behind me and slowly moved towards Dr. Q to force him out of the doorway and out of Drew's earshot. He might be sedated, but I knew Drew could hear everything. I did not want him to pick up any thought of death.

Dr. Q ignored my shushing and shouted a third time, "If we don't move him, HE WILL DIE."

I got it. He wanted him moved because he didn't want to have this death on his hands. I couldn't blame him, but all I could think was, *if Drew is in your care, then he will die.*

While a part of me was afraid Dr. Q was right, I did not believe that Drew would die in this hospital. The move to UHC was more likely to kill him.

Dr. Q left the room in a huff. I stayed with Drew the rest of the day. He was completely lifeless, so I made a lot of calls. I called Clinigen, the Aviptadil distributor, for an exact delivery date and left a message. Next, I called the IRB Chairman and gave him another update. *I'm the squeaky wheel*, I thought.

I called Dylan and told him that Dr. Q said Drew would die if he stayed at this hospital. Dylan said, "Mom, we need to change doctors." He said we needed a doctor who was confident he could save him.

Dylan was right. I walked to the main office and asked about switching doctors. The woman explained that there would be paperwork to fill out. I said that I would think about it and decide overnight.

Changing doctors was a big decision. On one hand, Dr. Q didn't have faith in Drew's survival. But on the other hand, Dr. Q was a good doctor, and I knew he cared about Drew. I decided to sleep on it. There was an even bigger decision to make at the moment, and that was the question of sending Drew to UHC.

As I drove home, I went back and forth in my mind. Should we allow the move to UHC for a lung transplant? You have to decide, Maria. NOW.

The fear of making the wrong decision ran through every fiber of my body. Who in the hell was I to argue with the doctors on this? What did I know about lung transplants? Why was I questioning Dr. Q, who obviously knew more than I did? But everything inside me screamed *No! Don't do it.*

I wasn't equipped to make this choice. I looked up to the sky, "Dear God, take this decision off my shoulders. Please make whatever is best for Drew happen."

I handed it over to the Universe, to God, to the angels. I decided not to decide and let fate play out. And, at that moment, I felt a release, a dark energy, leave my stomach. I took in a deep breath and let it go.

Later, I called the hospital to see if they had a date for the Aviptadil delivery. The nurse told me it was scheduled to arrive in three days.

Then she said, "I'm sorry. I have bad news. We just got word that UHC has changed its mind. They denied Drew for the transfer."

A flood of relief spread through my body. I looked up to the sky and said, "Thank you." The decision had been made by a higher power. It could only be the right one.

A heavy weight had been lifted off my shoulders. I could breathe now. No transfer, no lung transplant. It felt right.

I wrote in my Dear Drew Journal:

Drew, I miss you. And I'm exhausted. It's so much work to keep you alive.

41

BELIEVE

December 18, 2021, Saturday
Hospital Day 35, Ventilator Day 24

Drew looked worse today. At any moment, he could slip away. I heard whispers that the staff was expecting him to die because there was nothing else they could do for him.

Drew's face grimaced in agony. Even while sedated, he could feel when the nurses changed his PICC line or moved him too roughly. He was locked inside his body, unable to communicate, and it was torture.

His tongue was raw, swollen, and bleeding from the ventilator pressing against it. It was so deformed and gross that I had to look away so I couldn't feel it. I felt his pain, and sometimes, it got to be more than my body could handle. His condition worsened every day, and the only way I could keep my faith was to pretend I didn't see what I saw and keep praying for a miracle.

Believe he can come back from this, Maria. Believe it, I kept saying to myself over and over again.

Meanwhile, locals from Drew's hometown in Myrtle Beach, South Carolina, were rallying for him. A screen printing business did a fundraiser for us. They printed a tee shirt with one of Drew's most popular surf paintings with the words "Pray for Drew" and then Drew's favorite saying "Life is Good," emblazoned on the front. A surf shop was also holding a fundraiser for Drew. Knowing how much other people cared uplifted my spirits. I knew I wasn't in this alone.

People just wouldn't let us fail. I felt a curious mix of gratitude and unworthiness. I was learning how to let people help.

Andrea called, and I told her I was going to change doctors. She was irritated that I didn't trust Dr. Q and hammered me hard with a line of questioning. "Since I left, things got out of balance," she said. "You lost your trust in the doctors."

I had to be careful with how I answered her. She and I had different views, and I didn't want to fight. The truth was that when she was here, I went along with trusting the doctors because I was sick, and I leaned heavily on her to help me make decisions.

But now that I could think clearly, I knew that blind trust would not save Drew. Too many people died under the Covid protocol; that was evidence to me that we had to do something different, or he would die like all the others.

But I couldn't tell her all that because I didn't want to argue. No one could change my mind, anyway. I was on a mission. I told her I loved her, cut the phone call short, and drove to the hospital.

When I arrived, Paul was holding Drew's hand and praying. The sight of Paul in Drew's room gave me great comfort. He was the person I trusted the most with Drew's life.

I didn't see any of Drew's doctors today, but the nurse told me they decided to do the tracheotomy after all, and they were having a trauma surgeon evaluate the air in his chest. This was the best news I could hear as it was a big step up from the tube down the throat.

Dr. Stan called me that night. "Dr. Q said you were changing doctors." He urged me to reconsider. I wondered how Dr. Q got word on that so quickly. All I did was ask what the process was. I was learning that everything I said, no matter who I said it to, got back to the doctor somehow.

I told Dr. Stan that I wanted a doctor who believed in Drew's recovery. "If the doctor doesn't believe that Drew will live, he won't take the action required to save him, and Drew will die." It's a simple equation, really. Belief leads to action, which leads to results.

Because they thought he was going to die, they over-sedated him, which led to paralysis, worse respiratory failure, and new health problems we were now dealing with.

I said, "I am going to surround Drew with people who believe he will live."

"Dr. Q does believe in Drew's recovery," Dr. Stan emphasized.

I paused as I thought it over. I knew that Dr. Q cared about Drew. And now that UHC was off the table, maybe he would shift his strategy.

And maybe, just maybe, this whole thing was divinely orchestrated to lead Dr. Q to a greater level of mastery as a doctor. Through this ordeal, we all learned our hardest lessons in life. Drew was a patient like none he had ever had.

I made the decision on the spot. "Okay, then," I said. "We will stay with Dr. Q."

COVID A LOVE STORY

> Last year on New Year's Eve I was at my friends house right next to his studio. I never met drew before in my life and the conversation I had with him changed my life and how I saw my future. Not everyone will understand what I'm trying to say, so I'll keep it short. He understood what I was saying and said I can do it. He literally showed me on his hand how to accomplish it. I have been saying a prayer for him every night since I saw the first post and I know he will recover Better than ever. He is a true artist/human

One of many messages on social media

PART TWO
Rebirth

CREATION
Artwork © Drew Brophy

42

SLIDING DOOR MOMENT

December 19, 2021
Hospital Day 36, Ventilator Day 25

There are pivotal moments in life when you're given a chance to alter the course of your future. Some call them "sliding door moments"—brief, fleeting seconds where a decision can change everything. Take the opportunity, and your path shifts. Let it slip away, and it's gone forever.

This was the day we were given one of those moments—an opportunity to shift Drew's energy from the brink of death to the possibility of life. And I almost missed it.

It was early in the morning, when a new nurse leaned into the iPad. "Hello! My name's Frank. I lowered Drew's sedation, and if you give me a few minutes, I'll sit him up so he can see you."

Frank lifted the back of the bed so that Drew was sitting upright. It was the first time anyone had sat Drew up. Seeing Drew sit up gave me a tinge of hope. He was almost normal.

"Hi, honey. Welcome back!" I said, elated as if he had just returned from a long trip overseas. The drugs were wearing off, and as Drew's consciousness came back online, his eyes opened wider, and his face started to show expression. He was the most alert I had seen yet.

"You're the first nurse to bring him back to me. Thank you," I said, deeply appreciating this simple act of lowering his sedation.

Frank was a serious, older Polynesian man—tall, strong, and a former military nurse with plenty of experience. He exuded confidence in everything he did and would go on to become one of Drew's biggest angels.

An hour later, Frank reappeared on the iPad. "This man needs to move," he said firmly. "I'd like your permission to move him from the bed to a chair."

"Is it even possible?" I asked. "How exactly will you move him into a chair when he's got all those IVs and a ventilator down his throat?

Frank pointed to a harness hanging from the ceiling. He explained that it would be placed around Drew's waist, and with the help of a few nurses, they would transfer him from the bed to a chair. "I've done this many times. I know how to do it safely," he said with confidence.

And then he emphasized, "If we don't move him, he will not improve." Frank was insistent.

My fears shrouded my good judgment. A memory flashed in my mind of that horrible day back in the Covid Unit when the respiratory therapist moved Drew, and it almost killed him, as Andrea, Dylan, and I watched helplessly through the window.

Drew could "crash" again, and the thought terrified me. Now that the tracheotomy was scheduled, I was leery to do anything that would jeopardize that.

"No, it's too risky," I said. Frank tried to change my mind, but I was stubborn.

Then, fate gave me a second chance to take the opportunity when Kim called me from Drew's room. "Frank said you won't let them put Drew in a chair. Listen, sister, we've got to move him," she urged.

"It's too risky, Kim. He might crash, and then they won't give him the trach surgery."

"Sister, if you don't move him now, he may never move." She pushed harder. "I don't care if you hate me right now, but I'm not going to let this go. You have to let him do it."

I said reluctantly, "Okay, but only if you're there. Please, will you be there when it happens?"

She promised she would.

I called the nurses station, and Frank was happy that I changed my mind. While it was happening, I was at home with my stomach in a knot. *Dear Jesus, please guide the hands of the nurses.*

Kim watched as Frank and four other nurses placed a ceiling sling around Drew's waist and very carefully, in unison, moved him and all his tubes, IVs, and cords from the bed into a giant chair, where Drew got to sit like a human being for the first time in over a month.

Kim texted me a video of Drew in the chair, moving one foot and swinging it ever so slightly, with Kim's sweet voice in the background encouraging, "Yeah, Drew, yeah!" Then she switched to her drill sergeant tone, "Drew, are you ready to get the fuck out of here? Let's go, Drew!"

When I arrived later, Kim was still there. Since two visitors were not allowed in the room, I snuck in and closed the curtains so no one could see both of us.

There my Drew was, alert and awake, thanks to Frank giving him a sedation vacation—a short break from the induced coma. It was a beautiful moment. I FaceTimed Andrea, and she was ecstatic as Drew showed off for her, swinging his foot.

My excitement was dampened, though, by the reality of how impaired he was. I never knew that an induced coma would paralyze your body. The truth was, seeing him swing his leg as if it were a big deal showed me just how bad it was. What did I think, that he would come out of a coma after a month and just walk out the door?

Drew's feet were very swollen and red with edema. Kim said, "I can fix that!" And she made a plan for her next treatment.

Frank texted Dr. Q the good news, that Drew was in a chair and moving his leg. But it was much more than that. Drew was conscious, and putting him in that chair gave him hope—I saw a spark ignite in his eyes.

This marked a momentous point in time where Drew shifted, ever so slightly, from dying to living.

Sliding Door Moment

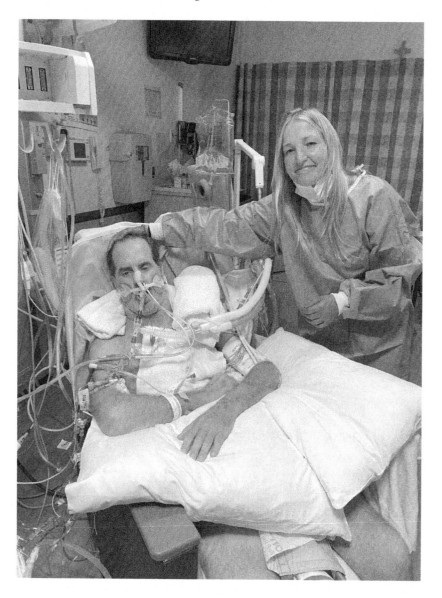

43

SO MANY ANGELS

December 20, 2021
Hospital Day 37, Ventilator Day 26

As the battle for Aviptadil continued, a new challenge emerged—they were reducing Drew's sedation again, and as a result, ICU Psychosis was setting in.

"Drew has been putting his hand on his chest in pain," the day nurse reported. I worried it was his heart, but she assured me that it was anxiety.

I asked, "Please ask Dr. Q what time the Aviptadil will arrive today." I wanted to make it clear to Dr. Q that I was not going to give up on this.

Then I called Clinigen to confirm that the Aviptadil was being delivered. But the woman who answered said, "We don't have any record of it being ordered."

I argued, "Dr. Q placed the order, and he said it's on its way. There must be a mistake."

She said, "We have no record of Dr. Q ordering it."

Now, I would have to confront Dr. Q again, and I was getting so tired of it. But I had to keep fighting. And I was getting better at it with practice, learning to push away the little voice in my head that says not to annoy the doctors. Drew's life was on the line, and my being disliked was not as important as saving his life.

Meanwhile, out in the Universe, our angels were doing the energy work for us. A local surfer named Tracy texted:

"My friends held a powerful 'Om' chanting circle this morning for Drew. As we focused on Drew's lungs opening and his health blooming, the cold air turned warm, and we could feel the energy from the sun flowing through us. Everyone sends their love."

More prayers were being sent by people we didn't even know, yet I felt connected to them through the shared faith in bringing Drew back to life. I was still working to shift my inner dialogue to allow the love in —to accept that, yes, we were worthy of it. Accepting help was something Drew and I both had to learn how to do gracefully.

And then a tiny miracle happened. When I arrived at Drew's room, he watched as I stood outside his door, putting on the blue gown and gloves. For the first time, he waved to me with the only body part he could move, his right arm. My heart leaped with joy. Though he couldn't smile with that tube in his mouth, his energy expressed that he was happy to see me.

Drew motioned for a pen. He tried to write, but all that would come out was a very messy "w." His eyes narrowed, frustrated.

"Are you trying to say you want to go home?" He shook his head. "Are you trying to say you love me?" He shook his head. Finally, I got to what he wanted to ask. "Do you want to know more about your tracheotomy?" Bingo. He nodded yes. When his sedation was turned down, Drew was fully aware of what was going on. I had to remember to give him information every day now.

I was learning a new language: how to read his eyes and energy. I began to sense when he was trying to communicate, understanding that it was up to me to pick up on those subtle messages. I noticed that the best nurses also tuned into Drew's nonverbal cues. Despite being on his deathbed, Drew somehow radiated an inner light through his eyes, making me love him even more.

Kim had warned me that we needed to move Drew's body daily. The only part of his body he could move was his right arm, and even that wasn't strong enough to hold a pen. The only thing I knew was to move Drew's arms and legs in a circular motion, and I did that for an hour.

I asked the nurse for a printout of all the medicines that Drew is on. "I can't do that," she said. So I sat next to her on her computer with my notebook, and she read to me, one by one, each medicine and dosage he was on. It took a long time; he was on so many drugs, including Fentanyl and Versed. This would become my routine every few days or so because they constantly changed.

The nurse started reading the notes on the computer. She read an entry from three weeks ago that stated Drew had less than a 20% chance of survival. I asked what his chances were now, hoping she'd say better. She said they were less today but wouldn't give me a number. Seeing the reality before me, I felt a bolt of fear but decided not to tell anyone. At that moment, I chose not to believe it and shook it out of my mind.

Dr. Q arrived mid-morning, a very different man from last week. He was extra attentive and spent more time with me. The weight of the transfer to UHC had been lifted, and now the focus was to save Drew, here and now. He told me that Drew had been approved for the tracheotomy, and he explained what to expect with the surgery. I liked this new Dr. Q.

I asked, "What time is the Aviptadil coming today?"

He glanced away as he said he was still working on it. I told him I was disappointed that it wasn't here. I reminded him that every day is crucial because this drug works best early on. He assured me it was coming, but there was more paperwork to do. "But, I thought it was all done?" I pressed.

After Dr. Q left, I called Chris for advice. He said, "I told you they would do everything they can to slow the process down. Don't give up."

Later that morning, they reduced Drew's sedation even further, and as the drugs wore off, he began to "wake up." His eyes shot open, and he looked at me as if to say, "Help me." It had been twenty-six days since Drew was placed in the induced coma, and they were slowly bringing him out of it. But Drew started to shake violently. Coming off the drugs wasn't going to be easy. Anxiety took over, and his heart rate spiked. I feared he might have a heart attack. I held his hand, speaking to him softly.

The anxiety escalated so much that the nurse had to increase Drew's sedatives again, knocking him out once more. As long as I've known Drew, he'd never experienced anxiety about anything. Later, I would learn that sedation can cause traumatic brain injury, and that many patients never fully recover from the anxiety that often follows.

Raz was the last to visit Drew. I asked her to do all she could to help his heart rate lower. She brought a crystal bowl into his room, sat on the floor, and played its soothing sounds. The nurse said this was the first time she'd ever seen someone bring a crystal bowl to the ICU, and she closed the door so the sound wouldn't travel down the hall.

Raz watched Drew's heart rate on the monitor as she played. Then, a song channeled through her in words she had never heard before. She sang as it flowed through her:

"Break away, break away, break away from fear now.

Break away, break away, break away from doubt. Believe you are walking out.

You will surf soon, for the ocean is calling for you to rise up now.

Believe, just believe you are healing now.

Hey ya, hey ya.

Perfect health surrounds you.

Vitality is within you now.

You are loved, and you are safe.

Find grace and patience, for you are coming home soon."

When Raz left, Drew's heart rate had lowered to 120.

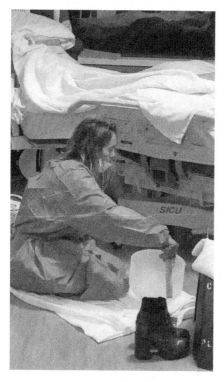

Raz singing to Drew

44

DREAMS

December 21, 2021
Hospital Day 38, Ventilator Day 27

Only one more day until surgery for Drew to get that horrible tube moved out of his mouth and into the front of his throat. If all goes well, he will be taken out of the medically induced coma for good. I sent a text to my prayer warriors, asking, "Please pray for Drew tomorrow at 7:30 a.m. when he gets his tracheotomy."

I wrote in my journal:

Today is December 21st, the Winter Solstice, the longest night of the year. Spiritually, it's a time of rebirth. Maybe that's why dozens of people sent me messages about their 'vivid dream' of Drew's recovery last night.

As if in a feedback loop, the energy people were putting out for Drew started flooding from the quantum field back to them, and many of them had dreams about Drew being healed.

It started in the morning when Dylan's friend dropped by the house. He told me, "I had a dream last night that I was driving past your home, and I felt Drew's presence. I looked into his eyes, and I knew, at that moment, that he was going to be okay."

Another friend dreamt that he ran into Drew at a party, and, shocked, said, "Drew, what are you doing here? Wow, you're recovered!"

Another dreamt that Drew was helping them paint a large canvas, and yet another dreamt of watching Drew surf.

Message after message poured in from people all over, each saying they had a dream of Drew doing something he loved. There were too many of them to ignore the magic of it.

But when I went to visit him, the reality was very different from everyone's dreams. Drew was completely unresponsive. They had increased his sedatives again, and he was lifeless. I moved his floppy arms and legs around, trying to get blood flowing for him.

When I saw Dr. Q, I asked about the Aviptadil. He said it was "being processed," and he changed the subject. Drew's heart rate was still high, and he advised against having Kim do any treatment today. One step forward, two steps back.

Dylan did the evening shift. He liked being there to hold Drew's hand at the end of the day. When I got home, a large bowl of homemade Brazilian chicken and rice soup was left on my doorstep by another angel friend. It meant that Dylan and I would eat again tonight.

I was heating up the soup when Dr. Q called. "I wanted to update you on the process for the Aviptadil," he said. "It's being reviewed by a panel of doctors tomorrow."

This was a great sign that he actually called me about it. Even so, the story had changed again.

"But I thought it was on its way. And, besides, it falls under the 'Right to Try' law," I said. "What changed?"

Dr. Q told me that the ethics team had to review the chart and discuss it with all of the doctors in his group. He assured me, "Once they approve it, the drug will ship that same day. It should be here by Friday."

We just lost another week! What happened to yesterday's shipment? Chris was right; this was a battle. They keep telling me one thing while doing another. We just lost more precious time to repair Drew's lungs.

I was so angry, and I felt like a fool, not knowing how to beat this impossible system. I had never been good at chess games. Why couldn't I figure this out?

Then I got a text from Dr. Stan that made me feel a little better. "Drew's surgery is first thing tomorrow, and my partner, Dr. Z., is going to take great care of him." For every complaint I had, there was an equal gift to celebrate.

Meanwhile, in the realm of the unseen, the forces of good were at work. Something big shifted for Paul. He later explained that he had always made a point of never bringing his work home with him, but he couldn't hide his sadness about Drew. Daylene had been telling him, "I know in my heart that Drew's going to pull through." But as a respiratory therapist, Paul knew that Drew's condition was terminal.

Then, that evening, on the longest, darkest night of the year, Paul had an unforgettable experience that shifted his belief. He had been distraught over Drew, and as he prepared for bed, he prayed intently for a miracle. In an instant, his heart was flooded with a deep knowing—a reassurance from God—that Drew would indeed live. Paul broke down and cried, and from that moment on, he never doubted it again.

3:15 PM

Hello just wanted to say that I've been praying 🙏 everyday for his recovery. I don't know him in person but his art changed my life. All I can give is hope and prayers 🙏 God is watching him and he'll be back to his family. Stay strong 💪 and happy holidays 🖤 God bless 🙌

🖤

45

TRACHED

December 22, 2021
Hospital Day 39, Ventilator Day 28

Today marked Drew's last official day in a coma—28 days in total. Early this morning, he was wheeled into surgery for his tracheotomy. I was consumed with worry, my teeth grinding again. Would he survive another day? I reminded myself that this was considered a low-risk procedure, but the reality was Drew was so fragile, there was still a good chance he might not make it through.

The sun beckoned me outside, offering a moment of calm. Dylan had refilled the birdfeeder in the yard, drawing a flurry of birds—gluttons, each one filling up on the seeds as they sang and chirped. The cool, wet grass soaked through my socks, but I ignored the chill as I lifted my eyes to the sky. "Please guide the surgeon's hand. Please let Drew respond well to this procedure," I whispered.

At 8:30, my phone buzzed with a text from Dr. Stan: "Drew did great.

No problems." Relief surged through me, instant and overwhelming. Dr. Stan had no idea how much peace those few words brought.

I wrote a list of things to do. Call Clinigen and ask if they heard from the hospital, ask Dr. Q about the Aviptadil delivery. Not one day was going to go by without me taking action on getting this drug.

On my drive to see Drew, I got a call from Mary, a longtime friend. Her sister was a nurse at the hospital, and she had heard that Drew was going into surgery. She bumped a travel nurse from the procedure so she could assist. She told everyone in the surgery room, "'This is my friend. Please take good care of him."

One of the medical assistants asked, "This is Drew Brophy, the artist? I'm a huge fan!"

"Drew was in good hands today, Maria," Mary assured me. "We all said a prayer before the surgery." So many people want to be a part of Drew's miracle.

Today marked a new phase of healing for Drew, and every phase had its good and bad. The promise of the trach was that it would allow him to speak and eat eventually. Now, the sores on his tongue could heal. He would be less susceptible to deadly infections. And his hands were now free to move easily. Once they get stronger, he would be able to work the iPad on his own. Oh, how I looked forward to not relying on the nurses to communicate with him.

When I arrived, Drew was in and out of consciousness, but his eyes lit up when he saw me. It felt so good to see him without that tube in his mouth. His eyes were greener today, the light from the window picking up a little sparkle in the iris. But his face didn't look like my Drew. His facial muscles were atrophied from having that tube strapped to it for so long. His expressions were not normal. I shrugged off a nagging worry that he would never look the same again. *Maria, stop being afraid. This is temporary.*

He had two new holes punched in his body. The first was in his stomach, for a feeding tube called a PEG, which feeds him liquid formula throughout the day.

The second incision was in the center of his throat, a new entry point for the ventilator. A strap holding the trach in place wrapped around his neck, like a dog collar. The site of both wounds was red and angry. His face winced in pain. He was suffering.

"Does it hurt?" I asked.

He nodded yes.

Dr. Q had already come and gone for the day. I left a message for him about the Aviptadil. I was determined to get it before Christmas, which was only three days away. I knew if it didn't come before then, it would be delayed even more because of the holidays. I put another call into the IRB office, asking for their help to push it along.

That night, I called Drew's iPad at 10:30 and could see that he was in pain. He never complained, but tonight, the grimace on his face said it all.

A new night nurse, Liza, walked in. I called her from the iPad and introduced myself. I told her he was suffering and asked to please give him pain medicine. She said she would.

But thirty minutes later, she still hadn't given him the medicine. So, I called the nurse's station and was told that Liza had gone on break. I begged the nurse to give Drew medicine, but she said that only Liza was allowed to do so. It was another hour before Liza came back.

When Drew finally got his pain meds, I could stop worrying, and we said goodnight.

As I lay down to sleep, I wrote in the Dear Drew journal:

I am so happy I can see your face now. And, there's only one thing I want for Christmas. I want to hear you say, "I love you."'

46

CHRISTMAS MIRACLE

December 23, 2021
Hospital Day 40, Ventilator Day 29

I didn't sleep last night because I couldn't get Drew's pained face out of my head. At 6 a.m. I made my usual morning call to Drew. Nurse Liza answered and refused to let me FaceTime him. "But I talk to him every morning at this time," I argued. She hung up on me. I felt a rush of anger mixed with separation anxiety.

The warrior part of me that had been newly awakened rose up. I had to protect Drew from anyone who did not care about him. I decided to make sure that Nurse "Ratchet" Liza was never allowed to see Drew again. I skipped the shower and put on my uniform of skinny jeans, black boots, and a v-neck sweater, and drove fast. I wanted to be there right when visiting hours started.

I went straight to the head nurse and made a formal complaint about Nurse Liza. The head nurse assured me that Liza would never be assigned to Drew again.

Drew was in more pain today. His face was contorted, wincing from his stomach tube and his trach, both fresh wounds. He had gurgling sounds coming from deep inside his throat. It was torture for him to endure, and I felt his pain.

I thought he would be able to talk now, but I was disappointed to find out that he was weeks away from that. Speaking required a special trach piece and a speech therapist. I wouldn't be hearing him say, "I love you," anytime soon.

Drew pointed to his stomach and winced. He was nauseous. I prayed he didn't throw up because if it got in his lungs, it would cause another infection—the kind that kills you. I asked the nurse to give him medicine for the nausea.

A new thing started happening. Drew would choke on mucus balls coming up from his lungs. It required the nurse to stick a long, skinny suction tube down his throat, into his lungs, and suction it out. It was horrific to watch. He gagged and convulsed each time.

When Dr. Q came in, he had a new energy about him. Something had shifted, and his voice sounded hopeful for the first time. He said, "All things considered, Drew is doing extremely well." He looked at me with intensity and declared, "It's a Christmas miracle."

I allowed that to soak in for only a minute. Yes, it is a miracle. But I can't rest now. There's still so much more to do.

I switched focus to my obsession, "Has the Aviptadil been ordered?"

I was a broken record with the Aviptadil, and every day, there was a different story. Today, Dr. Q's story was that the hospital had contacted the manufacturer, and it had been approved by the IRB, and they requested it from Clinigan. He said that it may ship today.

I wasn't taking any of this at face value since the drug has been "on its way" for a while now. I felt alone on the front lines of a big battle. It was little ol' me against a Goliath of a system.

After he left, I called Chris. "I'm not sure I'm smart enough to navigate what I'm up against. It's as though they are trying to stop me from getting this drug."

"Don't give up, Maria. Keep making phone calls. Don't let your foot off the gas," he encouraged. He gave me the push I needed to keep going.

Next, I called the IRB office. The receptionist knew me on a first name basis now. I asked her where we were with the ordering process. She said that the paperwork was in a "bottleneck" with the hospital administration. I told her that I needed help figuring this out. She gave me the number of a woman named Catalina, who was the Clinical Research Coordinator, and she was directly involved in processing the paperwork.

I called and was surprised when she answered. Her voice was friendly and kind. "I know of your husband's art," she said. "I heard about Drew's condition. I've been praying for him. I'm happy to help." This was a big win. Now, I had one person on my side who knew what was going on, and she cared about Drew. She ended up being my biggest ally.

On the drive home, I stopped at the mall. Christmas was in two days, but I didn't feel like celebrating without Drew. I knew I should try to make it nice for Dylan, so I bought him two long-sleeve shirts, a cute little black dress for Raz, and a pair of Olukai slippers lined with sheepskin and a nice pair of sweatpants for Drew.

When I got home, I checked the mailbox. A few pieces of junk mail, a bill from the Gas & Electric Company, a Venus Clothing catalog. Then I saw an envelope that had been hand-delivered. On the front it said, For Drew and Maria Brophy. I opened the mystery envelope, and inside was a check for $5,000 with a note attached that read, "We are praying for you and Drew."

I felt a deep gratitude. *What is it about this story that's inspiring so many people to help?*

It was a question I asked over and over again.

47

"I LOVE MY WIFE"

December 24, 2021
Hospital Day 41, Ventilator Day 30

At 6 a.m., the night nurse told me Drew's stomach was sick again. Through the iPad, I could see that his facial muscles were returning. Though he couldn't speak, he moved his lips slowly and deliberately, saying, "I love my wife. I love my wife. I love my wife." Christmas came a day early! This was all I wanted.

Today, Dylan gave Drew a black marker and white paper, and he wrote a big messy R, and then, because his wrist was weak, he wrote another letter on top of it, an O. Then on top of that, a C. Then a K. Next, Drew mouthed, "Rock." It took Dylan a moment to figure out that Drew was asking for the rock on the windowsill, the one Raz brought from the ocean. Dylan placed it in his hand, and Drew closed his eyes, smiling.

When I arrived in the afternoon, Drew was still holding the rock. I brought Christmas gifts for the staff. For Dr. Q, I brought a good bottle of Pinot, a red wine that one of the nurses had told me he liked. I included a "Pray for Drew" tee shirt in the bag and a handwritten note, "Thank you, Dr. Q, for caring for Drew."

For the staff, I brought a large box of mini surfboards and stickers with Drew's art on them. I placed the box on the nurse's desk outside of Drew's room and put a note on it that read, "A Christmas gift from Drew Brophy. Please help yourself." All day, the staff would walk by and happily grab goodies out of the box.

Drew was gagging on mucus bombs again today. The nurse showed me how to suction it, but I hated doing it. You had to shove it deep into the lungs to clear it out, and it was excruciating to put that thing down his throat as he gagged uncontrollably. It put me further on edge, my body being pushed past its limit of stress.

When Dr. Q came in, I handed him his Christmas present. He was surprised. "And all I want from you is that Aviptadil!" I half-joked.

"Well, then, Merry Christmas," he said, as he handed me paperwork to sign. It was the consent forms for the Aviptadil, the final step needed to order it. I was so happy.

What happened next surprised me. Dr. Q looked into my eyes and said, with great sincerity, "Thank you for being Drew's advocate. Thank you for fighting for him."

I couldn't believe that he was thanking me, even though I had been the biggest pain in his neck. But I knew he meant it.

That night, Raz spent the night so that we could all wake up together on Christmas morning. At midnight, my phone rang, "At last..."

The night nurse said, "Drew asked me to call you. But first...we had a setback. Drew threw up and some got past his trach. We had to raise his oxygen back up to 60%."

"What's causing this?" I asked. She didn't know.

"I Love My Wife"

Ever since he got the PEG, something was making him sick. But what?

The nurse set up the iPad. I asked him, "Are you in pain?" He shook his head no. I could see by the grimace on his face that he was lying.

I told him I was so happy he asked to call me. He mouthed back, "I love you."

I felt a little flutter in my belly; it reminded me of when we first met, and he could melt me with his smile. Only now, my love for him ran deeper than ever.

48

CHRISTMAS DAY

December 25, 2021
Hospital Day 42, Ventilator Day 31

Dylan woke up early and built a fire in the wood-burning stove in the living room. It set a nice mood for Christmas Day. When Dylan was just five years old, Drew taught him how to carefully stack the wood, add kindling and paper, and then light the fire. Most of our winter nights were warmed with a wood fire, and by age six, Dylan was in charge of building them.

At 8 a.m., Etta James' "At Last..." rang. I placed the phone on a tripod and set it on the living room table so Drew could watch the fire.

Dr. Q came into Drew's room and talked into the iPad. "We had a setback last night," he said, talking about the incident where Drew's throw-up got past the trach. He said they would run cultures and watch to see if Drew gets an infection in the lungs from it. I knew this could be serious, but I tried not to allow this bad news to ruin my day. Drew is healing, I reminded myself.

Dylan, Raz, and I opened presents as Drew watched on FaceTime. When we were finished, we got hungry, but everything in town was closed, so we foraged for food in the house. I picked oranges off the tree in the backyard and made fresh squeezed orange juice. Dylan whipped up some French toast, and Raz made a sweet potato dish.

It was now 1 p.m., and we still had Drew on the tripod. He motioned with his arm for me to come. He was tired of me taking my sweet time today.

"Okay, I'm coming now," I said.

When I arrived, Drew was shaking from an anxiety attack due to ICU Psychosis. I've lived with my own anxiety and learned how to deal with it without medicine, so I coached Drew on how to use his mind to calm down.

"Say to yourself, 'I am safe. Everything is going to be okay,'" I held his hand and stroked his head.

He mouthed, "I love you."

Dylan came, and the nurse looked the other way while we broke the "one person only" rule. We closed the curtains so no one could see the two of us in there.

Drew mouthed, "Call Mom." We called Drew's mom to say Merry Christmas. Then we called Andrea. It was her first time seeing Drew since the tracheotomy.

"I'm so happy I can see your face," she said.

Drew was exhausted after two phone calls and suddenly looked sad and defeated. Dylan sat on one side of the bed, and I was on the other, holding Drew's hands. We were quiet, but I could read Dylan's face. He wanted to make Drew feel better, but he didn't know how.

We were like three peas in a pod; Dylan went everywhere with us when he was little. We took him traveling all over the world on surf

Christmas Day

trips and even to our business events. Now, it felt surreal that our adventurous lives had come to this.

Drew's expression was somber. He motioned for a pen and paper and began writing messy letters, stacking them on top of each other. But we could make out the words, and it felt as though he was saying goodbye.

"Take care of Mom," his shaky handwriting read.

Dylan spoke softly, "I will, Dad."

Was he giving Dylan a final directive to take care of me? *Oh, hell, no.*

I said firmly, "No, Drew, YOU will take care of me."

49

THE OTHER SIDE

December 26, 2021
Hospital Day 43, Ventilator Day 32

When I arrived in the morning, Drew's mouth opened wide in a yawn. It was the first time I had seen him perform such a normal, human function in weeks, and it brought a small, unexpected burst of happiness.

But the relief was fleeting. He had thrown up again, and his fresh wounds were sore. And suddenly, he started to gasp for air. Something was malfunctioning and he fought to breathe. He was in agony, and all I could do was hold his hand, feeling helpless.

Like an angel, Paul walked in at the perfect time while on his lunch break. I waved him over in a panic to help.

Paul suctioned Drew's lungs and trach and fiddled with the controls. He discovered that Drew wasn't tolerating the normal ventilator settings. Paul was determined to figure out what would work. He spent over an hour trying different settings until he found one that allowed Drew to breathe, called CPAP. If it weren't for Paul, Drew might have died right then and there.

The CPAP setting was questioned by all the doctors because patients on high support like Drew aren't supposed to be on it. But it was the only setting that Drew could breathe easily on. Paul would argue, "Throw out your textbook. Drew isn't like all the other patients."

It seemed like all the things that didn't fit "the norm" were what was saving Drew. The therapists assigned to Drew never had enough time to fiddle with the settings to figure it out. And let's be honest, most people follow "the norm," not their own intuition. I'm not blaming them. It takes out-of-the-box thinking combined with absolute love to put that much effort into figuring it out.

Still shaking from the fright of being unable to breathe, Drew motioned for a pen. His handwriting was getting better. He wrote, "I'm dying."

"No, you're not," I said matter-of-factly, even though I was shaken up inside.

I looked at Paul, "Please give him proof that he's not dying." Words cast spells, and I won't let him use the D word.

Paul gave Drew the facts on his heart rate and oxygen levels, and he explained how the sedation was causing panic attacks.

Drew wrote, "Why am I paralyzed?"

Oh, my God— I suddenly realized he didn't know he had been in a coma for four weeks, and that the time spent in it had atrophied every muscle in his body.

Paul explained, "You were put on the ventilator a month ago."

Drew started to tremble. The realization that he had been in a coma for a month shocked him.

Afraid he would have a psychotic break over this news, I squeezed his hand and assured him, "It's okay, Drew. You have to get your mind to surrender to it. Can you do that?"

He nodded.

It was a rough afternoon. Drew complained about his stomach, and at times, his choking fits would be so violent that I feared he would die right then and there.

After some time, Drew's nausea passed, and his energy took a dramatic shift from being filled with pain to being filled with love. Now that he was feeling better, he started mouthing words as I read his lips.

"Tommy, Tommy, Love," he mouthed.

I asked, "Do you want me to tell your brother Tommy that you love him?"

He nodded yes.

Then he went on to say the name of every family member, ending with the word love.

"You will be able to tell them yourself very soon," I said.

Just then, Dr. Q came into the room.

Drew mouthed, "Tell Doctor I love him."

"Dr. Q," I hollered to the front of the room, "Drew said to tell you he loves you!"

Dr. Q hollered back, "I love you too, Drew!"

Then Dr. Q told us that he was going on vacation for a week and will be gone when the Aviptadil arrives. A Dr. Pittman would be administering it. I was disappointed to have a different doctor for something so important.

After Dr. Q left, Drew wrote, "I went to the other side. I saw everyone and everything."

"You had a near-death experience?" I leaned in closer.

"I saw Poppi. I saw everyone is one. All connected." He motioned with his hand and wrote that there were waves of energy and lots of colors.

He wrote, "No more anger."

I thought about Drew losing that edge of anger that he had. Most people weren't close enough to him to see it, but I knew it well. He got mad at the injustice in the world. If he saw someone being bullied, his anger would flare up, and he would protect them, even if he didn't know them.

His eyes started to tear up. "I saw all the prayers," he wrote. "I felt all the love." I wondered how it was possible that thousands of people had sent him healing energy, and he had seen it in his near-death experience. A little part of the miracle revealed itself to me.

He became very emotional and started to cry. I asked him if he was crying because of the intensity of the love he saw. He nodded yes.

50

FALLING IN LOVE

December 27, 2021
Hospital Day 44, Ventilator Day 33

I hired Ren's Tree Service to remove the bamboo that had been leaning against the backyard fence I planned to replace. That bamboo had been a source of argument between Drew and me for years. I wanted it removed but he refused. He had planted it to block out the neighbors, but the thing about bamboo is, it grows fast and is nearly impossible to control. What started as a little shoot had turned into a chaotic mass, pushing against our fence and the power lines above. It had to go.

Now that Drew was alert, he demanded that one of us be there every moment of visiting hours. Dylan was on the morning shift today. He brought Drew's favorite sore-muscle tool, the "pounder," as Drew called it—the Hypervolt, a percussion device used to massage muscles. Dylan gently ran it over Drew's thighs and calves.

Today, we had a new nurse, another angel. Tina had been saving patients for thirty years. This was her calling. She was a buxom brunette, strong and sure of herself. She never stopped smiling. When she spoke, she sounded like she was singing.

Nurse Tina introduced herself, "Helloooo, Drew," she sang. Drew raised his arm and waved.

Tina looked at all the photos on the walls and asked, "Oh, you're a surfer?"

I noticed immediately that she didn't talk to him like he was dying. She spoke of his life in the present tense, unlike the others.

He nodded. She pointed to the photo of him paddleboarding on the Colorado River. "Tell me the story," she said.

I told her about the time, back in 2011, when Drew and his friend, a whitewater expert, became the first people ever to stand-up paddleboard the entire 225 miles of the Colorado River through the Grand Canyon. Drew had no river or rapid experience, and that year was the most dangerous: the water was running at its highest in 28 years, and the rapids were treacherous. Park rangers tried to turn them away, but Drew and Seth went anyway. It took them sixteen days, sleeping in tents on riverbanks and paddling through some of the biggest water the Grand Canyon had ever seen.

Tina sang, "Drew, you are a serious athlete!"

Drew and I spent the rest of the day together getting to know each other in a new way. It was the first time we'd had this kind of quality time—no electronics, no people, no distractions. We were fully present with each other, and I was getting good at sensing his thoughts before he even wrote them down. I started to know what he wanted before he asked. For the first time, I was seeing Drew's true energy and soul—clearly and completely.

Even trapped in a broken body, Drew radiated a light that pulled everyone in. He wasn't the surfer or the artist he had once identified

Falling in Love

as—those things needed a body. Now, he was pure light. Pure love. And it couldn't be stamped out.

As the sun set outside the window, I felt full of love. For this tiny sliver of time, I was completely content. Drew meant more to me now than ever before.

I felt his hand rub my back, and my heart fluttered. It was the first time he had touched me since he got sick.

I was falling in love with him all over again.

Drew Brophy SUPPING Lava Rapids Colorado River

51

FIGHTS

December 28, 2021
Hospital Day 45, Ventilator Day 34

Drew and I spent the morning together on the iPad. I was getting better at reading his lips, and it felt like we were discovering each other all over again. I felt giddy, like middle school puppy love. I loved the attention Drew was giving me—right now, I was the most important thing in his world. And it felt really, really good.

I asked the nurse to leave a message for Dr. Pittman. "Please ask him to call me with the status of the Aviptadil delivery," I said. With Dr. Q gone, I had to start setting expectations with this new doctor.

Dylan went to Drew for the morning shift, and I went to the gallery to do payroll. Raz was receiving a huge commission check this month for all the art sold, and I gave her an extra bonus. We sold more art in December than we had ever sold in one month. Now that Drew was on his deathbed, the money was rolling in. It seemed unfair that he couldn't enjoy it.

It was now 11 a.m., and I still hadn't heard back from Dr. Pittman. I called Catalina, the Clinical Research Coordinator, and asked how the Aviptadil would be administered. She explained that it was a twelve-hour infusion by IV, each day for three days. She said that it was being delivered to the Pharmacist today and would be ready for Drew tomorrow. I was both excited and nervous.

Later, I went in to visit Drew. I was happy to see that Tina was our nurse again today.

"Good morning, Mrs. Brophy. Your man is doing great today," She sang in her sunshiny voice.

I pulled down my mask and gave Drew a big smile. "Hi, honey!" I said. He motioned for me to come over to him. When I did, he pulled me in and hugged me with his good arm.

Just then, Dr. Pittman walked in. He was a short man in his late sixties, with a Hitler-like mustache that peeked out from under his mask. His body was wiry, and he moved quickly, slipping on a blue gown and gloves with practiced speed. He stopped about five feet from the bed, gave Drew a quick glance, then walked over to the computer and started typing his report.

I waited until he was finished. "Good to meet you, Doctor. I'm Drew's wife, Maria." He didn't answer me back.

"I left you a message this morning," I said. "Can you confirm if the Aviptadil is coming today?"

He answered curtly, "Tomorrow." Then, he briskly walked out of the room. I had more questions, and I thought I'd ask when he came back. But he never came back.

Paul stopped in on his way up to the NICU. "What's up, Drew?" Paul asked. He pulled his blue gown down to show Drew what he was wearing. It was a Pray for Drew tee shirt. Drew gave him a thumbs up.

Paul read while Drew scribbled a description of his near-death experience on a piece of paper. His eyes were watering as he wrote about what he saw on the other side. He wrote "My true fear is being separated from source."

Nurse Tina updated me on Drew's status. Today, they removed his Arterial line, a tube that had been inserted in his groin so that they could take blood gas readings. They took him off of the fentanyl completely, a drug that really shouldn't be used long-term, though Drew was on it for weeks. Drew still had a chest tube, and it couldn't be removed until the air leak in his lung healed.

Tina told me that I needed to choose a Long Term Rehabilitation Center (LTAC) for Drew to go to next. The ICU at the hospital was only meant for short-term care, and it was time for Drew to move on. She handed me a list of local LTACs.

I told her I was worried he was developing drop foot and that Drew hasn't had any physical therapy except for Kim working on him. Tina said, "I'll see what I can do."

One hour later, two physical therapists showed up. They wrangled Drew and all the tubes and lines and IVs and lifted Drew up to sit on the edge of the bed. Drew's paralyzed stomach and neck muscles couldn't hold him up, and he flopped around like a rag doll. They held Drew on both sides as his head bobbled on his weak neck. They had him sitting up, though unsteadily, for five minutes.

That afternoon, I wrote a Facebook update. It took me an hour as I carefully thought out every single word I wrote. As usual, I made it sound like things were better than they actually were.

In the post, I recapped Drew's situation: "It's been 6 weeks since Drew went into the ICU. He now has a trach delivering oxygen, and he is being weaned off of heavy sedation. I was told Drew had a less than

20% chance to live, but six days ago, he turned a corner, and his doctor called him 'a Christmas Miracle.' Drew had a profound experience on 'the other side,' which gave him insight into how EVERYTHING in the Universe works. We have a ways to go, but Drew is getting better."

An hour later, Andrea called me. She was very angry about the post. "You never told me the doctor said he had a 20% chance to live," she yelled. "And how dare you put this on social media without telling the family first?"

She pushed, "Who said it? And when did you hear it? And why didn't you tell me?"

I wasn't sure how to answer. I didn't know why I never told her. It was probably because it was too terrible to say out loud. And the reality was, his chances were actually less than 5%. The 20% was sugar-coating it.

Her criticism brought back memories of being a kid and being yelled at for expressing myself. I felt shame like I had done something terribly wrong. As we argued on the phone, I quickly logged into my Facebook and edited out the sentence about the 20% chance to live.

Then, I got mad. I wanted so badly to be able to express myself in my own way.

I was tired of people bullying me into doing things their way. I was sick of the doctors pushing back on me. I was mad about how Dr. Pittman treated me. And right then and there, I decided I wasn't going to take it from anyone anymore.

My shame transformed into anger. I fought back, "I'm going to write whatever I want on social media. I'm tired of people telling me what to do."

We argued until we were exhausted. Before we hung up, we both said we were sorry. We needed each other. She was still my rock, even though we saw things differently. "I love you," we said before we hung up.

Raz called me from the hospital. She was the last visitor today. She pulled an oracle card for Drew, and it was the Trinity card. It read, "Everything happens in threes, and this season is coming to an end."

It was true. Drew was completing his first phase of his recovery process. The second phase would be the LTAC, and the third phase would be the rehabilitation of his broken body.

Tomorrow, the miracle solution of Aviptadil was coming. I declared out loud, "Dear God, I'm claiming the Aviptadil does remarkable healing on Drew's lungs, enabling his type 2 alveolar cells to repair in the most perfect way. I pray that Drew's lungs heal swiftly, easily, remarkably, and miraculously. So be it, and so it is."

52

AVIPTADIL DAY 1

Dec 29, 2021
Hospital Day 46, Ventilator Day 35

Today, the Aviptadil finally arrived, and I had a really good feeling—we were about to close part one of this terrible chapter in our lives. But my good mood didn't last long, thanks to Dr. Pittman.

Dylan had left early to do physical therapy exercises with Drew, but then he called me from the hospital parking lot.

"Dr. Pittman kicked me out of Dad's room," he said. "He told me, 'You don't want to be in here when this drug is administered. You don't want to see what it will do to him.'"

"What?!" I was baffled as to why he would say such a thing. "Sounds like he didn't read the studies on Aviptadil. If he had, he would know that there are only two possible side effects: diarrhea and a change in blood pressure." I was beyond annoyed.

"Okay, wait, don't leave," I said, thinking out loud. There was no way I was going to leave Drew unattended with Pittman there. "He can't kick you out. Go in there and tell him you insist on staying."

Dylan went back into Drew's room and calmly told the doctor he wasn't going anywhere. He watched as Dr. Pittman administered the IV with the wonder drug that I had fought so hard to get.

The Aviptadil drip started at 11 a.m. Dylan stayed with Drew for the next three hours, until I arrived. The moment I walked into the room, a speech therapist showed up to work with Drew. It was his first speech therapy session—terrible timing, but Pittman had ordered it.

The therapist, Rashid, put a speaking valve on Drew's trach so he could speak. "What's your favorite color?" Rashid asked, wanting a one-word answer to get Drew's voice box working.

"Blue," Drew whispered. His voice was weak, raspy, and soft.

Rashid asked more one-answer questions. "What's your son's name?" and "Where do you live?"

As Drew struggled to get the words out, I thought about what a bad idea it was to do this while the Aviptadil was being administered. Rashid had Drew talking for seven minutes, which wore him out completely. And then, just as Rashid was finishing up with Drew, something went terribly wrong. The ventilator started beeping loudly. Drew suddenly couldn't breathe, and his oxygen was not working.

The respiratory therapist came running into the room. She could not figure out the best setting on the ventilator to resolve it. I saw the fear in her eyes. Drew was drowning. She increased his oxygen to 100%. This was a massive step backward.

Drew mouthed, "I'm dying."

"No, you're not dying," I said, trying to calm him down. But I knew that he could be right, and I hid my fear from him.

Aviptadil Day 1

Frank administered Versed to calm Drew down and stop his struggling. Dr. Pittman walked in as the three of us were scrambling to resolve the issue.

I explained, "This is the second time this has happened this week. It's a setting on the ventilator."

The therapist checked the settings and found that someone had changed the setting off of CPAP, the only setting that allowed Drew to breathe comfortably. She changed it back and made other adjustments. Drew started to settle down.

Dr. Pittman said smugly, "It's the experimental drug causing this problem."

He talked down to me the way my misogynistic father did my whole life. For a moment, I was a vulnerable little girl again, staring up at an abusive authority figure. Then I remembered I'm a grown woman now, and I wasn't going to allow him to make me feel small.

"No, it's not," I said. "This exact thing happened a few days ago. It's the setting on the vent."

He said, "Well, you know how I feel about this drug."

I was startled. "No, I don't. How do you feel about it?" I asked.

"We were all against it," he said, speaking for the doctors on the team. Until that moment, I didn't know they were all railing against it. Dr. Q had been telling me all along they were supportive. But, of course, they were against it. Why else would they have dragged it out for weeks? *Wake up, Maria!*

"It's risky, and I recommend we discontinue it immediately," he pushed. He moved his face closer to mine, looked into my eyes, and said, "It could kill him. Give me approval to stop it."

His words dug deep into my fears of Drew dying and it being my fault. He was skillfully planting doubt in my mind, using words to cast spells. A form of medical voodoo. But I reminded myself I had already done the research and consulted some of the best doctors on it. Even so, Pittman was getting inside my head.

"Give me time to think about it," I mumbled. I started to wonder if I had made a mistake. Will this kill Drew? Should I stop it?

I called Paul. "Drew had another episode with breathing. Dr. Pittman says it's the Aviptadil. What do you think?" Paul agreed that the episode was the same as what happened days ago, caused by the vent setting.

I started to see what was really going on—this doctor was a misogynist. He had no respect for the nurses, for me, for my son, or even for my husband. And I didn't want to follow medical advice from someone who clearly didn't care about my family.

I decided to stay firm in my decision to administer the Aviptadil and would live with any consequences. And besides, all of the doctors who recommended it were people who loved and cared about Drew. I trusted them more than this guy.

Just a few more days, I thought, and Dr. Q would be back. Oh, how I missed him!

One by one, everyone left the room, and it was just me and Drew. I counted the medicine dispensers and was happy that Drew was down from eight drugs being dispensed into his IVs to only four now, plus the Aviptadil. I knew that with every drug removed, we were one step closer to Drew coming home.

I held Drew's hand and set the intention to be fully present with him. I closed my eyes, "Dear God, please let this miracle drug repair Drew's lungs. Please take it into his cells and regenerate them." I visualized the medicine filling up his cells and repairing them.

When I left the hospital, Drew looked very weak. He was still very much on the edge of death. We weren't out of the woods yet.

53

AVIPTADIL DAY 2

December 30, 2021
Hospital Day 47, Ventilator Day 36

A heavy rain tapped the roof, waking me out of a deep sleep. The sky was dark and foreboding. I felt uneasy. Even though I didn't trust him at all, the seed of doubt that Dr. Pittman planted was taking hold of my mind. Would the Aviptadil harm Drew?

I had already talked to all my doctor friends—even the IRB Chairman gave Aviptadil the thumbs up. But Pittman had put a voodoo curse of doubt on me. I lay in bed thinking, *Who else can I call?* I needed one more opinion. So, I called Debi—the crystal energy healer.

Debi tapped into her Spirit guides and relayed their answer in the simplest way so I could understand. "The Aviptadil is helping to clear the goo off of his lungs. It's causing his blood to rush faster and his heart to pump vitality. It is bringing blood to his brain and making him more vibrant. It's healing his lungs."

Next, she gave me insight into Drew's state of mind. "He is in and out of reality because of the drugs. He is worried he will end up in a wheelchair, and he's upset about losing his hair. He's anxious, not knowing where this is going to end."

She added two bits of advice, "No speech therapy today. And he doesn't know what is real. You have to tell him everything that is happening."

As always, Debi knew things she couldn't possibly have known—like the fact that he was losing his hair. And she never let me pay her for her readings. I felt lucky to have her. Her reassurance gave me exactly what I needed to calm my own mind.

I called and left a message for Dr. Pittman to continue the Aviptadil treatment and cancel the speech therapy. Nurse Frank answered, and I was grateful that he was there to protect Drew.

It was afternoon when I finally got on the road to the hospital. I turned on my windshield wipers and hit my brakes as bad drivers weaved in front of me. No one in California knows how to drive in the rain.

I dreaded seeing Dr. Pittman today. He was arrogant, and I was afraid that if I made him angry, he would hurt Drew. He had that power. I would have to pretend that I had respect for him to appeal to his big ego. Be nice but firm.

As I pulled into the hospital parking lot, a text came in from Chris. "Aviptadil made the mainstream news last night," he wrote, along with a link to the article. The headline read: "Patients treated with Aviptadil vs. placebo demonstrated a statistically significant increased odds of being alive and free of respiratory failure at day 28 and day 60."

The timing was nothing short of divine. After everything, the Universe handed me a final, crystal-clear confirmation that Aviptadil was the right choice. It was the exact shot of courage I needed to walk into that hospital and face Dr. Pittman.

But when I got into Drew's room, he had already come and gone. So I wrote a note, "Dear Dr. Pittman, here's the phone number of Dr. Melvin, a pulmonologist and expert on lung fibrosis and the use of Aviptadil. He can answer all your questions." I taped the note to the wall above the sink in Drew's room so he could not miss it. If Pittman wanted to do his job, he would make the phone call.

When I came over to Drew's bed, he was completely lifeless. I poked my head outside the room and asked Frank, "What's wrong with him?"

Frank said, "Dr. Pittman put him on Propofol."

"What's that?"

"It's the drug that killed Michael Jackson."

I felt a little fear rise up in my throat. Frank told me that Drew hadn't moved in three hours, and his blood pressure had dropped significantly. I went on the NIH website and looked up Propofol and found that it's one of the worst things to give a patient with respiratory issues. What was Pittman doing?

An hour later, Drew started to come out of his drug-induced slumber. He had a rash on his face, neck, and chest. He pointed to his thighs. I pulled the bedsheets away, and there was a raging, bumpy rash on his scrotum and inner thighs. It looked painful. This was the worst rash I'd ever seen.

At first, I worried it was that culprit they wanted to blame everything on–the Aviptadil. But no, I read all the side effects, and a rash was not one of them. Could it be the Propofol? Or the Prednisone? Whatever it was, he was clearly having an allergic reaction.

Drew's face winced in pain. He pointed to the table for me to grab a tube of lotion for rashes in your private parts. I squirted some of the white, pasty cream into my gloved hand. It was thick, and I imagined it would hurt going on, so I hesitated. Drew got frustrated, and for the first time in our entire marriage, he got mean. With a frown, he mouthed very clearly, "Put the fucking lotion on." So I did.

I talked to him about all the things Debi said he was worried about. I told him that he wasn't going to end up in a wheelchair. "You'll walk again, Drew," I assured him. "And your hair will grow back," I laughed. And I added, "You are doing so well. Look, you moved a leg today. That's a start. Tomorrow, you'll move it more. And next week, you'll be moving both legs."

He wrote, "Make them stop the drugs."

I nodded and tried to cheer him up, "You have come so far, Drew!"

He wrote, "We crossed a milestone."

"Yes, we did!"

That night, I got Dr. Gibbons on the phone. His practice was crazy busy now that Covid was rampant with the Omicron variant. I gave him an update on Drew's breathing episodes and about Dr. Pittman wanting to stop the Aviptadil.

Dr. Gibbons looked up Drew's medical records and saw a leak in the cuff of Drew's trach. This was probably causing the distress. I wondered why no one at the hospital told me about that.

I was so grateful for Dr. Gibbons being in my life. Oh, how I wished he were Drew's doctor.

54

AVIPTADIL DAY 3

December 31, 2021
Hospital Day 48, Ventilator Day 37

Another dreary, overcast day—perfectly matching my mood. As I left for the hospital, the fence guy was tearing out the old one. "You'll have a new fence when you come home today," he said. His words felt almost symbolic, like something old was being ripped away to make space for the new.

But when I walked into Drew's room, he was struggling to breathe. A nurse and the respiratory therapist hovered over the ventilator, adjusting settings, trying to stabilize him—again.

I stood there, silently praying this was just a healing crisis, one of those moments where things look worse before they get better.

"Dr. Pittman said it's happening because of the Aviptadil," Nurse Gwen said.

"So, the leak in the trach had nothing to do with anything, huh?" I asked sarcastically. She didn't know what I was talking about. It wasn't her fault, and I apologized for being snarky.

Drew was a vegetable again today, too drugged up to write or move his lips. The nurse told me that Pittman had him loaded up on Propofol again. "It's sending him backward. Can we please take him off of it?" I begged.

"I'll let the doctor know you requested that," she promised.

Then I noticed that his cheekbones were sticking out of his face. He no longer looked like Drew, except for his eyes. His shin bones were sharp and jutted out. I could put one hand, thumb to finger, completely around his thigh. He had gotten much skinnier in the last couple of days. How did I not see this?

Paul came in to say hello. This morning, they gave Drew another chest X-ray, and Paul looked up the results for me. "Good news, Drew's X-ray shows that he has less free air in his lungs from yesterday. It's a slight improvement."

Just then, Drew started choking. His eyes widened, and he put a hand to his throat. Thank God Paul was there again. He suctioned it out and cleared mucus from his lungs. Before he left, Paul held Drew's hand, and I bowed my head as he said a prayer.

That night, I came home to a beautiful new redwood fence standing tall in the backyard, and Dylan in the kitchen, cooking spaghetti.

I called a local landscaper to come plant a eucalyptus tree and some tropical greenery. That would complete Drew's new backyard—a sanctuary waiting for him.

No matter how bad things looked, I had to keep planning for him to come home. I had to hold the vision. I had to believe, no matter what.

55

A NEW YEAR

January 1, 2022
Hospital Day 49, Ventilator Day 38

It was New Year's Day, and my only resolution was to survive another week. The Aviptadil treatment was behind us, and now, all my focus shifted to Drew's reaction to the Propofol. I had been reading everything I could find about how the drug affects the lungs —how it can trigger coughing fits and make it harder to breathe. This was my new battle: to get him off it, fast, before it did any more damage.

I drove to the hospital in the rain, bracing myself for another fight with Dr. Pittman. When I arrived, I was happy to see Nurse Tina. Hearing her sing, "Good morning, Drew. It's a beautiful rainy day today," brought my spirits up.

But it was a rough day. Drew's heart rate was resting high, and at times, it spiked to 150. He had a fever, which was a sign of infection. And Drew was a lifeless vegetable again, thanks to the Propofol.

I asked Nurse Tina to give me a list of all of the drugs he was on. She read them off to me, one by one, as I hand-wrote them in my medical journal. Klonopin for anti-anxiety, Versed, Precedex, Levophed, and the dreaded Propofol. Tina and I both saw that the Propofol was making Drew sicker, but Dr. Pittman insisted on keeping him on it.

I was determined to find a way to resolve this. I sent a text to Dr. Stan, "Can you call me? I need help figuring out Drew's medications." But he texted back that he would be in surgery all day. So, I asked Nurse Tina to help.

Dr. Pittman made an appearance in the afternoon. Nurse Tina approached him with the confident tone of an experienced nurse. "I'd like to titrate Drew off the Propofol," she said, pointing out the reactions he was having. "He's unresponsive, and his blood pressure..."

Dr. Pittman interrupted her abruptly and said, "Keep him on it." She frowned and left the room.

That afternoon, Drew came out of his drug stupor and motioned for pen and paper. He wrote, "Lots of yellow mucus. Infection in lungs." I popped my head out to the nurses' desk and asked Tina to order a test to check for an infection.

Then he wrote, "Food making me sick."

I looked at his gaunt face, and it reminded me of old pictures of the starved survivors of concentration camps in Nazi Germany. Drew looked like a one-hundred-year-old man. How did I not see the severity of this until now?

"Tina, how many calories is he getting?" I called out through the door.

She put on gloves and a gown and walked over to the dispenser. "Right now, he's getting only about 600 because of his nausea." She answered.

"Six hundred calories, how often?" I asked.

A New Year

"Per day," she said.

That's not even a Starbucks drink. He was starving to death right before my eyes, and I didn't even notice, because I had been so focused on the other problems. I walked over to the bag of formula that flowed from a long tube into his stomach, put my glasses on, and read the ingredients.

"Oh my God," I said out loud to Drew. "No wonder your stomach is sick! This isn't even food." The ingredients were chemicals that I wouldn't feed to a stray dog.

"Tina," I called out, "What will it take to have this formula replaced with real food?"

"You'll have to meet with the dietician," she said. "I'll set up a meeting for tomorrow."

That evening, Drew and I watched the sunset through the window and held hands. Drew's medicine IV pump started beeping, and Nurse Tina came into the room to refill the containers. As she finished, she looked at me and announced, "By the way, Dr. Pittman is gone for the day. And I thought I'd let you know I'm titrating down the Propofol. Drew will be completely off of it by morning."

And just like that, the Propofol battle was over. This angel warrior nurse risked her job to protect Drew. I now understood how nurses save lives. The experienced ones trust their knowledge and take life saving actions, regardless of doctor's orders.

That night, I went to a sound healing class put on by Shaman Alicia and her husband. They set up four large gongs and a dozen crystal bowls in a yoga studio. Alicia was surprised to see me. She knew how bad things were.

The room was illuminated by burning candles. As people rolled out yoga mats, I made a little nest on my mat with a pillow and blanket and snuggled in. When the music began, I prayed for my own health. I felt my body vibrate as the beautiful sound filled my cells. A strong energy moved through me, up to my heart, my throat, and my eyes. I was lulled into a deep, restful sleep.

When it was over, I felt truly relaxed for the first time in a long time. Alicia hugged me. She said that while the music played, she saw my spiritual ancestors come into the room and take my burdens off of me. They cleared energy that had been stuck in my throat. *Maybe now I'll be able to speak up for myself even more*, I thought.

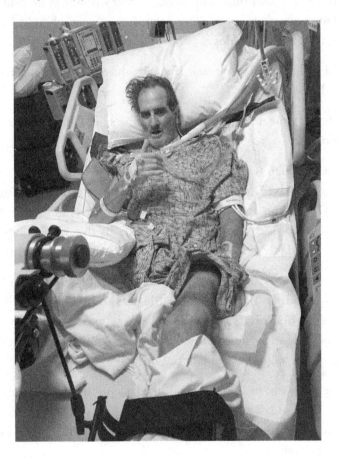

56

LET'S CRY TOGETHER

January 2, 2022
Hospital Day 50, Ventilator Day 39

The sun returned, and it brought me joy to wake up to the light streaming through my window. I snuggled under the covers and prayed, "Dear Jesus, please go into Drew's room and put a shield of protection around him."

I added, "And please give me the strength to face Pittman today."

My to-do list included meeting with the dietician and later shopping for furniture for Drew's new backyard.

We had a new nurse on duty. Sativa was a sweet, thirty-something brunette with an English accent. She was extra attentive to Drew and told me he'd been sick to his stomach again. "Dr. Pittman said the nausea is from the experimental drug," she explained.

I felt a surge of anger. What is Pittman's obsession with Aviptadil?

Why does it make him so mad that he has to lie? *Now I'm really pissed off. That's it. I'm going to set the record straight.*

Thankfully, I had recorded every issue with Drew and his stomach. I flipped through my medical journal and gathered the data proving that his stomach pain started long before the Aviptadil. Having the facts at my fingertips gave me confidence. I was going to show Pittman, once and for all, that it wasn't the damn experimental drug!

When Pittman walked in, I confronted him.

"Look, Doctor, here's a list of all the days *before* the Aviptadil when Drew was having stomach problems." I held up my notebook and read it out loud. "On December 23rd, Drew had severe stomach pain. On December 24th, the pain was so bad Dr. Q ordered an X-ray. On…"

Pittman barely looked at me as I read the data to him. When I was finished, he said smugly, "Well, we disagree."

"But you can't disagree with facts!" I stuttered.

As he walked out of the room, he got in the last word: "We disagree."

And he was gone. His arrogance was maddening. But I was proud of how I stood up to him. I liked this new Maria, who didn't back down. Even though he wouldn't admit it, we both knew the truth. You can't argue with facts.

I didn't want Drew to see how mad I was. I paced in circles in an attempt to release some of the bad energy that was just generated in that room.

Drew was alert today. Now that he was off the Propofol, his mind was clear. He wrote, "Up all night coughing up sticky stuff. No more drugs, please."

Suddenly, his chest heaved. His face twisted with pain. He scribbled frantically, "Something wrong. Can't breathe."

I hit the call button and begged for the respiratory therapist, Remmy, to hurry. It would take her forty-five minutes to come.

While we waited, I held Drew's hand and spoke to him in the calmest voice I could fake.

He gasped for air, struggling to form the words, "Help. I can't do this."

He was slipping. Right in front of me. Teetering at the edge of death again. He was shaking and struggling. I kept my voice steady, forcing myself to believe the words even as my heart pounded out of my chest, "It's going to be okay. We've been through this before."

Frantic, I texted Paul. "Are you at the hospital today?"

He answered almost immediately, "I'm at home with the family. What's up?"

"Drew's struggling to breathe again. Will you talk to the therapist?"

"Yes, call me when she gets there."

Remmy finally came in, moving slowly with no sense of urgency. She was a big woman who walked with a limp. She frowned as she assessed the machine settings. I put Paul on speaker, and he directed Remmy to try a few different settings. Then he asked, "It's still on CPAP, right?"

Remmy said, "No, Dr. Pittman ordered us to take him off CPAP."

"Well," Paul said, "Just like I said the other day, that's the only setting that works for Drew. You have to put it back to CPAP."

Remmy changed the setting, and, as Paul directed her, she fiddled with other settings. Drew started to breathe with more ease, and he settled down. It was working. Once again, if it weren't for Paul, Drew might have died right then.

Later, the dietitian showed up for our meeting. Her name was Princess, and she was all business. I explained that Drew was allergic to something in the formula because he had been throwing up since they started feeding it to him.

"Do you have a different formula that resembles food?" I asked, kind of laughing. She didn't see the humor in my joke. She handed me a brochure that showed several options.

I read through the ingredients of each formula and chose the one that appeared to be the most healthy, called Nestle Compleat. The label boasted, "...includes a variety of real food ingredients," with the words "real food" highlighted.

Princess prepared the new formula for Drew. "We will start it slow and then increase the calories as he can tolerate more," she explained. One more problem solved. It was like whack-a-mole around here.

A couple of hours later, Drew's stomach was feeling better, so I asked the nurse to increase the flow of food into his tube to help him get more calories.

I was so glad that we found the cause of the stomach issues, and it was so simple. Change the food formula, and the stomach pain goes away. I had to wonder why he had to suffer for so long. *I just have to always be here*, I thought.

It was becoming clear that I had to question every problem and then seek out a solution for it. I couldn't fully rely on the staff; they were too busy.

Drew was feeling a lot better, so he started writing. "I heard nurses say I wasn't going to make it," he wrote. Drew was cursed with ridiculously good hearing. This was the second time he'd overheard nurses outside his door, talking about how they thought the room would open up soon—because he was going to die any day now.

It made me sad. Drew's body was ravaged, but his spirit was strong. I started to feel a hint of the sorrow I'd been running from—a grief so intense I had to bury it deep inside me. That was my coping mechanism. If I let myself feel everything this ordeal brought up, it would crush me.

Drew's eyes teared up. His long lashes were wet. He wrote, "Can't believe this happened."

I reveled in the rawness of the moment. He was suffering—a prisoner in that bed. And me? I was fighting with every ounce of energy I had to try to save him. Together, we were more deeply connected than we had ever been.

"Do you want me to cry with you?" I asked. He nodded yes.

We'd never cried together before. Even when Poppi died and Drew was completely heartbroken, he stayed strong and never shed a tear.

But now, his tears were flowing. He couldn't be the strong guy anymore, and he surrendered to it. I looked at my once-Superman of a husband in his weak, broken body, and I felt so deeply sad. Out of habit, a sharp pain in my chest rose up to block my tears. But then, as Drew hugged me with one arm and gently patted my back, I absorbed his sorrow—and I surrendered, too.

We held each other and cried. I let my tears fall freely. In the letting go, Drew and I shared our utter despair, our helplessness, and the deep sadness for the life we once had. But we still had each other.

And in that moment, we became even closer—two halves of one whole. A complete heart.

57

FOOD WARS

January 3, 2022
Hospital Day 51, Ventilator Day 40

Drew's stomach tolerated the new food formula so well that today's nurse increased his calorie intake again. Another battle won, but the war wasn't over yet.

For the first time, I met the hospitalist—the doctor overseeing Drew's case. He was six foot five and towered over me like a redwood tree. I felt like a tiny little girl craning my neck just to meet his eyes as he spoke.

He handed me a stack of papers and a pen. "For you to sign," he said.

I saw the words "hospital transfer" on the cover sheet. My stomach dropped.

"Move him out of this hospital? Today?" I asked, alarmed.

"Yes. Dr. Pittman has recommended a transfer to a Long-Term Care Facility."

Just like that. No warning. No time to process. I hadn't even chosen a facility yet. Panic set in. More of the unknown, the next danger. A new battle.

Drew was still too fragile. There was no way he could survive a transfer. And suddenly, I started to see a darkness I'd been unwilling to face. But I wasn't the same woman I was a week ago. That version of me was gone.

Now, I was the unlikely warrior, David. And I was ready to stand up to Goliath.

I stood up straight and narrowed my eyes. I stamped a foot onto the ground. "No. This is not going to happen today," I said firmly.

I surprised myself with my newfound confidence. "He is not stable enough to be moved." I repeated, "No."

The doctor took a small step back, then reached for the papers. "We'll wait a few days, then," he said, before walking out.

I stood there, stunned. He didn't argue. He didn't push back. I exhaled a breath I didn't know I was holding, feeling like I had dodged a bullet.

Just then, Paul walked in. I was shaking.

"What's wrong?" he asked.

I told him that Pittman had tried to transfer Drew to an LTAC today. Paul agreed—Drew wasn't stable enough.

"I've been taking notes on some of the things happening around Drew's care. I'm going to make a formal complaint," he said, lowering his voice. It was a relief to know I wasn't the only one who saw it—that I wasn't crazy.

Paul suctioned Drew's throat, checked the ventilator settings, and held Drew's hand as Drew wrote about his near-death experience. Every day now, Drew wanted to tell us more about what he saw on the other side.

I stayed until the end of the day. As I walked down the hall towards the elevators, something made me glance back toward Drew's room. That's when I saw Princess walking in—carrying a bag of formula. My heart dropped. I recognized it instantly—the old formula that had made Drew throw up for days.

I turned on my heel and chased after her.

"Hi, Princess," I said, trying to stay calm. "What's going on?" I pointed to the bag in her hand.

She paused. "Dr. Pittman ordered me to switch the formula back. He said it's not the food—it's the experimental drug that's making Drew sick."

"That's not true," I snapped. I wasn't going to sugar-coat my words this time. "He's lying, and I can prove it." I grabbed my notebook and pulled out the medical study on the Aviptadil.

"See," I said, waving the study in front of her. "There are only two side effects. And he didn't suffer from either of those. Dr. Pittman didn't research it, so he doesn't know."

Then, I grabbed my medical journal and read the list of all the days that old formula made Drew sick. His problems started with the PEG and ended with the new formula.

"No. We keep the new formula. We are not changing it back," I said firmly, emphasizing it by stamping my foot. I was starting to enjoy this new bulldog side of me.

Princess stood still for a moment, wondering how to respond. She started to argue, "But Dr. Pittman ordered this."

"Well, I make the final decisions about his care. I say no to the formula that makes him throw up."

Princess grabbed the bag of that lousy formula and left the room. What if I hadn't been there? He would have started throwing up again, and that could cause an aspiration, which could kill him.

God, I wished Dr. Q were back.

Drew had witnessed the whole thing. He picked up his pen and wrote slowly, then held up the paper:

"I have protection around me. A light that keeps negativity away."

Maybe that's why we kept nearly missing disaster. Every time the darkness tried to take Drew's life, divine intervention stepped in. Every single time.

"I've been sending that protection to you every morning," I said. I felt elated and surprised, knowing that my prayers were being answered.

That night, Dylan and I talked about all the things that had gone wrong since Drew was in Dr. Pittman's care. Either Pittman was extremely incompetent, or he was evil. Either way, Drew was not safe with him.

Dylan Googled reviews of Dr. Pittman. There were many bad ones. "You should fire him, Mom," Dylan urged.

"There's no point. Dr. Q is back any day now," I said.

Later that night, after a long shift at her hospital, Dr. Sue called. She said, "This morning, I went deep into meditation and had a vision. I was shown that you were going to write a book about this, and the title was *Covid, A Love Story*."

I laughed to myself. Who would read a book with that title? It sounded like a goofy love story, with the horrible word "Covid" in it. That was the silliest book title ever. But I didn't tell her that. I felt honored that she was even thinking about me in her meditation.

"I can't even think about writing a book right now," I said.

She went on, telling me how heartbreaking it had been to watch so many Covid patients die alone.

"I don't know if I'll ever recover from the things I've seen," she said sadly.

"Maria," she continued. "Your story is hugely important. It will show people how to advocate for their loved ones."

Maybe she was right. Maybe this story would help others. But I still didn't know how it was going to end.

That night, I prayed to Jesus, "Please stay in Drew's room and protect him from any evil, malpractice, or honest mistakes. Please allow the new food to nourish him. And please, bring Dr. Q back."

58

CHANGES

January 4, 2022
Hospital Day 52, Ventilator Day 41

The night nurse, Andrew, called me early this morning with something wild. He held up a drawing Drew had made overnight—a rough, chaotic sketch of a tunnel in space with shapes flying through it. "He said it's what he saw during his near-death," Andrew told me.

Drew and I FaceTimed for an hour, then I hopped in the shower and hurried to get to the hospital before Pittman did anything stupid today.

I slipped into my usual hospital uniform: dark skinny jeans, ankle boots with a heel, and a red v-neck sweater. I'd learned that when I dressed well, the doctors treated me with more respect. Around my neck, I wore my long, black kyanite and moldavite necklace to protect me from negative energies, and a shorter, light blue Larimar stone necklace because it was pretty.

I walked into Drew's room at the exact same moment Pittman did. I braced for battle—but to my surprise, he was friendly. Word must have gotten back to him that I had been complaining. Hospitals are just like high school. You can't keep a secret in them.

He explained the issue with Drew's air leak in the lung. He said he had to put a water seal on Drew's chest tube so it would "stop sucking air" through it. Then, he joked, "I know you think I suck. But that's a different discussion."

"No, I don't." I lied, appealing to his ego. I figured he wouldn't kill Drew if I was nice to him.

He said, "I heard from Dr. Q that you had concerns about transferring him to an LTAC. I'm not in a rush to transfer him."

Oh, how the story keeps changing.

"Isn't Dr. Q coming back today?" I asked.

"Not until next Monday," he replied. Oh no, that's another week that we are stuck with Pittman. The Omicron variant was running through the hospital like wildfire, and I suspected that Dr. Q caught Covid on his vacation.

"I want to clamp the chest tube today, and in the morning, get a CT Scan and see if we can remove it." Dr. Pittman said.

As he walked out, he had to get one last dig in. "Now that the experimental drug is out of his system, he can start feeling better."

I wanted to yell, "Now that the Propofol is out of his system, he's doing better." But instead, I pretended I didn't hear him.

Physical therapy moved Drew from the bed to the big chair. The transfer was much easier now that he had the trach. But it was still strenuous for Drew—sitting up meant using neck and back muscles that had completely atrophied. I brushed his teeth, combed his hair, and rubbed his feet.

He wrote, "I woke up this morning thinking it was the day Poppi died."

He was right. It had been eight years to the day since Drew's father passed. I don't know how he knew that.

In anticipation of discharge, I started calling all eight LTACs on the list. To my surprise, only one allowed visitors. That was completely unacceptable.

I made an appointment to tour the only LTAC with visiting hours, Santa Ana. I kissed Drew goodbye and drove forty-five minutes north. The LTAC was in a seedy neighborhood where some of the buildings had bars on the windows. I parked behind the old LTAC brick structure that was built in the 1940s. I made sure to lock my car.

I was met by Danny, who greeted me with a big smile. His name tag had a red sticker that said, 'I've had my Covid-19 vaccination." He handed me a mask and led me down the halls.

Our first stop was the cafeteria—a sad little abandoned room with five tables, two vending machines, and a counter for ordering the meal of the day. "This is where you can eat your lunch," he said.

Then we continued down the hall to a room on the left. "This is our Respiratory team. Meet the head of RT, Jack."

He introduced me to a tall man wearing a name tag like Danny's—minus the vaccination sticker. We talked for a few minutes. Jack explained that their main goal was getting patients off the ventilator. I liked hearing that.

Next, Danny led me to the physical therapy room. It was empty except for an overweight man with an expressionless face. In the center of the room was a short runway with orthopedic parallel bars. Exercise balls were scattered across the floor, and a dozen oxygen tanks were lined up next to a small refrigerator. The floor looked dirty, or maybe it was just old.

Danny called out to the man. "This is one of our physical therapists," he said. "Meet Maria, her husband will be with us soon." The man nodded his head.

As we walked the halls, I glanced into the patients' rooms. Most were critically ill and on ventilators. A few were alert enough to watch TV, but most looked miserable—or comatose. I didn't see a single visitor.

Danny led me into the private office of the registered dietitian, a petite Spanish woman named Bernadette. Her office felt good; it was an island of its own, separate from the rest of the dingy facility. A warm light glowed from a salt lamp in the corner. On her desk, next to a computer, were three quartz crystals. I looked at her and said, "You're my kind of people!" She smiled.

Bernadette asked me about Drew. I told her I was worried about his weight loss and lack of nutrition. She assured me that he would be weighed regularly at their facility. I asked if I could bring in healthy smoothies and have them fed through his feeding tube. She said she would get approval from the doctor. "My uncle was in here with Covid last year, and I made him smoothies too," she said.

Despite all the questionable things about this LTAC, Bernadette—and the generous visiting hours—sold me.

The last room we peeked into was the ICU, where Drew would be, since he was still highly critical. It was dark and creepy, filled with bodies that weren't moving. Seven small rooms, each separated by glass, circled a nurse's station in the center. I shook off the feeling of dread. This wasn't a place I wanted Drew to end up, but I knew he would only be happy if Dylan and I could visit him.

As I drove, I forced myself to forget the bad stuff and focus on what I liked about the LTAC: only 60 patients, generous visiting hours, two visitors allowed at the same time, and best of all, I could bring healthy smoothies for Drew to start building his strength back.

Changes

I drove back to Hospital One. "Well, honey, I found the place I want you to be transferred to," I announced as I walked into Drew's room. I glanced out the window — the sun was setting over the ocean and the trees. I looked around at the big room Drew was in, the nice new equipment, his own sink and counter, and I felt a pang of sadness at the thought of leaving it behind for that other place.

"I have to warn you," I said. "This place is like a luxury hotel. The one we're moving you to... it's more like an old Motel 6. But it's the only place that will let you have visitors. Would you rather have a nicer place, or visitors?" I asked, letting him make the final decision.

He wrote, "I want my family." It was settled, then.

Dylan came for the night shift, armed with a razor. He shaved his father's face and neck, then used the pounder on Drew's back to break up the gunk in his lungs.

Drew was deep in thought about his predicament. He wrote, "I am letting go of years of disappointment and pain." Dylan didn't know what to say, so he held his dad's hand as they listened to a Tool album — a reminder of the good memories from the concert they went to together just a year earlier.

When the night nurse came in, Drew wrote sadly, "All I have is my wife, my son, and this window."

Drew was experiencing depression for the first time in his life. It was a realization that he had been stripped of everything, except, of course, the most important things.

That night, I reflected on all the crazy things that happened. I wrote in the Dear Drew Journal:

> *I thank Dr. Pittman for bullying me. He woke up my fierce, inner warrior. I no longer care what anyone thinks.*
>
> *Only one thing matters: you coming home alive. I'm not letting anyone get in the way of that.*
>
> *They will have to kill me first.*

59

THE LIGHT

January 5, 2022 Wednesday
Hospital Day 53, Ventilator Day 42

Drew had always been the giver. He had boundless energy and poured it into doing things for others. He loved being the man everyone could count on. But that man was gone now. His body was no longer his instrument. He would have to learn to master the energy flowing through it instead.

Even paralyzed, there was still a fire burning behind those green eyes. Drew's energy was so powerful, so alive, that the nurses started fighting over who got to care for him. I guess everyone wanted to be part of his miracle. It started with the night nurse, Andrew. And now Frank and Tina were fighting over the day shift. Today, Frank won.

Early this morning, the landscapers were clearing out the backyard planters. I sat at the kitchen table, making my list of things to do. Today, my focus was getting Drew's muscles working. Dylan and I had been doing our best, moving Drew's arms and legs every day, but we weren't therapists.

Until now, I hadn't faced the reality: Drew wouldn't be walking anytime soon. If ever.

I Googled, "How to recover from an induced coma," and nearly dropped my phone. For every one day of being immobile, it would take seven days of therapy to recover. I did the math. Drew had been bedridden for forty-one days. Forty-one times seven... 287 days of recovery. Over nine months.

A lump rose in my throat. Why didn't I realize this sooner? I felt the urgency flood me and called Kim.

"If he's going to beat this," she said, "he needs physical therapy twice a day."

Kim emailed me a printout of physical therapy exercises with diagrams. I took the printouts to Drew's room and taped them to the wall. Dylan and I made a pact that we would both do the therapy exercises with Drew every day.

The hospital was extra busy now that the Omicron variant was rampant. So many nurses and doctors were sick with Covid that the hospital was letting staff come to work even if they tested positive. And now, the cafeteria wouldn't allow visitors to eat there anymore, which meant I would have to leave the hospital if I wanted food.

Dr. Pittman came in and told me that he had removed Drew's chest tube. Then he lectured me for telling him how to do his job.

"Just like you wouldn't want Drew's clients to tell him how to paint," he said. I nodded to appease him. Dr. Pittman was unusually chatty as he told me how he collects and builds antique furniture. I was surprised to hear that he had a creative side to him. It made him seem a little more human.

The Light

Frank enlisted the help of a few nurses to move Drew into the big chair. Vertigo was another side effect of sedation, and sitting up made him dizzy and sick. But we didn't abort the mission because there was only one way to get stronger, and that was by doing the things that made one stronger.

Drew's head bobbled; his atrophied neck muscles weren't strong enough to hold his head up. He wrote, "How am I ever going to do this if I can barely sit up?"

Frank positioned the chair so Drew could see out of the window. I enjoyed every moment of it, knowing that our days of having a beautiful view would end soon.

We watched the light in the sky change from yellow to gold to red. We held hands and talked about Drew's near-death. He wrote, "We are creation machines. We are stardust, pure light, and love." It was strange for Drew to talk like this. And I was loving it because he was always all science and facts, and now he was seeing the world the way I did–through the eyes of Spirit.

He told me that during the many times he almost died in that bed, he would keep his body alive by saying to himself over and over again, "You can't kill me; I am the light. I am the light. I am the light."

60

FOUR GOOD DAYS

January 6, 2022
Hospital Day 54, Ventilator Day 43

A good day in the ICU was a day when there were no close calls with death.

We had now racked up four good days in a row—no emergencies. It was a record for us.

A new nurse joined in on the fight with Tom, Frank, and Tina to be assigned to Drew. Her name was Danielle, a sweet young redhead who was very attentive. She would ask Drew questions about his life, and then she would patiently wait for him to scribble out his answers. She joked with him, teased him, and flashed a big, warm smile that made his day better. Today, she won the spot as Drew's nurse.

Kim was now coming every other day to work on Drew. Though she has a slender frame, Kim is a strong boxer and a surfer and has a reputation as a healer among athletes. Drew's eyes would light up when she walked in; he loved his sessions with Kim. She was like a sister to him. And she was intimately aware of all of his past surfing injuries because she was the one who helped him heal from them.

Today, Kim worked on waking up Drew's diaphragm through massage and tapping. It was paralyzed too, another cruel side effect of sedation. If he was ever going to breathe on his own, the diaphragm had to come back to life.

Later, two hospital therapists came in. As they lifted him up to sitting, the ventilator tube popped out of his trach, and his air was cut off. Drew's eyes opened wide, and he thrashed his arms about, gasping for air. One therapist scrambled to shove the tube back in. Over the next ten minutes, the tube popped out three more times. Each time, my heart jumped out of my chest. After they left, Drew was exhausted. I was, too, wrecked from the stress of watching that tube pop out.

A few minutes of holding Drew's hand helped, but my nervous energy had me pacing the room, scouting for the next threat. I was always in fight-or-flight mode. I could never fully settle down.

I grabbed the iPad and said, "It's time for you to learn how to log into this thing so you can call me on your own!"

We practiced—slowly—Drew punching in the code to unlock it. I showed him how to click "Contacts," find "Maria Brophy," and hit the FaceTime button. Suddenly, my phone rang. Bingo. It worked. Drew's fingers were finally strong enough to FaceTime me all by himself. Freedom!

61

TRUST DANIELLE

January 7, 2022
Hospital Day 55, Ventilator Day 44

At the crack of dawn, my phone rang. It was Drew—calling me all by himself for the very first time, no help needed. I felt a surge of joy... but it was crushed the moment he held a piece of paper up to the iPad. "Tube came out of trach last night. No one came. I fixed it."

My stomach dropped. He told me he had hit the call button over and over, but no one came. Alone, gasping for air, he somehow managed to reach for the ventilator tube with his weak arms and jam it back into his trach. He scribbled more words on the page. "It popped out at midnight. I thought I was a goner."

I was horrified. I pictured him—desperate, struggling, like a fish out of water, fighting for air. One slip, and he could have been gone in minutes. "You have angels looking out for you, Drew," I said.

At morning shift change, we were still on FaceTime when Danielle came into the room. "Frank and I fought over who got Drew today. I won again," she gloated.

From the iPad, I heard Danielle ask the night nurse, Tom, to help her before he left. They pulled the chair lift from the ceiling and started the process of moving Drew into the chair. I called out nervously, "Um, Danielle, maybe we shouldn't do this without Frank."

Danielle popped her face into the screen and smiled, "I can do this!" She was overly excited to put Drew in a chair. She wanted to be just like Frank.

I didn't want her to. Frank was the only one I trusted with the chair lift. All of the other nurses were afraid of it because it was so risky. What gave her so much confidence? She was so young and had no experience. Drew was anxious, also. But then, I felt a word whispered in my ear, "Trust."

I reluctantly surrendered. Okay, I'll trust. I took a deep breath to calm my nerves. I watched through the iPad as the two nurses put the strap around Drew and precariously lifted him out of the bed, with all his tubes and IVs flying through the air toward the chair. "Please, God, guide their hands."

One of the IVs in Drew's arm got stuck in the corner of something, about to get yanked out, and I heard myself gasp. But Danielle, with her youthful confidence, quickly moved it as she guided Drew's body, suspended high, to the chair.

A few minutes later, Drew was safely seated. We both sighed with relief. Danielle smiled big, proud of herself. This was a defining moment for her. She had just up-leveled as a nurse and a healer.

When Kim came for her session today, Drew was dizzy with a bad case of vertigo, but he pushed through it and did the therapy movements anyway.

Kim called me with an update, "I kept telling him over and over, 'You are a badass, Drew. You're coming off of some big drugs, brother.' We are taking big steps. I'm so proud of him." Her enthusiasm gave me hope.

When I arrived that afternoon, piles of scribbled notes were stacked on Drew's side table. I read through them, piecing together a conversation between him and Kim. "One of the nurses said no one thought I would survive. They all have been working so hard for me. Dr. Q said not many people come back from where I went."

I did a physical therapy session with Drew, following the exercises on Kim's printouts. I lifted his leg, bending his knee and pulling it gently toward his chest, then guided it outward. I encouraged Drew to help with the movements. He tried, but he could barely move a muscle. This would become my favorite exercise—the one Dylan later named "Flyboys."

When I got home, our new Costco outdoor furniture had been delivered. Dylan was sitting on the grass, surrounded by open boxes, building chairs, ottomans, and a couch with Drew's old toolkit. Drew had taught him how to build things when he was just a little boy. My vision for Drew's backyard sanctuary was coming to life.

That night, I wrote:

Dear Drew,

You don't know it, but you're impacting people as you lay in that bed. Today, Danielle became a more skilled nurse, putting you in that chair. And Dylan has stepped up to the role of being man of the house.

As for me, I'm learning to trust and surrender even more.

62

HOW I FEEL

I went to Ralph's grocery store to pick up bananas and frozen blueberries for my smoothies, the only food I ever had time to make.

A nurse who had been following our story on Facebook approached me in the produce section. "You don't know me," she said, pulling me into a hug, "but I've been praying for your family."

Then she asked, "How are you feeling, Maria?"

It caught me off guard. People usually asked about Drew. No one ever asked about me. I didn't know what to say. I had been on autopilot for so long that I didn't even know how I felt anymore.

I paused and thought about it. My emotions were permanently switched to the "off" button. My cries had been stuck in my throat. My hearing was getting worse, and my vision was blurry. My body had subconsciously turned down all my senses because I didn't want to see or hear any more bad news.

How do I feel?

I felt afraid. Drew was Superman, who was taken down by an invisible virus and the brutal treatment meant to save him.

I felt deep sorrow for the widows who couldn't even say goodbye.

I felt grief for those who died alone, scared, locked away from the people who loved them.

I felt anger—for the doctors trapped by a system that punished them for questioning the rules.

I felt betrayed by a medical establishment that was supposed to protect us.

And yet, despite it all, or maybe because of it all, I felt strong. I had become a warrior on the front line of a battle I never signed up for. But I wasn't sure yet how this story was going to end. Would Drew live, or would he die?

I dropped the bananas into my cart, forced a smile, and said, "I'm doing great. Thanks for asking."

63

NEW HOSPITAL RULES

January 8, 2022
Hospital Day 56, Ventilator Day 45

When I arrived at the hospital today, a big sign was taped to the door: "New Visiting Rules effective immediately. Only one visitor a day. New hours are 10-8."

My heart sank. This meant Dylan, Kim, and I would have to take turns each day. With only one of us allowed in, that one person would have to stay with him all day long. No more taking shifts, no more back up. I texted Kim, telling her she had to cancel her visit with Drew today. When I broke the news to him, the disappointment on his face crushed me.

And it only got worse from there. Drew had vertigo and was in agony when I walked in. His body shook. His face was pale and he had a stabbing pain in his side. He scribbled on his notepad: "I'm fucked up." Then another: "I'm suffocating."

He was slipping backward again. The nurse explained that the dizziness was vestibular dysfunction—damage to his inner ear from being immobile for so long. As for the sharp pain in his side, she wasn't sure what was causing it. She quickly texted Dr. Monty, the doctor on call, asking him to come right away.

While we waited, I tried to make Drew as comfortable as possible. The nurse showed me how to turn on the CPM percussion on the bed. It vibrated Drew in the bed gently. I tapped on his back and massaged his stomach. As a last resort, I ran "the pounder" gently over his colon. But nothing. Drew continued to cry in pain, and I was suffering right along with him.

It was now noon, and Dr. Monty still had not come. The nurse texted him again.

I skipped lunch because I was afraid to leave Drew. At 3 p.m. I asked the nurse to text the doctor again. Ten minutes later, she reported back, "The doctor said he's too busy to talk to you."

Seven hours after I arrived, Dr. Monty was still a no-show. Drew was still in excruciating pain. And now, visiting hours were over. It broke my heart to leave. He looked so miserable as I walked out.

On my drive home, a text from Dr. Gibbons popped up. "I just read Drew's chart. He developed a significant bacterial pneumonia on January 1. This means he aspirated."

I was shocked. No one told me that Drew had tested positive for a new infection. I let out a heavy sigh. I hadn't wanted to admit that the hospital was not treating Drew properly. I felt guilty even thinking it because so many of the staff loved him. But too many mistakes had been made. He was denied treatments that would have helped. He was given paralytic drugs for weeks that were only safe to be given for days. Dr. Pittman nearly killed him. Drew had lost half his body weight, and now, he was in so much pain, yet the doctor on duty refused to see him.

New Hospital Rules

I felt so helpless. I needed a professional to help. I begged Dr. Gibbons to take Drew on as a patient, but he said he couldn't.

That night, I watched a video by Lee Harris, a spiritual leader. It was as though his message was meant for me. He said, "Fear disables our power. Allow the fire of creativity to move through you, clear things out, and come through the other side to see what was burned down. Then you are able to rebuild."

I thought about how Drew and I were going through a massive transformation. We were being challenged in every way. Him, physically. Me, mentally. Both of us, spiritually. We were suffering and growing at the same time.

But I couldn't see how this was going to end. Will he make it? Will life for us be a terrible battle forever? Will we ever get through this?

One day at a time, one day at a time. *Don't think about the future, only today, Maria.*

I was on the last page of the journal. Tomorrow, I would begin a new one.

Dear Drew, I am praying for your pain to stop. I pray you sleep well.

And as we end this last chapter in this journal, my love, tomorrow we will start again.

64

SWEATPANTS

January 9, 2022
Hospital Day 57, Ventilator Day 46

Drew called early this morning with a very strange request. "Bring sweatpants and shoes," he wrote.

Without questioning, I grabbed Drew's new Olukai slipper shoes and his fleece-lined sweatpants and threw them in a bag.

When I arrived, I knew it was going to be a good day because Frank was our nurse today. I put on the blue gown but didn't bother with the gloves. Frank wouldn't hassle me about it, and I liked holding Drew's hand, flesh to flesh.

Drew pointed to the bag and motioned for me to put the shoes on his feet. I slid them on, and a big smile spread across his face.

Frank came in, "I want to check something," and he lifted Drew's blanket. He inspected Drew's condom catheter, a tube that fits on the penis like a condom, to collect urine and funnel it into a bag that's strapped to the side of the bed.

"It's not good to have this on for too long. It can cause problems with the skin," he said as he removed the catheter. Frank handed Drew a urinal jug. "You can use this from now on."

Frank knew that independence leads to recovery, and for Drew, this was a big step forward.

After Frank left, Drew pointed to the bag again and motioned for me to put the sweatpants on him. I looked around and mischievously laughed, "We will get in trouble for this!" I pulled the curtains closed, then slipped the sweatpants over his ankles and carefully worked them up to his waist. It was not easy since he couldn't lift his hips to help. He giggled, and seeing Drew wearing sweatpants and slippers made me a little giddy. It was almost like he was normal, and we were children having fun.

When Frank walked back in, he saw the sweatpants and stopped in his tracks. Drew and I were giggling. Frank joked, "I was going to put a diaper on you, but hey, that works!"

Later, Frank moved Drew into the chair, and this was the first day I wasn't afraid of it. Drew wore those sweatpants all day. It made him feel like a man again. We watched the sunset through the window, and I reminded Drew that we needed to really enjoy this because soon, we would move to a room with no windows.

He wrote in his best penmanship yet, "We don't know what's next, but we will take it as it comes. Life is still good," and then he signed his name to it as if it were a letter. How funny it was that this silly little act of putting pants on him lifted his spirits so high.

When it was time for me to go, I pulled the sweatpants off of him and put them back in the bag. Drew quickly switched from happy to agitated. He angrily banged his hand on the side of the bed, making a loud noise. Then, his eyes welled up with tears.

Sweatpants

It was as though the pants represented him being normal, and me taking them away put him right back into his helpless state.

"Let it all out, honey," I encouraged. "Let it out." I held his hand, and we both cried as we looked into each other's eyes. We took a moment together to share in our disbelief that our lives had turned into this hell.

That night, I started a new Dear Drew Journal. On the front page of the book, I wrote:

Chapter 2, We are Healing.

Life is Still Good, Drew

65

ICU PSYCHOSIS

January 10, 2022
Hospital Day 58, Ventilator Day 47

Dr. Q is back today. Hallelujah. I never knew I'd be so happy to see him. Goodbye, Pittman!

Drew woke me up at 5:30 this morning, filled with anxiety. Drew's sedation was being turned down, and the nurse warned me that it could cause him to act erratically.

"Dr. Q is back today. Life is going to be easier for us," I said, trying to soothe him.

Drew wrote, "Come here now."

"They won't let me in this early. And anyway, I have to meet the painter at the gallery. I have a surprise for you when you come home," I said.

I was redecorating Drew's office at our gallery. In the last year, his office had somehow become an overflow for storage with boxes all over the floor. Raz and I moved all the stuff out, I hired a guy to repaint the walls, and we put new furniture in there. We ordered a faux-leather brown couch, decorative pillows, and a carpet. I also bought Drew a new leather chair for his desk, one that was extra comfortable for his injured back.

We hung two of Drew's guitars on the wall and a sequence of three photos of Drew surfing a huge wave at Pipeline. The other walls were decorated with Drew's vintage paintings from the 1990s. His office has a sliding glass door that leads to a back patio, and Raz and I decorated that with plants and an outdoor rug. We finished it off with new gold curtains.

When I arrived at the hospital, I was happy to see Dr. Q. It was his first time with Drew in two weeks, and he was surprised at how well he was doing. Dr. Q stressed that we needed to move Drew to an LTAC this week because his hospital wasn't equipped to get Drew walking and talking again.

He warned, "If we don't get him moved to an LTAC soon, he will go directly to a nursing home." Drew frowned. Dr. Q explained that if that happened, Drew may never walk again because nursing homes don't do rehab.

Despite that frightening thought, Drew and I had a fun day together. He was working on his dexterity to hold the pee jug. We cracked jokes about it. Then I put toe-spacers, used for pedicures, in between his toes on both feet. Kim told me this would be good for him. He thought it was stupid, and we giggled about that, too. Drew's ability to laugh showed that he was reaching the next level of healing. It helped him forget about the pain.

After doing flyboys with his legs, he was tired. "Listen to this; it will help you heal," I said. I played a meditation by Dr. Joe Dispenza called "You Are the Placebo." It guides people to use their minds to create healing. Drew fell into a deep sleep at the end of it, and I left to get lunch.

I picked up a chicken salad at a restaurant down the street. While I was gone, the speech therapist woke him out of a deep sleep, and he was disoriented. When I came back into Drew's room, he was having a psychotic episode.

He wrote, "They are trying to kill me."

"No, honey, they aren't killing you. It's the drug withdrawals that are making you think that," I said, trying to reassure him. Just then, Paul walked into the room.

"You're experimenting on me," Drew wrote, accusing Paul of being in on the killing. He thrashed around in his bed, flinging his arms in frustration.

Paul stayed calm. "Drew, I'm your friend. I'm here to help." But it only made Drew more paranoid.

He started to cry in frustration. Then, to my horror, Drew reached for his trach and violently ripped the tube out of his throat. He couldn't breathe—it was suicide.

Paul, cool as ever, stepped in and calmly popped the tube back into Drew's trach.

"Drew, why would you do that?" I yelled, terrified. "Don't ever do that to me again. That's not fair to me," I pleaded.

Drew scrawled, "He's using me as a test dummy."

My voice went stern. I never wanted to see him rip his tubes out like that again. "Drew, do you trust me?" He wouldn't look at me.

"Drew," I said, louder now and right in his face. "Do you trust me?"

Finally, he nodded yes.

"Then trust me when I tell you, Paul is here to help you. He's the best friend you have right now. Don't piss him off!"

Paul stood steady at Drew's bedside, unfazed. He'd seen this many times before.

Eventually, Drew calmed down, the psychosis melting away into clarity. But when it was time to leave, I was still rattled. Watching him rip that tube out of his throat traumatized me. What if he did it again and we weren't there to stop it?

When I got to the parking lot, I found a giant crack across my windshield, stretching right through the driver's line of vision. Everything was breaking. I felt completely defeated.

66

HOPE AND MIRACLES

January 12, 2022
Hospital Day 60, Ventilator Day 49

I kept posting updates on social media, asking people to "visualize Drew as healed." To my surprise, hundreds—maybe even thousands—of people did exactly that. Messages poured in from those who wanted to be part of the miracle. Many started with, "You won't believe this, but I had a vivid dream about Drew, and he was back to his healthy self."

While some were doing the energy work, Drew's other angels were "boots on the ground." Behind the scenes, Paul was quietly taking action—steps that would later become an important piece of the miracle.

Since the doctors had no hope for Drew, they hadn't even tried to wean him off the ventilator. So, Paul took it upon himself to start spontaneous breathing trials. Drew wasn't even his patient, but Paul knew that if someone didn't take action now, Drew would be stuck in that hospital bed until he died.

During his lunch breaks and off-hours, Paul would come in and give Drew short trials off the ventilator, putting him on high-flow oxygen instead. The first time, Drew lasted ten minutes. The next day, Paul pushed it to fifteen. Then, one day, thirty. It was brutal for Drew. With a paralyzed diaphragm, he could barely breathe. He would gasp and fight for every breath. When Drew thought he couldn't go another second, Paul would lean in and say, "Just a little longer, Drew. Just a little longer."

This was a huge step. It meant that maybe—just maybe—Drew had a chance to get off the vent. What I didn't know then was that once you pass sixty days without weaning, the chances of ever getting off a ventilator drop dramatically.

Drew was now only allowed one visitor a day, but Dr. Q gave us special permission for Kim to do therapy with Drew without being counted as a visitor. Dylan and I took turns every other day. On Dylan's days, I would give him a to-do list, which included physical therapy and things like, "Call your grandmother," and "Shave him." Dylan was so easygoing—somehow, he managed to juggle a full-time job while being at the hospital all day, and he did it all with a smile.

Today was my day, and I brought a nail kit and gave Drew a pedicure using a plastic bucket filled with hot water and a little sea salt so he would feel like he was in the ocean. I had fun spending time with Drew doing things we had never done before.

Then, Drew asked Frank for a bedpan. After he used it, he hit the call button. I said, "Don't bother Frank, I can figure this out." I've never been the caregiver type. But I thought, how hard can it be?

It was harder than the nurses made it look. I had to roll Drew off of the metal bedpan carefully so it wouldn't dig into his skinny body and bruise him. It was like moving a 110-pound baby; Drew's body was limp, and he couldn't move his hips to help. I wasn't strong enough, but I managed. Then, I cleaned him up with wipes. I never liked changing diapers on babies, and doing this for a grown man took a special kind of person.

"I just wiped your ass!" I joked. "Oh my God, now we are really close!" We both laughed.

That evening, Joan brought dinner over, and Kim joined us. We sat on the couch, and I confessed that I was afraid of how this was going to end.

"What if he never comes home," I whispered, scared to say the words out loud.

Joan didn't even hesitate. "Drew is going to show us a miracle," she said, her words steady and sure, because she could already see it.

Kim's voice was fierce and protective. "We won't let him slip away, sister."

Then Joan asked if she could lead us in a prayer. I had never prayed with friends. But there we were, the three of us holding hands on my couch, bowing our heads.

Joan spoke with authority, directing the reality we wanted to create. "Dear God, we know that there is a miracle coming. We command that Drew will walk again, surf again, paint again. We command that he will live a long life. And so it is."

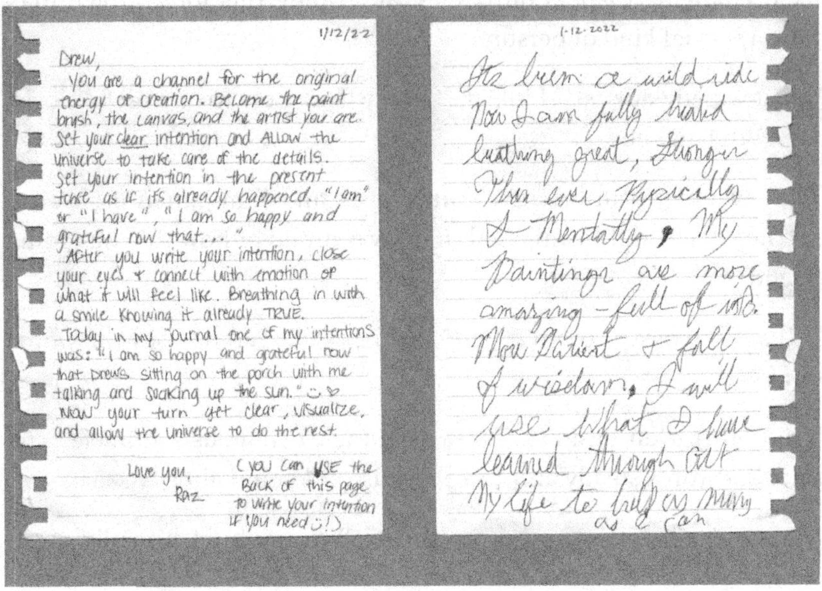

COVID A LOVE STORY

[Handwritten note 1, dated 1/12/22]

Drew,

You are a channel for the original energy of creation. Become the paint brush, the canvas, and the artist you are. Set your clear intention and ALLOW the universe to take care of the details. Set your intention in the present tense as if its already happened. "I am" or "I have", "I am so happy and grateful now that..."

After you write your intention, close your eyes & connect with emotion of what it will feel like. Breathing in with a smile knowing it already TRUE.

Today in my journal one of my intentions was: "I am so happy and grateful now that Drews sitting on the porch with me talking and soaking up the sun." ☺ ♡

Now your turn — get clear, visualize, and allow the universe to do the rest.

Love you,
Raz

(You can USE the BACK of this page to write your intention if you need 😉!)

[Handwritten note 2, dated 1-12-2022]

Its been a wild ride. Now I am fully healed — breathing great, stronger than ever Physically & Mentally. My Paintings are more amazing — full of info. More Patient & full of wisdom. I will use what I have learned throughout my life to help as many as I can

67

TRANSFERRED

January 13, 2022
Hospital Day 61, Ventilator Day 50

After two months in the ICU, today would be Drew's last day at Hospital One. The news came out of nowhere. Kim was finishing a therapy session with him when Dr. Q walked in and said Drew had been accepted into the Santa Ana LTAC—and would be transferred today. When Kim called to tell me, I dropped everything and raced to the hospital, desperate to be there when it happened.

We waited all day for the ambulance to arrive for the transfer. I was nervous. What if his life support fails on the drive? What if there's an accident? What if. What if. What if. Thank God Frank was Drew's nurse today; that made me feel better.

Drew wrote to Frank: "I am stoked to be leaving but sad that I will not see you again."

"I'm going to miss you, too, Drew," Frank said, and he meant it.

I faked excitement for the move. I didn't want Drew to worry. And I warned him, one last time, "It's an old, dingy hospital. It's not five-star like this place. But they have physical therapy, and you'll be walking soon." I kept my voice optimistic.

Paul came in to say goodbye. "I heard the news. Drew, I have friends in Santa Ana, and I've already asked them to look out for you." He promised to visit, but we both knew we'd see way less of him. And I was sad about that. Paul was the one who always swooped in and saved Drew when he was teetering on the edge of death. Now, who would I be able to count on?

I took down all of the photos from the walls and put them in a bag. Frank printed me out a list of Drew's medicines. It was ten pages long. Finally, I got a printout and didn't have to write it by hand.

Just before sunset, a crew of EMTs arrived and moved quickly to load Drew onto a rolling stretcher. "Be careful. He's very critical," I pleaded, afraid they would be too rough. And then I felt silly for being the worried little wife.

"I'm Drew's wife, Maria," I said, making sure to use Drew's name so they would see him as a person, not a patient. "What's your name?" I asked, locking eyes with each one as I said their name back to them to make sure they knew that I was watching.

As they wheeled him out of his hospital room, I felt sad, saying goodbye to the ocean view and the nurses who fell in love with Drew. We were saying hello to a new hospital, far from home, where we would have to start all over again.

Drew was strapped down on the gurney and waved goodbye to Frank with his good arm. Frank told me they had never seen a patient in Drew's condition leave this hospital alive. He said, "Get your phone out. You'll want to film what's about to happen."

As Drew's gurney turned the corner, I froze, stunned by what I saw. The hallway was lined with dozens of nurses and staff members, shoulder to shoulder, clapping and cheering for Drew, celebrating his "graduation."

Tears fell from Danielle's long lashes. She reached out to touch Drew's foot as the gurney rolled past her. Tina smiled big and sang, "We'll miss you, Drew!"

Drew's lips trembled, sad to say goodbye. He swung his hand back and forth, waving as he was pushed down the corridor. From behind us, Frank called out, "The miracle man!"

For a moment, I didn't want to leave these people who lovingly cared for Drew. The new place held so many unknowns. I felt a mix of deep appreciation and sadness. "Bye, Danielle. Bye, Tina. Bye, everyone! We will miss you," I called out. The love I felt was overwhelming. With tears in their eyes, they clapped louder as Drew disappeared into the elevator.

Outside, the light blinded Drew's eyes. He smiled and lifted his face towards the setting sun, eyes closed. I watched as they loaded him into the back of the vehicle. *Be careful with him*, I thought. I closed my eyes and said a prayer, asking my angels to ride with Drew in the ambulance.

I followed behind them on the freeway to Santa Ana. When we arrived, Danny greeted me in the lobby and led me to Drew's new room. It was small and ugly, with old yellow walls and barely any space to move around his bed. But he didn't have a roommate, and that was one good thing about having a contagious infection—you get a room all to yourself, in isolation.

There was no chair to sit on. I wandered until I found a folding chair near the nurse's station and, without asking, carried it into Drew's room. I texted an update to the family. "Drew is getting settled. There's no window. But I'll hang the photos, and we will make the best of it."

Dylan came and helped me tape the photos to Drew's new walls. We hung memories of Drew surfing, paddleboarding, family photos at the beach, and crayoned pictures that kids made, wishing him well.

Drew's new nurse, Peggy, was busy and unfriendly. That bothered me, but I didn't let Drew know. She held a clipboard, weighed Drew on the bed, and I watched her write "110 pounds".

"Is that accurate? That doesn't seem right." I said, alarmed. "He normally weighs 220."

She assured me the scale on the bed was right. That meant that Drew had lost one hundred pounds since November, the weight of an entire person.

By now it had been hours without his medicine, and Drew started getting agitated. He was going through withdrawal symptoms. It started with anxiety and then grew into full-blown panic. "Peggy," I called out to the nurse. "When will Drew get his meds?"

She said that she was still processing him and had to get the doctor to sign off on the meds, then order them from the pharmacy, and then she could administer them.

"How long will that take? Because he's really suffering," I pleaded.

"It will take as long as it takes," she answered. I didn't like the sound of that. We were getting off to a bad start.

Drew's panic escalated to a severity I had never seen. Beads of cold sweat dotted his forehead, and his eyes were not focused. He clutched at the sheets, white-knuckled, bracing himself against the agony inside him.

Dylan knelt down on Drew's left side and held his hand. "Dad, it's going to be okay. We are with you."

Drew mouthed, "Heart attack."

I held his right hand. "Honey, this is drug withdrawal. It will pass." But, I wasn't totally sure. I tried getting Peggy's attention again, but she waved me away.

As the clock ticked closer to 7:30, I felt my own anxiety rise. I knew that as soon as the nurse shift happened, we would lose another hour.

"Please," I called out to Peggy. "Please give him his meds before you leave!" Now, she was ignoring me. And, just as I predicted, the shift change happened, and the night nurse came on duty. It would be another hour of torture.

The night nurse's name was Marigold. She was Eastern European and didn't speak English very well. With the mask muffling her voice and her strong accent, I couldn't understand a word she said. Now I hated this new place.

Drew's entire body was trembling uncontrollably like he was having a seizure. His heart rate climbed. He clutched his chest in pain. "Now we know why it's so hard for people to quit heroin," I said out loud to no one in particular. "The pain is too much to bear."

We thought Drew might die right then and there. Dylan and I did everything we could to calm Drew down. I put a sound healing song on. Dylan massaged his back, and I rubbed his feet. Nothing helped. Did we move him too soon? I started to question why Dr. Q was in such a hurry to get Drew out of his hospital. This transition took Drew into the bellows of hell.

All three of us were exhausted. Drew's crazy panic attack was the hardest thing we endured together as a family. Dylan and I were still holding Drew's hands when visiting hours were over. Marigold came in and told us we had to leave.

"We aren't leaving until he's given his meds," I said firmly, stamping my foot. There was no way I was going to leave him like this.

Finally, Marigold gave Drew a dose of Ativan. It calmed him enough to where we felt it was safe to go. I set up his iPad and put on a Dr. Joe Dispenza healing meditation for Drew to listen to, and then Dylan and I kissed him goodbye.

We got home after ten, and neither of us had eaten. Dylan said goodnight and went to bed. I turned on *Sex and the City* and opened a bottle of wine. The red medicine started to relax me. Thank God for wine and *Sex and the City*. Otherwise, I'd have killed myself by now.

In the middle of the night, Drew called, eyes wide, having another panic attack. He held the paper up to the iPad. "Can't sleep."

I calmed him down with the softest voice I could muster, "You are safe. This new place is where you are going to get your body back. You'll get through this."

We hung up. And then he called me back two hours later. It was a repeat of the earlier conversation.

Early in the morning, I woke up to a crow screeching outside my window. "Kakaw, kakaw".

I threw the covers off in anger; I hadn't slept all night. My body felt like I had been running a marathon for 61 days. I didn't have anything left in me.

In the Dear Drew Journal, I wrote:

> *I'm exhausted and tapped out.*
> *I can't do this for much longer.*
> *Something needs to change.*

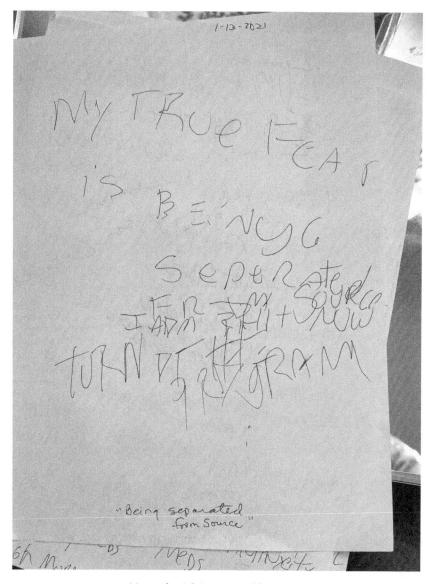

My true fear is being separated from source

68

SANTA ANA

January 15, 2022
Hospital Day 63, Ventilator Day 52

It was Drew's third day at Santa Ana, and his healing was slipping backward in a terrifying way. The infection in his lungs was highly critical, and he was back to dying at any moment. His temperature spiked high, and it came with unbearable hot flashes.

Some say that a Long-Term Acute Care Facility is "where people go to die." And though Drew's prognosis was as grim as death itself, and the new place was dark and dingy, I clung to the hope that Santa Ana was the second phase of his recovery.

We met Drew's new Pulmonologist, Dr. K. He was a slender man in his mid-forties. You couldn't miss him because he had long black hair tied in a ponytail. Dr. K worked at several hospitals and had his own practice, so he was busy. Even so, he would take time with Drew and was patient as Drew wrote down his questions.

Today, Drew held my hand all day. He was in a lot of pain. In all our years together, he never liked holding hands, but now it gave him comfort. I had a hard time leaving because he was so miserable.

On my drive home, I listened to *Walking Home from the ICU* podcast. As I learned more about how the induced coma caused Drew's paralysis, I became more regretful. If I had known this sooner, I could have stopped it. What else am I missing? What else do I need to stop from happening?

I have to do more. I have to pay attention to every detail. I was feeling desperate and weary. I was mentally and physically exhausted, and the pain in my throat never stopped.

When I got home, the house was filthy. Piles of unopened mail cluttered the kitchen table. All my clothes were dirty. I didn't have the energy to do anything. And tomorrow night, I'd be hosting a women's circle at the gallery—and I still hadn't prepared for it. My chest hurt from the stress.

There was a knock at the door. It was Joan, dropping off dinner again. As she stood in the doorway, she read the desperation on my face and asked what she could do to help. "My throat hurts. My house is a mess. Drew is dying, and I'm worn out," I sulked.

Just saying the words out loud made me feel sorry for myself. I was carrying a heavy burden, and there was no end in sight. I felt like giving up but didn't even know how to do that.

Joan grabbed my shoulders, looked into my eyes, and said intently, "You are strong enough to do this. Drew is going to recover. I know it to be true."

It was good to have a friend who believed in the impossible.

An hour later, I received a text from a lady who said, "Joan hired me to clean your house. What day can I come?" Gratitude flooded my heart. This kind gesture made my night a lot brighter.

Santa Ana

That night, I wrote:

Dear Drew,

Today I felt like giving up. But then Joan reminded me to keep the faith.

So much support is coming to us.

It gives me the strength to continue this fight.

69

FULL MOON

January 16, 2022
Hospital Day 64, Ventilator Day 53

Today, I was making Drew's first smoothie—the first real food to go into his body through his stomach tube. It felt like a turning point, something I could do to help him heal. My friend Nikki in Tennessee had connected me with Dr. Bill Sears, the famous nutrition expert. I got him on the phone and he guided me in choosing ingredients to help rebuild Drew's body. The recipe was packed with healing: MCT oil, avocado, kefir, vegetables, wild blueberries, pomegranate juice, and fresh ginger. I mixed in a handful of vitamins to strengthen his immune system, plus mullein for his lungs. I blended it all together, filled an eight-ounce jar with my "special smoothie," and handed it over to the nurse, who fed it carefully into Drew's stomach tube.

Now that Drew was allowed multiple visitors, I organized a list of who was coming every day. Dylan and I took the morning or evening shifts, and I scheduled friends to visit in between.

At noon, I met with Drew's medical team in the conference room of the LTAC. I came prepared with a list of questions. But the most important thing on my mind was getting Drew back to breathing on his own. I asked, "What is your plan to get him off the ventilator so he can come home?"

They all looked at me, astonished, as if I had two heads. Someone on the respiratory team said, "We've never gotten anyone off a ventilator after this long." Another therapist at the table agreed, saying it wasn't possible with Drew's lung infection, as he was too critical. They tried to gently explain to me that people in Drew's condition don't go home; they end up in a nursing home. I pretended I didn't hear that, rejecting that horrible outcome from my mind.

"Let's give him another round of high-dose Vitamin C infusions. It knocked down his last infection." I said, offering a solution. Everyone went quiet, and I felt a weird energy in the room. Finally, someone said in a quiet voice, "We will have to ask the pharmacy about that." Later, it became clear that none of the doctors at Santa Ana would sign off on the high-dose Vitamin C, though I fought for it for many weeks.

That afternoon, Drew's nurse put a condom catheter on him. "Why are you doing that? He doesn't need it," I protested. She insisted that this was better for him. We are going backward a few more steps, I thought. I made a note to fight this on another day; today, I didn't have the strength.

Just then, Drew's new internist came in, bringing a dark cloud with her. Dr. Kamatow was a tall woman with a permanent frown on her face. She introduced herself to Drew, and he wrote, "How much longer on the vent?"

She gave a grim answer, "Oh, you won't be getting off the ventilator. But don't worry, Drew, you will adjust."

Full Moon

"Well, he has to get off of it," I argued, pointing to the big machine by Drew's bed. "We can't take that thing home with us."

"He will be moved to a nursing home from here," the doctor said matter-of-factly. And then, as if it would cheer us up, she said, "Many patients live a good life in a nursing home."

Hearing this for the second time today brought an avalanche of fear and anger over me. It was too terrible to even think about.

I stared at Dr. Kamatow with contempt. How dare she assign my husband to live out the rest of his life in a nursing home, not even knowing Drew's will to survive. She hadn't even spent time with him yet.

When she left the room, I turned to Drew and said, "Don't listen to her. You're getting off this thing." He nodded in agreement. When I drove home, I felt defeated and depressed again.

It was a full moon, and I was co-hosting a women's circle with my friends Andréa and Raz. We were in our second year of leading women in a sound bath, meditation, and energy healing once a month. I had considered canceling until Drew was better, but I needed one thing that made me happy, and these events uplifted me.

I mentally put away my worries and switched my focus to making the circle a place of peace for our guests. The three of us prepared the gallery with flowers and crystals and placed lit candles around the room. Andréa brought her big gong and crystal bowls, we saged the room, and together, we said a prayer for our guides to help us make every woman who arrived feel loved and peaceful.

Eighteen women gathered, and for two hours, I forgot about my troubles as Andréa played her instruments, Raz did energy healing, and I guided a heart-opening meditation. Some of the women had no idea what was going on in my personal life, but a few who knew hugged me before they left. "I don't know how you are doing this with Drew in the hospital," one said with compassion.

"I needed this probably more than anyone here," I said. And I did. My spirit had been fueled enough to get me through another day.

70

BREAKING POINT

January 19, 2022
Hospital Day 67, Ventilator Day 56

Santa Ana was draining the life out of me. It was getting to Dylan, too. The drive was too far, and it was a dark, depressing place.

Today, Drew's condition was visibly worse. The infection in his lungs had gone without treatment for too long, and he was tormented with choking and nausea. Dr. K addressed it with new meds, but Drew's hot flashes never stopped, and we had to put ice packs on his head and shoulders constantly.

When I arrived, Drew wrote, "I saw them take a body out last night." He pointed to an area that Dylan and I called "the death-corner" because it was where they put critical ICU patients when they didn't have an empty room. The corner had three beds lined up next to each other. Today, one of the patients had his feet hanging out of the covers, flopping with drop foot. It made me sad that this person would never walk again.

Drew had his brother Jamie on FaceTime. Drew wrote, "I need you here." Drew never asked for anything from his family. But now, he needed them. And no one, except Andrea, had come, though he had been on his deathbed for months. I felt resentment grow inside me. If they aren't here for him when he's dying, then when?

Visiting hours were almost over, and I kissed Drew goodbye. Drew held my hand and wouldn't let go. He didn't want to be alone; he feared the nights at Santa Ana. The night nurses were rough, and nighttime was when people died. He was distraught, so I stayed until the nurse kicked me out. When I left, I felt terrible.

The darkness at Santa Ana put me in a gloomy state of mind. I couldn't stop thinking about Drew's fate, as promised by Dr. Kamatow, "He will be moved to a nursing home."

I decided to tell no one about this. I did not want anyone, not even Dylan, to think for a minute that Drew would end up in a nursing home. I didn't want to give that terrible fate any energy because energy leads to reality. I had to make sure that everyone believed he was coming home, especially family.

It took all my might to keep these things to myself. Overwhelm hit me hard as I walked to my car. I had nothing left inside of me—no more light, no more positivity. The pain in the side of my neck flared up, and I tried not to swallow because that made it hurt more. I couldn't take one more day of this.

Suicide would be easier. For a moment, I considered it. I'd take one too many sleeping pills, or I could drive on Ortega Highway's twisty roads and just keep driving off of a cliff. But then, what would happen to Dylan? I couldn't leave him without his parents. And what if Drew came home, and I wasn't there to care for him? I was trapped. I couldn't even kill myself. I was stuck in hell.

Until now, my texts to the group of 14 family members had been positive. But today, I felt abandoned. I was mad that no one was here for Drew, and he was nearly dead. Where is everybody?

I got in the car and texted a plea for help. This time, I was brutally honest:

> I've reached a breaking point.
> I'm not sure how much longer I can do this.
> My biz is going to fail. I don't feel well, and there is so much to do for Drew.
> So many problems to solve.
> I need help.

I drove the car like a crazy person, weaving in and out of traffic, slamming on the breaks, speeding up. I thought about crashing into a pole and ending my pain. I was having a nervous breakdown.

Drew's Mom read the desperation in my text and called me right away. My voice was distraught, and I admitted that I was disappointed in the family. If any of them were dying, Drew would have been there for them. My despondence turned to anger, "If we are on our own, then I'm just going to cut everyone off," I blurted.

Mom was upset and started to cry. "Please don't cut us off."

A shot of guilt went through me. She was hurting just as much as I was. It was her baby boy that was dying. And she was in her 80s and couldn't fly out here by herself. It wasn't her fault. "I'm sorry, Mom, I just don't know what to do."

Andrea called me next. "We feel abandoned, Andrea. We can't do this alone. It's too hard." She could hear the desperation in my voice. She sprung into action, teaming up with other family members. They organized an online meal train and a shared website for me to ask for help. Andrea sent out a family text, laying it all out. And the text ended with, "Maria, we love you and all you are doing for Drew."

I felt better that they heard me. I knew they cared. But I needed more. I needed bodies here, boots on the ground.

COVID A LOVE STORY

I wrote in my Dear Drew Journal:

You need your family here, and today, you asked them to come.
You never ask them for anything.
I hope they listen.

71

IT'S OK IF I DIE

January 20, 2022
Hospital Day 68, Ventilator Day 57

It was Raz's birthday, and she asked me to spend the day with her at the luxury Waldorf Astoria day spa in Laguna Beach. I didn't want to go because I'd worry about Drew the entire time. But Andrea talked me into it. "You need a break," she said.

So I did. But first, I organized Drew's visitor lineup for the day. Our website manager Cory, who just flew back from Denver; our friends Craig and Denise; Kim; and then Dylan. Cory was on the morning shift, so I put him in charge of the smoothie and packed it on ice. "Ask the nurse to feed him the second you get there," I instructed.

Raz and I spent the day getting facials, sitting in the steam room, and writing in our journals. I pretended I was having fun, but deep inside, I was miserable. I kept texting each person as they were visiting Drew, asking how he was. I hated being so far away from him. Raz took pictures of us in our fancy robes for her Instagram as I forced a smile.

That night, when Dylan came home, he looked very depressed. It worried me because, normally, he was a happy kid. I said, "Son, you are going to have to go home soon. You can't stay here forever."

He said, "Mom, I'm not going anywhere until Dad is home."

Though we tried to hide it from Drew, he sensed that we were at a breaking point. He FaceTimed Andrea and wrote, "Need help. Maria's exhausted. Come see me here, not on the iPad." Andrea didn't hesitate–she booked a flight immediately.

That night, over FaceTime, Drew held up his paper, "Don't let them forget about me." He was losing sight of his old life, the one full of people and places and adventures.

He started to have another anxiety attack, and this time, I calmed him down by talking about happy memories we had over the years. "Remember when we were in New Zealand, and we took Dylan on a boat through the glowworm caves?" I recounted every detail of the trip. Drew nodded through the pain.

Then he wrote, "It's ok if I die. My life has been great."

"You're not going to die. We have many more adventures to come." I said, trying to convince both of us.

That night, I thought about how everyone was celebrating the fact that Drew survived, but they didn't know that he was still inches from death. Keeping that secret was wearing on me.

My own life force was dimming. My ability to smile through the fear had weakened. I wrote in my Dear Drew Journal:

> *I felt guilty not being with you today.*
>
> *Dylan's stressed, and I'm always on the verge of tears.*
>
> *But we will keep going.*

72

TALKING

January 21, 2022
Hospital Day 69, Ventilator Day 58

Dylan was out test-flying drones, his favorite part of his job as a software engineer. I was on the morning shift with Drew. When I arrived, the speech therapist was putting a Passy-Muir valve on Drew's trach, a part that enabled him to speak, just for a few minutes.

He waved to me, and I heard his voice say, "I love you, Spunk." It was a weak, raspy whisper, but I felt my heart jump, hearing him say my nickname for the first time in months.

Then, he called out to the nurse, "Thanks for taking care of me." Next, he called his mother on the phone so she could hear his voice. It was just like Drew, always thinking of others.

When we were alone, all he wanted to talk about was his near-death experience. He described how he had left his body and floated away in a river of light and how he had become a part of everything all at once. He had so much more to tell, but he was getting worn out, and the therapist came back and removed the speaking valve. And just like that, he was mute again.

Being able to speak gave Drew a renewed sense of hope, and he wrote out a list: "Goals: Sit on the side of the bed all by myself. Control my breathing. Visualize being strong and healthy." I taped the list to the wall where he could see it.

Drew asked me to reposition his legs for him. I looked down the hallway and saw a patient in his bed, a fit, forty-ish aged man. He was on a ventilator but was wide awake and sitting up. I watched him lift one leg and casually cross it over his other leg as he read a book. I felt a tinge of jealousy. I wished Drew was strong enough to cross his legs. He couldn't even lift them.

Later that afternoon, Drew's case manager came to me. She said, "The next step for Drew is to be moved to a sub-acute facility. You need to choose which one you want him to go to."

I asked if that was a rehab place where he would learn to walk again.

"No," she answered. "It's a nursing home."

Oh, hell no, I thought.

"Well, that's not going to happen," I told her. "What's another option?"

She repeated three times that there weren't any other options for Drew. But I kept pressing until she finally gave in and said, "Well, there are facilities where they rehab the patient to get ready to go home. But Drew is definitely not a candidate for that."

Ok, I thought. *We will do what we need to do to make him a candidate for rehab.*

Talking

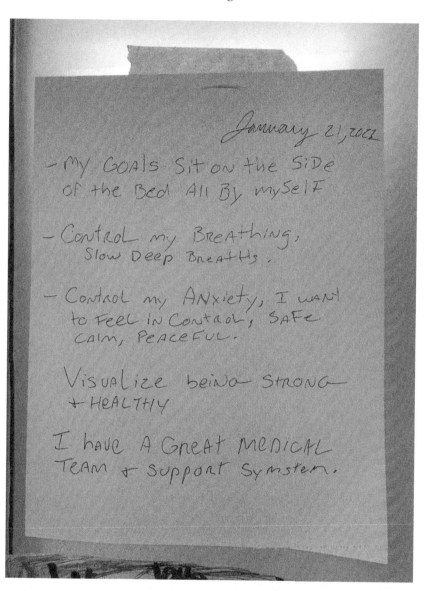

January 21, 2002

- My goals sit on the side of the bed all by myself

- Control my breathing, slow deep breaths.

- Control my anxiety, I want to feel in control, safe calm, peaceful.

Visualize being strong + Healthy

I have a great medical team + support symsten.

73

ANGEL

January 22-25, 2022
Hospital Day 73, Ventilator Day 62

For three days, Drew had massive amounts of blood filling up his urine bag, but no one at Santa Ana knew why, and quite frankly, they didn't care. It was scary, and I was in a state of shock over how bad things had gotten. I called Drew's cousin, who is a nurse. She suggested I raise hell and get the doctors to do something. But I didn't have the energy for another battle. My body was almost as limp as Drew's; I could barely drag it out of bed.

Drew was given another round of antibiotics for the lung infection, and that created stomach distress. They gave him a Scopolamine patch for the nausea, but he had a terrible reaction, and it made his vision blurry. It was another round of whack-a-mole. Every time we solved one problem, two more popped up.

One morning, Drew was suffering worse than ever. He had cold sweats, shaking, nausea, and pain from head to toe. His hand shook as he wrote, "I'm dying."

I was distraught; the staff expected Drew to die, and they had given up on him. That's why I couldn't get them to investigate the cause of his bloody urine. It all seemed so hopeless. I was losing a battle that I wasn't equipped to fight. I held his hand and prayed, "Please, God, send someone to help us."

It was as though I had placed an order, and the Universe delivered—because not even an hour later, a human angel walked into Drew's room. She was a bright light emerging through the darkness, and the room seemed to illuminate around her. She had sparkly blue eyes, long blonde hair, and a warm smile behind her mask. Her name tag read: "Alicia, Respiratory Therapist."

She knelt down to be at eye level with him and said, "Hi, Drew, I'm Alicia. How are you feeling?"

Alicia's eyes emanated love, patiently waiting as he wrote answers to her questions. She was serious and soft-spoken. She made Drew feel important.

There was something about him that made her believe in him. Maybe she saw his bright energy, trapped in a broken body. I found out later that, soon after meeting us, she had already started making a plan to get Drew off that ventilator.

Looking back on all that happened, I now know that Alicia was the reason we ended up at Santa Ana. I was divinely guided to choose that dingy hospital over better places so that she would help us make a miracle.

I don't blame those who couldn't believe it. It did seem hopeless. He was as critical as those who died around him. Drew could only move his arms slightly. His muscles were atrophied so badly that he couldn't sit up by himself, and that had to happen before he could get

Angel

in a wheelchair, and that had to happen before he could walk. Like a baby, he couldn't even roll over by himself. It all seemed impossible.

Drew's mental strength was impressive, though. He had a strong will to live. The near-death experience made his mind clearer than it ever was before, and he was able to reflect on the impact his illness had on everyone. He saw more love in the world now, and it was filling him up with the energy he needed to keep fighting.

Our friend Rich called from his house in Costa Rica. "When Drew's well enough, I want to fly you here. Maybe in the fall. It will be healing for both of you."

I said, "Yes, we will come." I didn't tell him that Drew was so sick he may never travel again. But, the promise of going on an adventure gave us something to work towards. What I didn't know at the time was that our future trip to Costa Rica would bring this entire ordeal to a close.

I wrote in the journal:

> *Dear Drew,*
>
> *Today we met another one of your angels, Alicia.*
>
> *She was attentive and seemed to care.*
>
> *There's something very special about her.*

74

GOOD IS COMING

January 25-26, 2022
Hospital Day 74, Ventilator Day 63

Andrea flew back in from Atlanta for the week. Now that she was here, things would be easier for Dylan and me. But this time, I am a different Maria. The needy, scared little girl Andrea left back in December had gone. I was now a strong woman, confident and unwavering in my decisions.

Andrea spent all of her days with Drew. She hung a large calendar on his wall to track his accomplishments. She got to witness Drew sitting up on his own for the first time. And she watched as the therapists lifted him on a board to slide his butt from the bed into a wheelchair. Even though it took two people to do it, we celebrated. Andrea recorded on the calendar, "January 23, got in a wheelchair."

Drew's infection was clearing up, and he was getting stronger. I increased his smoothies from one jar to two. He gained a pound, then another. Speech therapy was three times a week, and for those short sessions, Drew was able to speak.

When we talked to his medical staff, we'd say things like, "When Drew comes home, we're going to do this... or that..." Even though everyone kept telling us he would live the rest of his life in a nursing home, we kept envisioning him back in his own house. We were planting the idea in the minds of anyone who would listen: someday, Drew would come home.

That relentless optimism got to Alicia. She began to believe it too—and quietly devised a strategy. She would start Drew on breathing trials off the ventilator to see if he could be weaned off it for good. The plan was to begin with short stints: three hours, then six, gradually increasing. If he could work up to breathing on his own for three full days, then home wouldn't just be a dream—it would be a real possibility.

But not everyone shared her faith. One day, Drew overheard Alicia arguing with Dr. K about her plan.

"No. It's too risky," the doctor insisted.

Alicia's own boss—the head of Respiratory Therapy—was no more supportive. "It won't work. It's been too long," he said, shaking his head.

But Alicia didn't give up. She got two other therapists in on it with her, and the three of them believed enough in the possibility that they finally convinced Dr. K to allow them to try. Elated, Alicia ordered a t-piece, a special part that is used with the ventilator for spontaneous breathing trials.

On the first trial, Alicia had Drew breathing on the t-piece for three hours. It was incredibly hard on him—his chest heaved in and out violently, and he struggled for every breath. But he made it through, and that was a good sign. The head of the respiratory team was impressed and said, "I have to admit, Alicia was right."

To get Drew off the ventilator for good, he would have to prove he could breathe for 72 hours without it. He would still need an oxygen tank, but he could go home with that; no nursing home needed.

We had a new goal now: increase the time on the breathing trials each day until he was strong enough to reach 72 hours. Goals always kept Drew motivated. As weak as he was, there was a spark of fire in his eyes—fueled by the promise that one day, he might be breathing on his own.

Besides worrying about Drew, I was deeply worried about money. With neither of us working, the business was suffering. If I didn't get cash rolling in soon, I'd have to shut down the gallery—and then what would we do?

I had a meeting with Cory and Raz, and we hatched a plan to release art prints of Drew's last painting before he got sick. Coincidentally, the name of the painting was *LIFEFORCE*. The plan worked—the prints sold like wildfire, and we made enough to get through a few more months.

For the first time in weeks, I checked our post office box. Buried in a pile of mail was an envelope from Native Sons, with a big check from their "Pray for Drew" T-shirt donation drive. Later that night, a friend stopped by the house and handed me an envelope full of grocery and gas cards.

"I know you're burning up a lot of gas driving to Santa Ana every day," he said. "Maybe this will help."

Good was flowing to us in so many ways. I wrote in my Dear Drew Journal:

So many people are looking out for us. They refuse to let us fail.

75

OUT OF ICU

January 27, 2022
Hospital Day 75, Ventilator Day 64

The hardest part of weaning off a ventilator is being able to control your mind. Patients become attached to the machine — it's their lifeline. A primal panic takes over at the thought of not being able to breathe. Even a year after coming off the vent, many members of my Ventilator Survivor Group still suffer extreme anxiety around the fear of losing their ability to breath on their own.

Drew felt that panic when Alicia started the breathing trials. His heart would race, and he would gasp for air for hours. He often wanted to quit but pushed himself because he knew that it was the only way to get back to his life. Luckily, Drew had mastery over his mind; surfing big waves taught him how to manage fear.

Alicia had arranged her schedule so that she could work with Drew every day. Yesterday, she had him breathing off the vent for five hours, his longest stretch yet. Today, her eyes sparkled as she announced,

"I'm going to take a more aggressive route now." I was on board with anything she said. She was one of the few people that I completely trusted with Drew's life.

Today, Andrea flew back home to Atlanta. Before leaving, she made a huge batch of homemade chicken soup and spinach egg muffins with bacon and froze half of it. Now, Dylan and I would eat for a couple of weeks. We were sad to see her leave. The house would feel empty again.

My friend Ashley asked to bring her boyfriend, a physical therapist, to see Drew. Even though he didn't know Drew, Tan said that he "felt called" to work on him. When they arrived, Ashley tried to hide her shock at how emaciated Drew was. Tan secretly told Ashley that in his line of work, he never saw someone in that bad of shape ever recover. Still, they began visiting a few times a week to give Drew therapy, and I started to realize just how many people it takes to help one person come back from a coma.

The belief in Drew's recovery was not just spreading; it was inspiring people to take action. Drew's team of angels was growing. People were praying. Friends were visiting. Healers were showing up to give him treatments. And now, three of his respiratory therapists were pushing the limits beyond what was normally done for patients. Everyone wanted to be a part of it. And it took all of them to make a miracle.

That night, Kim called me from the hospital. While she was treating Drew, the staff suddenly moved him out of the ICU to give his bed to someone in more critical condition. Thankfully, Kim was there to pull the photos from the walls and pack up Drew's belongings for the move.

Even though the transition was unexpected, I knew this much: every time Drew moved from one room to another, his healing leveled up.

76

THE GOAT

January 29, 2022
Hospital Day 77, Ventilator Day 66

Drew's new room was big with two beds, and because of his history of infection, still no roommate. He had a window now, looking out over a grassy area with trees. It was quieter here, away from the frantic bustle of the ICU. Sunlight poured through the glass, warm and gentle, and for a moment it felt like we had finally stepped out from under the dark cloud of death that had hung over him for so long.

But the peace came with a cost.

On this new floor, Drew was mostly left alone. When he pressed the call button, help rarely came. One nurse explained that many of their nurses had recently quit to work for a bigger hospital offering a $30,000 signing bonus. "We are terribly short-staffed," she complained.

Physical therapy was making only the tiniest bit of progress. Drew was still a double assist and he continued to suffer from terrible vertigo. He wasn't able to put weight on his feet. It seemed impossible that he would ever walk again. But the head therapist, Bill, was a drill sergeant. Word in the hospital was that if anyone was going to get Drew walking, it would be Bill.

I'd been warned that even if Drew did walk again, he'd need an oxygen machine and a walker for the rest of his life. The picture painted in my mind of Drew, being a frail old man at 50 years old, was horrific. I put it out of my mind and chose not to accept it.

We had become the talk of the staff at Santa Ana. We weren't like the other families. I was practically living there. Raz would meet me for business meetings in the cafeteria. Drew refused to wear his hospital gown, and his room looked like a college dorm, with photos covering the walls. Some days, he had as many as eight visitors—most of them there to give massages and therapy.

Alicia told me later that whenever she walked into Drew's room, someone was always there rubbing his feet or telling jokes and laughing with him. She said the positivity of his friends and family was inspiring. They all believed he was coming home, and that belief planted a seed of hope in her, too.

Drew's visitor list kept growing. My morning routine of coordinating Drew's lineup for the day got complicated as I scheduled each person so Drew would never be alone. I remembered Dr. Q telling me that the ventilator survivors tended to be "the people who have family who are always there."

Having visitors gave Drew a stronger will to live. When you're in a hospital for too long, surrounded by beeping machines and strangers in masks, you become institutionalized, and your mind starts to fail. Visitors keep you connected to your life and remind you of why you must fight to come home.

The GOAT

Drew was one of the few patients at Santa Ana who had visitors. I felt sad for the others. Where are their families? Why are they left alone?

When I arrived today, there was a crowd gathered around Drew's bed —Alicia and her fellow therapists. My heart dropped for a moment, fearing something had gone wrong. But as I got closer, I was relieved to hear laughter and conversation.

"Are you guys having a party?" I joked. They were all captivated by Drew as he wrote stories about surfing big waves in Hawaii.

Alicia had extended his breathing trial today—six full hours. Drew's oxygen saturation dipped a bit, but Alicia was pleased. His body was adapting more and more each time, and she could see the progress.

Today was the big World Surfing League contest. Drew was excited to watch it live on the iPad, as many of his friends were competitors. The event was held at the world-famous Bonzai Pipeline, a wave on the North Shore of Oahu, Hawaii, where Drew lived before we met. It was his favorite wave to surf. Pipeline is every surfer's dream, but only a small percentage is skilled enough to surf. It's a huge, powerful wave that breaks over a shallow volcanic reef.

One of the contestants was Kelly Slater, the reigning world champion. He and Drew used to compete in surfing contests as teenagers. Drew had once dreamed of becoming a pro surfer too, but in his twenties, he realized he wasn't competitive by nature. He chose a different path and became a professional artist. Kelly kept going, eventually becoming a multiple-time surfing world champion.

I climbed into the hospital bed and lay beside Drew. His eyes were glued to the contest. I felt his thigh, bony and fragile, against mine. I wanted to rest my head on his shoulder like I used to, back when there wasn't a dog collar and a ventilator tube in the way. I hated how that thing chained him to the bed.

We watched as Kelly's body flexed with feline grace, catching his last wave of the heat, his strong legs carving the board perfectly on the face of the wave. He was graceful, free, and strong, in sync with the ocean. Drew's eyes teared up, remembering himself on that beloved wave not so long ago.

The judges announced the winner: Kelly Slater. At forty-nine, he became the oldest competitor to ever win—a feat almost unheard of in surfing. He was "the GOAT," the greatest of all time.

It was surreal for Drew to see Kelly in his athletic glory while Drew himself lay paralyzed, reduced to a bag of bones with ice packs on his head and a dog collar on his neck, tied to the bed by a ventilator tube.

Drew was living his worst nightmare as he watched Kelly's dreams come true. With a weak smile, he wrote, "I'm happy for Kelly. What a different reality we are living."

I looked at Drew's broken body and tried to imagine him surfing again. I couldn't visualize it. All I could see was a frail old man.

And then, as if the Universe knew I needed a reminder to keep my faith, a bright light entered the room. Alicia bounced in, her face lit with joy.

"Congrats on the six-hour trial, Drew," She beamed. She was more talkative than usual, her eyes sparkling with excitement.

She leaned in, lowering her voice as if she were sharing a secret. "We have big plans for you tomorrow, Drew."

I felt the energy in the room shift. Something was about to change.

77

THE TEST

January 30th, 2022
Hospital Day 78, Ventilator Day 67

Alicia kept her promise. She and her respiratory therapy dream team, Cho and Sheldon, started a 24-hour trial with Drew off the ventilator. It was an aggressive move because most weanings take weeks. We were attempting it in just a few days. They shut off the ventilator and put him on high-flow oxygen, delivered through nasal cannulas.

That evening, as I sat with Drew, Sheldon said in an excited voice, "Now, let's see if you can go all night. If you make it to 72 hours, you're off the ventilator for good."

A surge of excitement—and fear—rushed through me. This was Drew's one shot, a chance Alicia had fought fiercely to secure. It felt like the biggest surfing contest of his life. But this time, his opponent wasn't another surfer—it was the machine. And the wave he had to ride was his own breath.

If Drew passed this test, he would advance to the next step in his recovery. If he didn't, then he would never come home.

I took my shoes off, climbed into Drew's bed, and snuggled against him as we watched an episode of Yellowstone. His chest heaved in and out with each breath. It was violent—the way he had to jerk his body just to pull air into his damaged lungs. Each inhale and exhale was a battle. We both silently wondered how he was going to make it through the night.

I stayed long past visiting hours. Finally, around midnight, a nurse peeked into Drew's dark room and caught me. "You must leave now," she barked in a sharp German accent.

As I was putting on my coat, Sheldon came in to check on Drew.

Drew looked uneasy and said, "It's hard. I might die in my sleep."

Sheldon took his hand and sat in the chair beside the bed. "Drew, I'll be with you the entire night. I won't let anything happen to you."

The next morning, when Drew opened his eyes, Sheldon was still there. "Congratulations, you made it," he said proudly.

78

48 TO GO

January 31, 2022
Hospital Day 79

I barely slept, my mind racing with fear that Drew wouldn't make it through the night. The worst-case scenario looped in my head—he'd suffocate, and no one would be there to save him. But then, just after sunrise, my phone rang. It was Drew, holding a piece of paper to the screen: "I survived." Relief flooded me. Two more nights like this, and he'd be off the machine for good.

Drew's older brother, Jamie, was flying in tonight from South Carolina, and Drew was very excited to see him. I organized the visitor lineup for the day: Ashley and Tan, Maria, Dylan, and Jamie.

When I arrived at Drew's room, I noticed he was still on the condom catheter. I checked my medical journal—eighteen days. That was far too long. I asked the nurse, "Let's remove this and let him pee in a jug."

The nurse said no, but I pushed. I knew that the more Drew did for himself, the stronger he got. And as silly as it sounds, peeing in a jug would make him feel more human and lift his spirits.

Reluctantly, the nurse removed the catheter and hung three pee jugs off the side of Drew's bed. It was a small step, but an important one toward independence. I was learning that every little thing made a difference.

Later, Drew and I watched an episode of *Yellowstone*, and I pretended we were in our living room on the couch. Out of nowhere, Drew grabbed my boob. It surprised me—just like old times! A good sign that my Drew was coming back.

"When you get a woody, that's when I'll know you are really going to be okay!" I joked.

He laughed, then his expression shifted. His face turned serious. He picked up the paper and wrote slowly, deliberately. He held the paper up to me.

"You saved my life."

He looked straight in my eyes and mouthed the words again: "Thank you."

For a moment, time stood still. A strong wave of gratitude flowed from his heart to mine. We were perfectly in sync on that hospital bed, experiencing life at its rawest. It was painful, but also strangely beautiful. Sacred, even. It felt like we had done this before, in another lifetime.

Our devotion was unshakable. Right there, in the middle of living everyone's worst nightmare, I realized something wild—I was actually lucky. I was part of a love story most people only dream about.

That evening, Dylan picked Jamie up from the airport and drove him straight to the hospital. I stayed home to clean and do laundry.

Halfway through the cycle, the washing machine made a loud banging sound, then one final *boom*. It was broken.

One more big problem I don't have time to solve, I sighed. I pulled the wet clothes out one by one and washed them in the bathtub, feeling sorry for myself.

Afterward, I sat down and wrote in my Dear Drew Journal, listing the things I wanted to happen next. I closed my eyes and visualized each one coming true.

I'm calling in the manifestation of Drew breathing without a ventilator, the house being in great shape when he comes home, and all broken things being fixed. And most importantly, Drew is home for his birthday. And so it is.

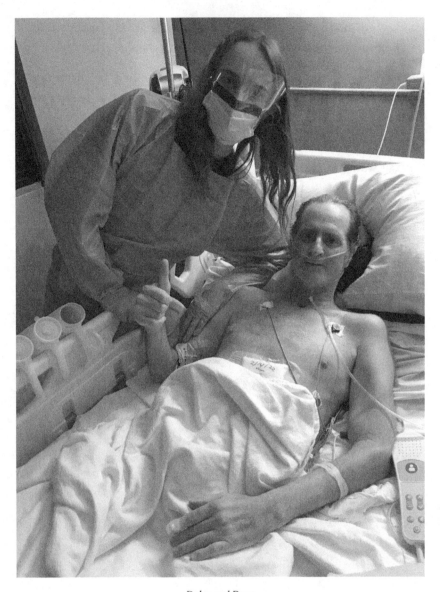
Dylan and Drew

79

MILESTONES AND LIES

February 2, 2022
Hospital Day 81

Jamie must have been a good luck charm because Drew hit a lot of milestones while he was here. It was his first time ever visiting us, and I was grateful for the chance to get to know my brother-in-law better. He spent every day with Drew, giving Dylan and me time to get caught up on our jobs. He had the gift of optimism—always smiling, always upbeat—and that energy was exactly what Drew needed.

We put Jamie in charge of smoothies, and Dylan taught him how to do flyboys with Drew. He'd arrive at the start of visiting hours and stay all day, laughing and talking with Drew, reminiscing about childhood adventures, and deepening their bond in a way they never had before.

Jamie recorded Drew's accomplishments on the wall calendar. He was there when the speech therapist gave Drew his first taste of real food—applesauce. And when Drew got his first sip of water, he told Jamie that the simple joy of it was indescribable. Jamie also witnessed a big moment: the first time Bill got Drew standing up, even though it took two people to hold him steady.

When I FaceTimed Drew, he complained, "You miss all the good stuff." He was right. A wave of guilt washed over me. I felt like a working mom whose babysitter got to witness the baby's first steps.

Then came the biggest milestone yet—Drew reached the 72-hour mark off the ventilator. Now, we anxiously waited for Dr. K to give the green light to remove the trach and dog collar so Drew could finally speak again.

I called one of the doctors at Santa Ana to review Drew's medications. I wanted to know what was causing his intense hot flashes. She pulled up his medical records from Hospital One.

"A Dr. Pittman wrote that Drew had a reaction to the Aviptadil," she said.

A flash of anger surged through me. I was shocked—Pittman had actually written a lie into Drew's official medical record.

And suddenly, I had a horrible realization. Anyone can lie in a medical report, even a doctor. And once it's written, it becomes fact. Even if it's not the truth.

80

LOVE VS. EVIL

February 3-4, 2022
Hospital Day 83

Drew had been off the ventilator for four days, and he was begging to have the trach removed. He said that it felt like he was breathing through a straw—it cut his air supply in half and forced his body to contort with every inhale. But Dr. K wouldn't remove it just yet. He thought Drew would crash and end up back on the ventilator. So, the dreaded dog collar stayed.

I finally got to see Drew stand up for the first time. Two therapists assisted as he held onto the walker, placed his feet flat on the floor, and with his entire body shaking, he pushed himself up to standing. He did it two more times before collapsing in exhaustion. Watching him struggle to stand made one thing painfully clear: I'd been fooling myself thinking he'd be walking anytime soon. The moment was sobering. I felt a wave of urgency rise in me. We needed new answers.

There had to be someone out there who knew how to speed up Drew's recovery. I searched online for patient advocates familiar with critical Covid cases and set up a consult with a nurse named Aaron.

Aaron didn't sugarcoat anything. He warned me that time was critical—if Drew didn't get moving soon, there was a real risk he never would. "Honestly," he said, "I don't know of a single patient who's been through what Drew has and lived. People who survive this are in the single digits. I've never personally seen it."

His words woke me up out of a stupor. In my attempt to convince everyone that Drew was not dying, I had been living a fantasy. Now, with Drew no longer on his deathbed, I could finally face the truth.

Nurse Aaron said that the high-dose Vitamin C and the Aviptadil were likely the reason Drew survived. He explained that a handful of doctors were quietly using alternative therapies—outside standard hospital protocol—to save critical Covid patients. He said, "The protocols actually cause more harm than good."

"What do you mean?" I asked.

He lowered his voice, "Let's just say there are financial incentives for hospitals to over-medicate and ventilate."

A chill ran through me. Something clicked. I didn't want to believe patients were being hurt by the system meant to save them—but it explained why I had to fight so hard for the treatments that kept Drew alive. A kernel of terrifying truth was beginning to form.

Resentment welled up inside me. My heart pounded as I thought of all the patients who'd died sedated, paralyzed, and alone—without their families allowed in to hold their hands or ask questions.

But who was I even mad at? Where did the protocols come from? How do you get doctors to follow orders without question? How many people died that didn't have to?

It was too much to handle. I felt despondent, helpless, caught up in something evil. I had to get control of my emotions. I couldn't let this distract me from my mission of getting Drew home. There would be time for grief and fury later, when this is over. I pushed it to the back of my mind, in that mental compartment where I keep the things too dark to deal with.

I suddenly felt a new appreciation for everyone who had dared to go against the "orders" to save Drew. A wave of gratitude washed over me for all the angels who had conspired to save him—Dr. Gibbons, Frank, Tina, and Paul, who stepped in when the machines failed over and over again. Dr. Q, who desperately tried his best. Alicia, Cho, and Sheldon, who pushed to wean him off the vent. And our friends and family, who kept showing up. The prayers. The love. The donations.

And the divine moments—those perfect interventions when something terrible was about to happen. Like the time I caught Princess about to feed him the wrong formula. The Aviptadil article that landed right when I was doubting it. The timing of it all was too perfect to ignore.

There was more love here than I ever imagined was possible. It shone a bright light over the darkness.

Love was winning over evil. For now, I would stay focused on the love.

81

CHESS MOVES

February 7, 2022
Hospital Day 86

Jamie had just flown back home to South Carolina, and things began to shift again. Drew had now been off the ventilator for a full week. Alicia dropped his oxygen to ten liters, and I set a new goal: get him down to three liters before he comes home.

When I walked into Drew's room, I wasn't expecting what came next.

"Howdy, Spunk. I got my voice back," he said, grinning.

He sounded like Clint Eastwood, tough and raspy, and it was beautiful to hear. "I can't wait to get this dog collar off," he added.

He still had the trach in, but Alicia put a "cap" on it, allowing him to speak. No more scribbled messages on paper. Now he could talk, drink water, and start eating blended food again. This was a major step toward freedom.

But then, Bill warned me that Drew would be discharged soon, and I had to decide where he was going next. We had a few options–take him to a nursing home, a sub-acute care facility, an in-patient rehab center, or bring him home.

Every decision was like playing a game of chess, except each move had dire consequences. I thought back to the bad moves I made that almost killed him, like waiting too long to get medical attention and allowing the Remdesivir. And then, the moves that led to survival, like the Vitamin C and Santa Ana, where they got Drew off the ventilator. It was up to me to make the right choices.

According to Bill, for Drew to recover, he needed physical therapy every day. Most of the options only did therapy once or twice a week.

I considered bringing Drew home, but our tiny house didn't have doorways big enough for a wheelchair, and I wasn't strong enough to carry Drew from room to room. When Dylan went back home, it would be just little ol' me. It would be like caring for a baby, except that baby weighed 120 pounds.

The only viable option was an in-patient rehab center. But they were expensive, and Drew would have to meet certain physical requirements to be accepted, and he was nowhere near that right now.

When I got home, I went to the backyard and put my bare feet in the grass. I was exhausted with decision fatigue. Drew still wasn't strong enough to make these decisions, and ultimately, I had the final say.

I thought about what Drew and the survivors in my Ventilator Survivor Group had in common. The miracle stories had a few similarities: families who refused to give up, something to live for—and prayer. Lots of prayer.

I'm not religious. I never thought that prayer could bring someone back from the dead. But now I was seeing things differently.

Drew's survival made no sense. He should be dead, according to every statistic. He survived sepsis, aspiration, drug reactions, a collapsed lung, and over two months on a ventilator. It was impossible for anyone to survive all that.

So what saved him?

And then, a vision popped into my head—thousands of people sending healing intentions and prayers, all forming a glowing web of light, each thread connecting to Drew. It was a powerful, collective force that literally willed him to live. That energy, poured into the field, became so strong it filled Drew's body with just enough life force to pull him back from the edge.

As more people prayed for him, the energy amplified, rippling through the quantum field and shifting the outcome, one small moment at a time—like chess pieces moving across a board. The girl who told me about the Vitamin C. Finding Dr. Gibbons, who led me to Aviptadil. Choosing the worst LTAC, only to meet Alicia there, who was hit with the burning desire to wean him off the vent.

And there were so many near-misses where Drew was saved moment by moment. He was protected by a force so powerful that it altered the outcome of his fate.

"So this is how it works," I said out loud, beginning to understand. It's all energy.

That night, I posted an update on Facebook. For the first time, I shared a photo of Drew in the hospital. Until now, I hadn't let anyone see him like that. I didn't want people picturing him on his deathbed. But now that he was on the other side of dying, it was safe to show the truth.

In the photo, his emaciated body lay in his hospital bed, his cheekbones jutting out of his face, his eyes hollow, his hair gray and thinned. He didn't look like Drew; he looked like someone's great-grandfather in their final days. It was shocking.

82

DOG COLLAR GONE

February 8, 2022
Hospital Day 87

When I first met Drew, he was twenty-five and had a list of goals taped to his bedroom mirror. It read: "Become the world's best surfboard painter. Travel the world with a wife and kids. Surf big waves across the globe." Check, check, check—he did it all.

Now his goals were far less exciting: "Stand up by myself, take five steps on my own, and get the trach removed." I hung his list on the wall—not just for him, but for the staff, too—so they could align with his dreams.

My sister Christine and her daughter Sophia flew in from Delaware, bringing fresh energy and love to our home. Sophia was a nurse, and she and I had a lot in common. We both loved meditating and self-improvement books. On their second morning, Sophia and I sat in the backyard, writing in our journals together. We could hear Christine in the kitchen, talking and laughing with Dylan. She was enthusiastic and loud, a trait that runs in my family. It was comforting having them there.

Meanwhile, Drew was already texting "Who's bringing my smoothies?" Christine was first on the lineup, and then Sophia, Dylan, and I.

Christine arrived just as visiting hours opened, cracking jokes and making Drew laugh. He needed cheering up. His nose was clogged, and breathing was still a struggle because the trach was cutting off half his air supply.

When Dr. K walked in, he was startled to hear Drew call out in his raspy Clint Eastwood voice, "Hey, Doctor." It was the first time he'd ever heard Drew speak. Watching Drew fight for each breath, he suddenly realized just how much the trach was torturing him.

Without hesitation, he said, "That's it. I'm taking that out." He called for the respiratory team. Minutes later, the dog collar came off, and Dr. K pulled the trach right out of a hole in the center of Drew's throat. Drew took in a deep gasp of air, and instantly, he could breathe and talk almost normally. It was no longer sitting on his vocal cords and obstructing his airway.

The trach was surprisingly huge and covered in blood and mucus. A raw, gaping hole remained where it had been, but Dr. K said it would close up on its own. No stitches needed—just a gauze pad to cover it.

Drew looked up and said, "Holy shit, why did you leave that in for so long?" He felt like he had just taken his first real breath in months. The dog collar gone, the throat pain gone, the block to his airway, gone.

Now that he could breathe better, physical therapy would be a little easier. This was one more big step toward recovery.

This surprise visit from Dr. K was another display of divine timing. Drew had an important interview scheduled with Carol from Restore

Rehab, our top pick for his next phase of care. She would assess whether he qualified for their program. Our challenge was that Restore only accepted patients who had already reached a certain level of rehabilitation, and Drew wasn't there yet. We would have to really impress her.

83

HATE MAIL

February 9, 2022
Hospital Day 88

Carol from Restore came to assess Drew. She didn't ask questions and she didn't talk much, she was only there to observe how well Drew did with physical therapy.

To be accepted by Restore, you had to be a "single assist," meaning that Drew would only need one person to help him stand or walk. But Drew was still a "double assist." I prayed she'd see Drew's potential and bypass the requirements. If she could just witness how hard Drew fought in therapy—how badly he wanted this—maybe she'd bend the rules.

Carol watched Bill help Drew into the wheelchair and followed as Drew wheeled himself down the hall to the physical therapy room. There, two therapists lifted him out of the chair and into position between the parallel bars. She saw how hard Drew fought his dead weight to stand up, shakily holding onto the bars while being spotted by the therapists. He was determined.

She smiled and said, "I'm going to make my recommendation and will let you know."

Everything hinged on her decision. If Drew was not accepted into Restore, I had no idea what we'd do. There was no Plan B.

That night, Drew and I snuggled under a fleece blanket I brought from home, one with his art printed on it. He was in pain from head to toe.

"This is so hard," Drew said, and he started to cry. He was facing the reality of his life and wondered if he would ever be normal again. Drew rarely showed his frustration, and I didn't know what to say, so I just held his hand and listened.

On the way home, I stopped at the gallery. There was a letter hand-addressed to me, with no return address. The stamp was from South Carolina. On the back of the envelope was scrawled "God Bless," with a smiley face. The moment I started reading, my stomach turned. The letter was filled with hate—riddled with run-on sentences, misspellings, and missing punctuation. It was messy, chaotic, and unmistakably hostile.

It began with: "Maria Brophy, you have some nerve. You came to the hospital with an unvaccinated husband." I felt sick to my stomach. This was a far contrast from the hundreds of loving messages I'd received. It was the yang to the yin. The dark to the light. I put the letter down and didn't read the rest.

But later, curiosity got the best of me. As Christine, Sophia, and Dylan made a late-night meal, I picked up the letter and read it out loud. This person had been stalking me online. She knew everything about me.

"How dare you go to the Waldorf Astoria spa, as your husband lay dying," she wrote. Then, she claimed she had reported me to the IRS because, "We all know you have insurance. You have zero reason to be accepting donations."

And then it got weirder. "I ran the numbers on all your art print sales and you make a lot of money." *Well, yes, we sell art. It's what we do for a living.*

Next, she accused me of secretly getting vaccinated, "Do you think people are stupid and don't know how many vaccines you need to travel to Egypt."

At that point, we must've been delirious, because as I read each ridiculous accusation, Christine, Sophia, and I laughed harder and harder. But when I got to this line, we howled so loud we nearly peed our pants: "Your crystals and bowls won't save you from the IRS. I hope you have to pay all of it back."

The letter was not signed, of course. I couldn't imagine how disconnected from humanity this person was to send hate mail to a woman whose husband was dying. It would have hurt my feelings had it not been so outrageous.

I ended up making a snarky rebuttal video on Instagram, just for her. I knew she would see it, since she watched my every move. Sophia tried to talk me out of giving her any energy, but I wanted to have the last word.

84

GENEROSITY

February 10-13, 2022
Hospital Day 92

It was another week full of milestones. Drew's oxygen had been lowered to four liters, and Alicia removed the bandage from his trach wound. We were surprised that the hole had closed up completely and in its place was a small scar. It's amazing how our human body is designed to heal itself.

Drew walked his first eight steps, holding onto the bars in the physical therapy room. In occupational therapy, he managed to put on a pair of shorts all by himself. It might sound small, but it was a big deal.

Dylan, Tan, Ashley, and I continued to give Drew therapy. Christine would spend all day with Drew. Sophia would shave Drew and comb his hair. Kim came at night to give him treatments. Raz sang to him. We all laughed, imagining what the nurses must think, watching a revolving door of pretty women fussing over him.

Drew had his first meal: pureed turkey, potatoes, and carrots, the Thanksgiving dinner he'd missed. Now he could drink my special smoothies through his mouth. No more having the nurse feed them in his stomach tube.

One morning, Dave Talbot called. I hadn't seen him since that day at church back in November.

"I hear Drew might be coming home soon. You're going to need a ramp for your front door. Do you want me to build one for you?" He asked.

I took in a breath. Needing a ramp to get Drew up three front porch steps put an image in my mind of him coming home in a wheelchair. *But really, Maria, what did you think would happen?*

"A friend gave me a bunch of birch wood, and it's been stored in my backyard. I was wondering what I was going to do with it. Now I know." He said.

Another divine gift, I thought. "Yes, that would be great, Dave. Thank you," I said.

Later that day, I got a text from an old friend, a general contractor named Rick, "I want to help. Let me know if there's anything I can fix at your house."

This was an answer to my prayer that things would be fixed before Drew came home. "I definitely could use help," I answered.

"Make me a list," he texted back.

I wrote out a list and had it waiting for him: fix my washing machine, the light fixture in the kitchen, a door jam, and the kitchen sink molding. Rick came over with his toolkit and a big smile. I left him the house key and went to work.

At the gallery, another friend, Gary, made a huge Welcome Home banner for Drew. Raz organized a banner signing event, and dozens of people came to sign it.

Generosity

When I got home at the end of the day, it felt like I had walked into a brand-new house. Rick hadn't just fixed everything on my list—he'd gone above and beyond, repairing things I hadn't even mentioned.

The biggest surprise came when I opened the laundry room doors: my twenty-year-old washer and dryer were gone, replaced with brand new units. I felt like I had won the lottery.

It was as if the entire community had conspired to make life easier for us. It was humbling. And beautiful. Drew's illness had opened the floodgates of generosity, and I was learning—sometimes uncomfortably—how to receive it. Letting people show up for us was part of the lesson we were living through.

That night, I wrote in the Dear Drew Journal:

All your good deeds are coming back in full force, Drew. The world loves you.

And I'm grateful to be a part of it.

85

VALENTINE'S DAY

February 14, 2022
Hospital Day 93

Sophia and Christine had flown back to Delaware, and the house was quiet again. Too quiet. It was Valentine's Day, and I hadn't gotten Drew anything. In all our years together, we rarely celebrated it. I never cared much for commercial holidays—and besides, we didn't need a day to remind us. We knew we loved each other.

I sat in the morning dewy grass and tilted my head back so the sun could warm my swollen thyroid. I hated how I'd neglected my body and all of my projects, my podcast, my writing. I hadn't done anything fulfilling in so long.

And now, I was dreading another long day in that horrible, dank old hospital. I felt so sad and lonely, completely depleted of all my energy, like there was nothing left inside me. No one knew how I felt, and they never would, and that was the loneliest part of all.

So many people were helping. And still, no one could do this job for me. The weight on my shoulders was so heavy. I felt sick all the time. But I had to keep going. There was no other choice.

Or was there?

The sun warmed the top of my head, and a new thought came in like a whisper: *What if I chose to see the beauty in this tragedy?*

What if I saw it as an adventure—one where Drew and I get to experience the full spectrum of life? Where we witness both the worst and the best in people. The raw pain and extreme gratitude. We get to explore the rough edges of life that most people never touch.

This tragedy had brought unexpected gifts. Drew and I were more in love than we'd ever been. We'd discovered who was truly there for us. We had friends we had grown closer to than ever before.

We were being tested in the most brutal way, and one day, I knew we'd look back and say, "We made it." And maybe—just maybe—we'd even be proud of who we became because of it.

I felt a new, positive energy rise up in me. I put on my shoes and got ready to make the drive to Santa Ana. I had many things to deal with, and I decided that today, I would do it all with gratitude and strength.

Just as I stepped outside, I saw a bouquet of red roses waiting on the front porch. The note read, "Happy Valentine's Day, Spunk." My heart leaped, like it used to when Drew and I first met. He had arranged for our friend Denise to deliver the gift. Even now, he was thinking of me.

When I arrived at the hospital, Drew was sitting up on his own. His back and ab muscles were getting stronger. He was burning with hot flashes, and I refilled his ice packs and put them on his bare chest, shoulders, and head.

Dr. K was there. He told us that his group was going to conduct a medical study on Drew. "We want to know why he survived," he said.

Valentine's Day

After he left the room, I turned to Drew and said, "Just watch. Once they figure it out, they'll scrap the study. No one wants to put on record that what saved you was everything they fought against."

Just then, my phone rang. It was Carol at Restore with exciting news. Drew was approved, and they would admit him in two days! I let out a big sigh of relief.

Bill got Drew into the wheelchair and followed as he rolled to the therapy room. Two therapists got Drew in between the parallel bars– one spotting behind him, another in front. I counted as Drew struggled with all his might to take steps forward. Five, six, seven... I watched the monitor as Drew's heart rate went up higher and higher. Drew pushed himself to take one more step, and his entire body shook before collapsing into his wheelchair. His heart rate was spiked to a frightening 170, and his oxygen levels dropped below 80. It was terrifying. Just eight steps and his body gave out.

We got him back to bed quickly. I watched the monitor, willing his numbers to settle as he lay there, breathless. I was breathless, too— trying to recover from the fear of watching my husband's heart nearly give out in front of me.

That's when Dr. Kamatow walked in. She abruptly announced, "Drew, you're being discharged today."

I felt a tinge of panic set in. I said, "Whoa, wait a minute. He's not scheduled to leave until Wednesday."

She kept her back to me, as if I was invisible, and addressed Drew. "Restore has a bed ready for you right now."

Memories flooded my mind of the late afternoon move to Santa Ana last month and how Drew nearly died, suffering from drug withdrawal because it took hours to get meds that close to shift change.

I had just watched his heart rate spike and his oxygen levels dip. I wasn't going to risk another traumatic late-day move.

"No," I said in a stern voice. "We are not moving him this late in the day. We can do it tomorrow."

Dr. Kamatow made a huffing noise through her mask and stormed out of the room. It was settled then. He would move tomorrow.

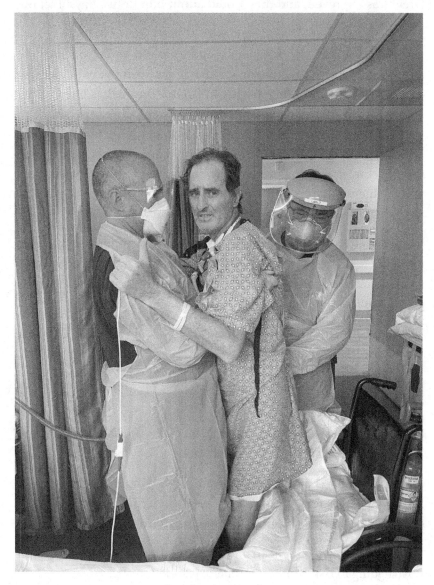

Drew, learning to stand up

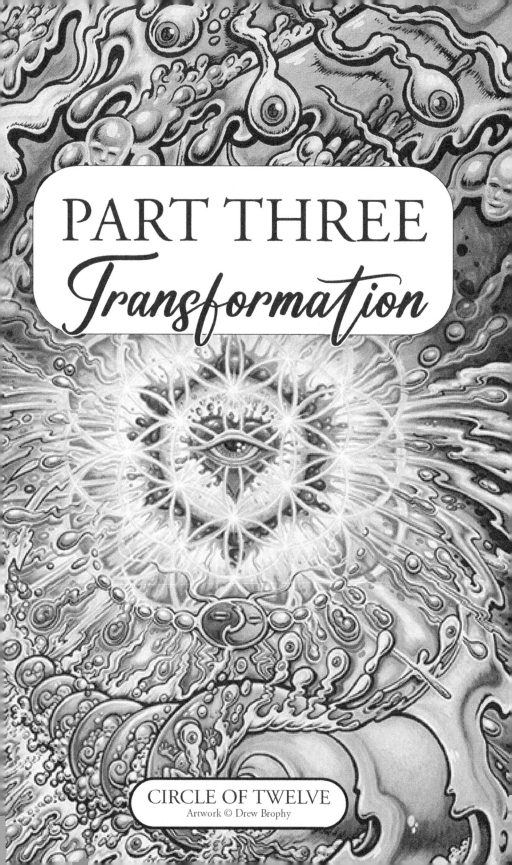

86

RESTORE

February 16, 2022
Hospital Day 95

It was an absolute miracle that Drew was accepted at Restore. For one thing, he didn't meet their requirement to be a single-assist. And the staff had to vote to accept a patient, and one of them, Dr. Wong, voted no. She said Drew was too sick and would end up back in the ICU. But, she later changed her vote, thanks to Dr. K, who convinced her to give him a chance.

Today was the big move. It was emotional for Drew and me to say goodbye to Alicia, Cho, Sheldon, Bill, and the other angels in Santa Ana. As the EMTs wheeled him out, Drew waved to his medical team and promised, "One day, I'm going to come back and walk through these doors on my own two feet."

I followed the ambulance to Restore. This new place was fresh, shiny, and new. There were nice chairs with padded seats, and the staff was friendly and unhurried. It was a stark contrast to the darkness of Santa Ana.

Drew's room was tucked away at the end of the second-floor hallway—a private space, because of his history of infection. For that same reason, I was required to put on a gown and gloves before entering. The blue gowns here were made of actual fabric, much nicer than the cheap plastic ones at Santa Ana. I felt guilty having to throw it away every time I left the room–it was so bad for the environment.

The room was bright with a large window and a mountain view, and the bed was big and comfortable. I began taping photos to the wall, one by one. I wanted the new staff to see the real Drew—a surfer, a father, a family man—someone they should care about.

The nurses got Drew settled into his new bed. It was different here. There was an expectation of recovery, of independence, of survival. They didn't hook IVs up to him, pumping drugs. There were no constant beeping noises. And he was not tethered to the bed by any cords or tubes. He was almost free.

I pulled a surprise out of my purse. "Here," I said, handing him his phone and wedding ring—two things I'd been holding onto since the day he was placed on the ventilator at Hospital One.

"To celebrate new beginnings."

Until now, his fingers hadn't worked well enough to use a phone, but today he was ready. I slid his platinum wedding ring onto his finger and smiled, "Will you marry me again?"

The nurse came in and weighed him using the bed scale. She read out loud, "127.5 pounds," and wrote it on a chart on the wall.

"Fuck." I said under my breath. My big, burly husband and I weighed the same now. I felt a shot of guilt. *I should have made sure he got nutrition from day one. I should have insisted he be weighed. I should have fought harder. I shoulda, woulda, coulda.*

I attempted to shake off these thoughts and be present, in the moment, and enjoy this new phase with Drew. This place had a vibration of hope around it. No one was dying here. People came here to get better.

Outside, a rare lightning storm rolled through the Southern California sky. The moon was almost full and a feeling of transformation filled the room. Drew asked the nurse to move his bed towards the window so he could watch the lightning flash behind the mountains.

That night, I tossed and turned in bed. Even though Drew was in a better place now, I couldn't stop obsessing over his weight loss. I was furious at the negligence. Nutrition is basic healing 101, and they'd failed him.

But anger was better than despair. It was more empowering than grief, and it gave me the fighting spirit that I needed, even at this stage of the game.

When I woke up the next morning, I saw in the mirror a new, deep line in the center of my eyebrows. I looked haggard. I grabbed my journal and walked barefoot into the backyard. The grass was still damp from the storm.

I prayed, "Please release all anger and fear from my heart. Please help me do something good with all that I've learned."

A crow called out in the distance, "Kaw kaw, kaw kaw."

Other people need to know, I thought. They need to know there are things you can do to keep your loved one alive, even when it looks impossible. That there is always room for a miracle.

I started writing a list in my journal:

How to Keep Your Loved One Alive in the ICU

Be there day and night.

Insist on nutrition and weigh them frequently.

Never give in to the demand for a quick decision. Research first.

Limit Sedation as it can cause brain damage.

Hold their hand and comfort them with positive words, especially when in a coma.

And never, ever, let them feel alone.

87

BELIEF

February 17, 2022

We had entered part three of the trinity of healing. Restore took Drew's recovery to the next level. And because they weren't sedating Drew, his mind was clear and he had more energy for therapy. For the first time, the focus wasn't just on keeping him alive. It was on getting him strong enough to go home.

Everything they did was designed to foster independence. Drew was expected to eat his meals sitting upright in a chair. He wheeled himself into the bathroom and brushed his teeth over the sink. The staff gently pushed him to do as much as he could on his own. Just being surrounded by people who believed in him made a difference. His recovery started to accelerate in ways that surprised all of us.

Drew got his first shower in three months. He was embarrassed because it was a young, pretty nurse who stripped him down and set him on a bench in the shower. He got a glimpse of his nude body in the mirror. It shocked him to see how emaciated he was. He remembered himself as a big, strong athlete. Now, he was a skeleton with no muscle or fat.

She handed him the water nozzle and showed him how to clean himself. He was too weak to maneuver it, and the activity spiked his heart rate. The nurse wanted to pull him out, but he begged for a few more minutes.

The shower washed away the grime and darkness from the two previous hospitals, and Drew's spirit was renewed. It's amazing what a shower can do for the soul.

Only one person a day was allowed to visit, so Dylan and I took turns. On day one, I climbed into Drew's bed and pulled the curtains shut. We snuggled. We laughed. For the first time, Drew used his phone and made a few calls to friends. It felt good to see him doing normal things. His voice was getting stronger. Now, when we did the flyboy exercises, he was able to do them on his own.

Physical therapy happened daily in the gym with Oliver and Nicole, his therapists. Now, Drew was strong enough to scoot his body from one side of the bed to the other, and he was taking steps, unassisted, with a walker.

For Drew, the hardest part of relearning to walk was mastering the simple movement of going from sitting to standing. It's something most of us do without a second thought, but when you're paralyzed, you quickly learn just how crucial muscle strength is for balance.

The first time Oliver guided him through it, he encouraged: "Alright, Drew. Sit on the edge of the bed, feet flat on the floor. Lean forward. Trust your feet — and if they don't catch you, I will."

Drew hesitated, leaning forward awkwardly. He almost collapsed as he struggled to get his balance. Trembling, he reached for the walker and forced himself upright, legs quaking beneath him.

Every day, Oliver made him do it again and again.

Belief

Restore and Santa Ana shared many of the same doctors and one day, Dr. Kamatow came to assess Drew. He was excited to tell her about the great progress he'd made, and he told her that his next goal was to wean off of the oxygen.

But she quickly shut him down with a sharp tongue. "Drew, you have severe fibrosis. You will be on oxygen forever. But don't worry, you will learn to live with it."

I'd had enough of her bad attitude. "No, he won't," I said, annoyed. "You can't surf with an oxygen machine."

I looked her straight in the eye. "And you said the same thing about the ventilator. He WILL get off the oxygen."

She left the room without saying goodbye. She didn't like me, and the feeling was mutual.

That night, her words haunted me, like an evil spell trying to take hold. *You'll be on oxygen forever.* What if she was right? I pictured Drew living with an oxygen machine, like an old man, never able to surf again. Our fun adventures would be over. We would spend the rest of our lives confined to watching TV on the couch. It was a terrible thought.

"No," I declared out loud. "That's not going to happen."

I thought back to all the miracles: how Drew beat death, then the ventilator, then paralysis. Each one began with a belief in the impossible. We could beat the oxygen, too. And we'd surround ourselves with others who believe as well.

88

FIRED KAMATOW

February 21, 2022

Dr. Wong was having Drew evaluated for a second week at Restore. I told her, "I don't want him to come home until he's walking. A wheelchair won't even fit in our tiny house."

What I didn't say out loud, but felt very strongly, was my fear that he'd come home as an invalid, and the medical system would give up on him. I needed them to fix him now, before he was discharged.

Even though he no longer needed it, the doctors had left the PEG tube in his stomach—the one they used to feed him back when he had the trach. I remembered another patient's wife telling me how hard it was to take her husband to a doctor to get his PEG removed after coming home. I decided that wasn't going to happen to us.

"Please make sure his PEG is removed before he leaves," I asked Dr. Wong.

"We don't do that here," she replied.

"But he doesn't need it. Why keep it in?" I pushed, and she finally said she would make a note for the doctor.

Every day, Drew made more progress. His oxygen was down to 3.5 liters. He could now stand and walk with a walker, sit on the edge of the bed unassisted, and even put on his pants and shirt by himself.

At the end of the first week, Dr. Kamatow came to check on him. Drew wanted to impress her, and he told her how he was taking steps on his own with the walker. But in her usual negative demeanor, Dr. Kamatow wouldn't celebrate his wins. Instead, she urged him to get vaccinated.

"How safe is it, now that his heart is compromised?" I asked. "I've read it can cause heart attacks."

She ignored me, turned to Drew, and warned, "If you catch Covid again, you will die."

I pressed on. "Some ventilator survivors I've talked to ended up back in the hospital after the shot. Can you guarantee that won't happen to Drew?"

Her face turned red. "Do you want to kill your husband? If he gets Covid again, he will die."

I flinched at her sharp words. "Can you guarantee it won't cause a heart attack?" I asked again, this time not hiding my frustration.

She refused to answer, exhaled a dramatic *huff*, and walked out.

Drew was mad at me for arguing with her. "I just can't handle the fighting," he said, his voice heavy with exhaustion.

"Look, I'm not taking a chance of you ending up back in the ICU," I said. "She has been wrong about everything. Why should we trust her now?"

I was afraid that if he took it, he would end up back in the ICU, hooked up to machines again, and I couldn't handle that. Now that he had immunity, it was not worth the risk.

"Promise me you won't get the shot," I pleaded.

"I won't," he promised.

He then made a formal request to never see Dr. Kamatow again. And we never did.

89

PROGRESS

February 22, 2022

As Drew's discharge date crept closer, the reality of him coming home started to scare me. I began to dread the stress that would come with it. I couldn't go back to work—Drew couldn't be left alone—and that would only add to our financial strain. I worried I wouldn't be able to care for him properly. He was still so frail, and I wasn't strong enough to lift him if he fell. I prayed the insurance would approve a couple more weeks at Restore—just enough time for him to get a little stronger, a little more independent.

Still, he was making progress. Drew could now walk 100 feet with his walker, unassisted. He was transferring himself from the wheelchair to the toilet without help. We recorded every small victory on his wall calendar, right next to his new list of goals: *walk without help, be independent, get off meds*.

I had pestered Dr. Wong for days about getting Drew's stomach PEG removed before he came home. Finally, one of the doctors came into

Drew's room and said, "I hear your wife's insisting this comes out. Do you want it gone?" Drew nodded yes.

The doctor grabbed the tube, yanked it out, slapped a piece of gauze over the hole, and handed it to Drew. "Here—hold this," he said, then walked out.

Drew kept his hand on the gauze and waited for the doctor to come back. An hour passed, and he finally asked one of the nurses, "Where's the doctor?"

She said, "He's left for the day."

I realized the entire staff was sick of my demands. But I didn't care if it gave Drew what he needed.

That night, our artist friend Chris Dyer called me from Peru to tell me about a spiritual message he received during his Ayahuasca plant medicine ceremony.

"I saw spirit guides surrounding Drew," he said, pausing as he searched for the right words. "He was given the gift of crossing to the other side and being reborn. He returned with insight meant to serve the collective."

Goosebumps rose on my arms. I was beginning to see that Drew's miracle had stirred something in everyone who knew him. Even Kim had told me she felt it had sparked a community healing. Still, I was only starting to glimpse the true magnitude of what had been set in motion.

90

100 DAYS

February 24, 2022

We hit Drew's 100-day mark in the hospital. The physical therapists at Restore fell in love with him because he was one of the few patients who pushed himself past the limits. Drew wrote a new goal, and I hung it on the wall: "Be home by March 8, my 51st birthday."

Kim had her first visit with Drew since Santa Ana. She called me with excitement, "Sister, his muscle mass is coming back!" She worked on the muscles between his ribs so he could take deeper breaths, and she tried waking up his still-paralyzed diaphragm. "If we open up his back, we can get him breathing better," she said with determination.

She spent the whole day with Drew, and they reminisced about the first time Frank had lifted him into a chair. They cried together—over the pain, the miracles, and just how far Drew had come.

Drew's sister, Julie, and their mom flew in from South Carolina, and I rented them an apartment right next door to the gallery. They visited him every other day, alternating with Dylan and me. I even got special permission for Julie and Mom to visit him together since mom couldn't drive on her own.

I was still making smoothies for Drew, supercharged with vitamins. I added a new favorite recipe–a virgin mojito with coconut water, hand-juiced limes, maple syrup, pineapple, and fresh mint leaves I picked from the backyard.

In physical therapy, Nicole was a drill sergeant as she pushed Drew to step up and down three stairs, walk one hundred feet down the hall with a walker, and get in and out of bed on his own. She was preparing him for real life again—for home.

I barely spent time with Mom and Julie because one of us was always with Drew. Dylan and I would meet them for dinner most nights, usually late, because whoever was with Drew wouldn't get home until after 9:00 p.m.

Dave Talbot came and built the ramp onto our front porch. It was a beautiful, dark wood ramp with railings on both sides. He tied a colorful Mexican scarf to the end of it for decoration.

I was relieved to hear that insurance had approved one more week at Restore for Drew. Now, it looked like he might come home on his actual birthday.

91

THE NEW NORMAL

March 7, 2022

Drew was scheduled to come home the next day, and I knew that I should have been dancing with joy, but I felt the burden of being responsible for keeping my frail, weak husband alive when he came home. *What if he stopped breathing in the middle of the night? He could still die. Dear God, please don't let me screw it up.*

Preparing for Drew's homecoming reminded me of when we had a baby on the way. Except this time, instead of baby bouncers and onesies, I was buying a foldable walker, a blood pressure cuff, a geriatric shower chair, a cane, and a gel-seat butt pillow because Drew had no meat left on his booty. And, I ordered three portable urinals, also known as pee jugs, complete with glow-in-the-dark lids.

He was still too weak to go from "sit to stand" from the deep, squishy couch in our living room, so I bought an outdoor recliner and decided to set it up inside for now. When he was "back to normal," we could move it outside. I also ordered an ugly, plastic folding dinner table, the kind my grandparents had. It would hold his drinks, pulse oximeter, and whatever else needed to stay within reach. And for a little joy, I bought a 20-pound bag of birdseed so Drew could watch the birds flock in our backyard.

Even a common cold could kill him now, so I stocked the kitchen with all the immune-boosters I could get my hands on: povidone-iodine nasal spray, elderberry syrup, Quercetin, Vitamins D3, K2, and C, mullein tea, and Zinc.

But the most important delivery was the oxygen concentrator. It was a monstrosity of a machine, a big blue block on wheels. A fifty-foot tube snaked from the machine to the cannulas that would go into Drew's nose, delivering oxygen around the clock. I plugged it into the wall in the living room, the center point of the house. The fifty-foot cord would allow Drew to move from the living room to the kitchen, to the bedroom, and to the bathroom while attached to it. This was the advantage of having a very small house. Fifty feet was all we needed.

The delivery guy's instructions were simple: one switch to turn it on and off and one dial to adjust the oxygen. Dylan set it to three liters. The man also left a portable aluminum tank—containing two hours of backup oxygen in case the power went out.

Suddenly, it hit me: *If the electricity goes out, Drew could die.*

"What should we do then?" I asked.

"Take him to the emergency room," he said casually.

I pictured a storm knocking out the power, me scrambling to get Drew in the car, rain pouring, wind howling, lightning overhead. Then getting stuck in traffic, cars backed up on the freeway, Drew's oxygen running out as I watch him die, helplessly, from the driver's seat.

"Can you leave a few extra tanks?" I asked, wanting to avert that nightmare.

The New Normal

He did. I would keep one in the trunk at all times, even though I knew it wasn't safe to have a flammable oxygen tank in the car. But it felt safer than being without it.

"No flames near the oxygen," he warned. That meant no candles. No burning sage. And no heat, because our heater ran on gas and sat smack in the middle of the living room. I wrote out a sign in red ink that read, "Caution: Flammable. No heat, no smoking, no flames." I taped it to the wall of the living room. Then I put tape over the "on" switch to the heater.

Next came the delivery of the wheelchair. I tried to put it in the trunk of my car, but it was too heavy and bulky; it was like wrestling an alligator. Dylan helped me break it down and wedge it next to the oxygen tank.

I shuddered at this new way of life. I had to find a way to surrender to it. This is temporary, I told myself. *You can do it, Maria. It won't be long before he's back to normal.*

For moral support, I joined a group called Protocol Survivors, led by a woman who survived critical Covid pneumonia. Most of the members were widows. Some were survivors. I attended their weekly meeting on Zoom, where four widows were given twenty minutes each to tell their story. All had lost their husbands around the same time Drew got sick.

One woman from Michigan told us about her forty-year-old husband, a rock climber, who deteriorated quickly. "They wouldn't let me in to see him," she said, tears streaming down her face. "But they told me that if I signed a DNR, they'd let me in to say goodbye." After three days on the ventilator, a doctor told her, "He's suffering. You can stop his pain by letting us remove life support." She gave permission. Her husband died. "I feel so guilty," she sobbed.

I felt her pain deep in my soul. I wanted to reach through the screen, hug her, and tell her it wasn't her fault. I felt so grateful that I did not consent to pulling life support when those exact words were spoken to me. If I had, Drew would be gone. I would have never known he would have survived.

The next three widows' stories were eerily similar. Different states, same script. It was as though there was a secret handbook for doctors titled, *What to Say To A Covid Patient's Family*.

That night, I crawled into bed, feeling so sad. The widows' grief was unbearable, and the realization that I had come so close to being one of them was sobering.

92

RELEASED

March 8, 2022

Drew finally came home on his fifty-first birthday. It was the goal he had written down a month earlier, and like every big goal he's ever set, he made it happen. Coming home marked a new chapter—one that would become the biggest challenge of his life: getting his body to work again.

Dylan and I drove to Restore early in the morning to pick him up. Julie and Mom stayed behind, decorating the kitchen with helium balloons and "Happy Birthday" banners.

We hung out in Drew's room and waited for the discharge process. A nurse came in with a syringe, pulled back the bed sheet, and gave Drew his daily shot of blood thinner in the stomach. I hoped they didn't expect me to do that to him at home.

A few minutes later, Drew's hot flashes kicked in, and Dylan put ice packs on his shoulders and chest. After months of watching him suffer through these torturous waves of heat, I suddenly realized—they always came right after the blood thinner shot. I asked the nurse to check with Dr. Wong about discontinuing them.

Drew hadn't worn anything but a hospital gown in months. I brought him new clothes, small sizes he hadn't fit into since he was in high school: 28" waist sweatpants, a small white T-shirt, socks, and pull-on shoes.

Oliver, the Physical Therapist, leaned in the doorway and asked, "Drew, what's next for you?"

"I'm going to get back to life," Drew said. "Play guitar, garden, draw. Learn how to drive again."

"Well, let's do one last thing before you go," Oliver said. Drew got in the wheelchair, and Oliver led us into the gym.

"Let me show you a technique to get back up if you fall," Oliver said as Dylan and I watched.

"Oh, he's not going to fall," I said confidently. I was naive and couldn't imagine a scenario where that would happen.

Oliver smiled and continued, "Drew, this is what you do if you end up on the ground. Roll over and lean on something. Use your elbows to pull yourself up from there."

He motioned for Drew to pretend to fall. Oliver guided him through the technique. I watched as Drew struggled to get up from the ground, something that should have been so easy.

Drew eventually got himself back up to standing, holding onto a walker.

"You're going to do great," Oliver said, hugging each of us goodbye.

I followed as Drew rolled his wheelchair into Dr. Wong's office to sign the discharge papers. She handed me a long list of meds that Drew was taking and a bag with all the bottles. I was relieved when she gave the okay to discontinue the blood thinner shots.

She looked at Drew and said sincerely, "I'm sorry I denied you at first. It's just that you were so sick. You've surprised us all. I'm so happy to see how far you've come." She hugged him with tears in her eyes.

Drew's discharge instructions were listed alongside his medications—what pills to take and when. But there was nothing about how to get him walking, how to wean him off the oxygen, or how we were going to live our new lives with him this way.

I packed up Drew's room into a giant shopping bag: his iPad, phone, a book he never read, and the photos we'd taped to the walls. Nicole walked us to the car, Drew in the wheelchair with the oxygen tank, Dylan carrying the bag, and me lost in my thoughts, ruminating over scary things that hadn't happened yet. But on the outside, smiling and looking happy because I was supposed to.

Drew wasn't strong enough to swing his body into the front seat of the car from the wheelchair. It took both Dylan and Nicole to get him in. Now, where to put the oxygen tank? It didn't reach the back seat while connected to his nose, so we straddled it between his skinny legs on the floor. Just getting him in the car was difficult. Was I capable of caring for him? More doubts flooded my mind.

"I've been released from prison," Drew said to Nicole, laughing.

She leaned in and hugged him. I promised Nicole I'd call her later to make a plan to do physical therapy at our home.

Dylan drove, and I watched from the backseat as my son stepped into Drew's role as the strong one. He cracked jokes to keep the mood light. Drew stared out the window at the sky, the sun, and the trees as if seeing everything for the first time.

"This is amazing. So amazing. Take me by the ocean," he said, in awe.

Dylan took the exit onto Pacific Coast Highway, and Drew's eyes stayed fixed on the ocean. "I can feel myself getting better just looking at the waves," he said.

A wave of gratitude washed over me. My son. My husband. My ocean view. I felt it in my soul, this deep experience I was living. It was raw, intense, and filled with love, sorrow, and mystery. I felt like I was living out a Hallmark movie.

First day home

93

HAPPY BIRTHDAY

For over twenty years, Drew and I had the same routine whenever we came home from a trip. He'd pull into the driveway and joke, "This is a cool little house. Wouldn't it be great if we lived here?" Then we'd unload our surfboards, wetsuits, beach clothes, and sandy flip-flops, chatting about our adventures as we slipped right back into daily life.

But today, our homecoming was very different. Drew waited in the car while Dylan and I unpacked a wheelchair, a walker, an oxygen tank, and a big bag of pills, anxiously stepping into a life none of us had asked for.

Mom and Julie were waiting for us in the front yard. Gary's huge banner hung between two posts, covered in artwork and dozens of signatures. It read, "WE LOVE YOU, DREW."

Drew looked around in admiration at the house we'd lived in for two decades, and the lush front garden he had grown with his own two hands. He loved this place. It was his first time home in four months, and the only visible change was the giant wooden ramp that now took over the entire front entrance of the house.

Dylan helped him out of the car, and Drew insisted on using the walker instead of the wheelchair. He stood at the bottom of the ramp and stared up at the steep slope. It was going to be harder than we thought—Drew hadn't practiced walking uphill. I spotted him just as Oliver had taught me. We had a gait belt around Drew's waist, and I slipped my hand under it at his back, just in case he lost his balance. Dylan followed behind, dragging the oxygen tank, while Drew slowly pushed the walker up the ramp, winded with every step. The three of us moved together, step by shaky step, until we reached the front door.

At the doorway was another obstacle—a high lip between the living room floor and the outside porch. Drew wasn't strong enough to lift his foot up and over it. I was puzzled as to how we would navigate that.

Drew had an idea: go in backward. He turned around, set the walker behind him, and managed to drag one foot over the lip. But he had no feeling in his feet—a side effect of the drugs—and as he tried to lift the other foot, it caught on the ledge. He lost his balance and wobbled backward in slow motion.

I watched, horrified, as he crashed to the floor with a sickening thud. I was helpless to stop it because I was standing on the wrong side of the walker. Rookie mistake.

Dylan, Mom, and Julie all gasped. He lay there, struggling to catch his breath. I was frozen in shock. *Did he just break a hip? Why did I let this happen?* Oliver's voice in my head, "If he falls..."

I knelt beside him, heart racing, and put the pulse oximeter on his finger. It read 88–not good. He lay on the carpet and gasped in deep breaths. I watched the numbers climb as he slowed his breathing: 89, 90, 91. When his oxygen reached 92, we recounted Oliver's instructions. Drew rolled over to the ottoman and leaned on it with his elbows. We helped him push up and get into the recliner. He was beyond exhausted. I ran my hands over his hips and legs to check for

Happy Birthday

broken bones. "It's a good thing my bones don't break," Drew said breathlessly.

An hour later, I was still shaking. If he'd broken a bone, it could've killed him. I felt like the worst caregiver in the world. My mind spiraled—replaying it over and over again, berating myself for letting it happen.

That night, Drew requested his favorite meal: meatloaf, mashed potatoes, and green beans. Mom mashed the potatoes, and I cooked my delicious, homemade meatloaf. Julie brought dessert: a chocolate birthday cake that read, "Happy 51, Drew."

Drew wanted to sit in his recliner in the living room and eat off of the folding table, but I insisted he push his walker into the kitchen and sit at the table. "If you're ever going to walk again, you have to keep moving," I demanded.

After dinner, we had cake and sang Happy Birthday. Drew tried to blow out the two candles shaped like a "5" and a "1," but he couldn't blow hard enough, so Dylan blew them out for him. Mom and Julie left soon after. We were all worn out from an emotional day.

94

GOING TO BE OK

Even the simplest things were hard now. Just getting Drew into bed was a challenge. Maneuvering a walker through our cramped bedroom was tricky. To get to his side of the bed, Drew had to squeeze through a narrow space between the mattress and the dresser, then make a tight turn. At the same time, I had to spot him with one hand to keep him from falling, while using the other to hold the oxygen tube, making sure it didn't catch on any corners.

Three pee jugs hung on our metal headboard above his head where he could reach them in the middle of the night. I hated it. The thought of him accidentally spilling it in our bed was awful, but navigating the bedroom obstacle course in the dark was just too risky.

Getting into bed was exhausting, and Drew was winded when he lay down. As he caught his breath, I put a fleece blanket over him. His emaciated body disappeared underneath like a little child. I noticed how much the ventilator had aged Drew. Most of his hair had fallen out, and what was left had gone gray in just four months, even the hair on his chest. His face was gaunt, his neck skinny, and the scar on his throat, left by the trach, was a forever reminder of the hell he survived.

Finally, I had what I'd been praying for—my man, home in bed beside me. Yet everything was so strange now.

I brought him a glass of water and his nightly cocktail of pills—Trazodone and Temazepam. He leaned forward, too weak to sit up, and swallowed them one by one. Then I climbed into bed and curled up beside him.

I closed my eyes and tried to picture him as the big, strong Drew I once knew. But the sound of the oxygen machine interrupted my fantasy. *Whooosh. Wheeee.* Over and over again. His stomach heaved deeply in and out in a dramatic, unnatural rhythm with every breath. I put a hand on his heart and felt it beating fast. I clipped the pulse oximeter on his finger. Resting heart rate: 120. Not normal. I felt a flutter of worry in my stomach. *We need to fix this,* I told myself.

I hated this new reality. I wanted my old life back, the one where Drew would cook dinner, lift heavy paddleboards, and take me on adventures. The life where I felt safe, knowing that if there were an intruder, he would protect me.

I was grieving the loss of the life we once had while also being in charge of a new game—one whose rules I didn't yet understand. Could I handle it? The image of Drew falling in slow motion as I stood by helplessly played in my mind over and over again.

I looked over at him, his eyes closed, chest heaving in and out. I didn't want to feel sorrow. I switched my thoughts to notice the beauty of this moment: he was home. He didn't die. I placed a hand on my heart and took a few deep breaths until I felt gratitude well up inside me.

"Thank you, God, for bringing Drew home. Thank you, thank you."

With this new energy, I turned to Drew and said cheerfully, "I'm so happy you're home!" I rubbed his chest and added, "I'm so glad to have my husband back."

Going to be OK

"It feels so good to be in my own bed," he mumbled sleepily.

Then, as my hand slid from his heart to his stomach and kept going, I felt a strong erection. I froze, then burst out laughing. That part of him was working. That was a very good sign.

"Honey," I laughed, "I think you're going to be okay."

95

MOUNTAIN TO CLIMB

I got my husband back—sort of. But Drew was no longer my Superman, who took care of all the things. This new Drew was fully dependent, an invalid. All the simple things he once loved had been stripped away from him.

Covid had ravaged his lungs, but the coma completely destroyed his body. His muscles were so atrophied that he was in constant pain from head to toe. His nerves were damaged, leaving him with neuropathy in his tongue, hands, and feet. Walking without tripping was nearly impossible. Electrical shocks ran through his body, and he had violent, unpredictable coughing fits. And still, Drew rarely complained. I'd see him wince and ask, "Does it hurt?" He'd lie and say, "No."

Bathing him was impossible. I wasn't physically strong enough, nor did I know the technique to safely get him into our tiny shower and on the plastic chair. If he fell, it could kill him, so we had an occupational therapist come twice a week to shower him.

Drew's world was confined to his fifty-foot oxygen hose inside our small, 930-square-foot house. He couldn't be left alone, which meant I was also a prisoner.

On Drew's third day home, he asked Dylan to take him into the backyard. This was another puzzle. How do we get him out there?

Drew couldn't navigate the three steps off our back porch, so we wheeled him out the front door, down the ramp, and around the side of the house. But the fifty-foot tube would not reach all the way around to the backyard.

Dylan and I made a plan. He pushed Drew in the wheelchair as far as the tube would reach, halfway around the house. Then, he pulled the cannulas out of Drew's nose, ran as fast as he could into the house, handed them to me, and ran back out. He quickly pushed Drew to the back porch, and I ran through the back door towards them, with the cannulas. I quickly put them in Drew's nose before he gasped for air. It worked.

Drew sat with Dylan, admiring his garden, lush with life. I made tuna fish sandwiches with orange slices on the side. We had been eating meals on this porch since Dylan was a baby, and as I carried the plates out, for just a moment, things felt normal.

But after only a few minutes, Drew shifted in his seat and said he was in too much pain. He needed to go back inside.

He couldn't even enjoy his garden.

All I could think was: *How do we get him back into life?*

We had a huge mountain to climb and no path to follow. We would have to find a way.

96

NICOLE

Drew set a new goal: get back into the ocean. The dream of returning to his life as a waterman lit a fire in him. He even pictured himself surfing again one day. I had a strong feeling that the salt water could heal his body and give him something to be excited about. I just needed to figure out how to make it happen.

But, the doctors were clear. Drew would never be able to live without the oxygen machine. And you can't take that big blue monster into the ocean. So, Drew and I decided to reject the notion he'd always need the machine.

Now that I believed in miracles, I had a steely determination. The plan was simple: first, get Drew walking on his own. Second, wean him off the meds. And third, the impossible: wean him off the oxygen. If we could do that, maybe—just maybe—he'd surf again one day.

To pull off another miracle, we had to believe that it was possible, even if no one else had done it before. And we needed to find a therapist who believed in it with us.

In Drew's second week home, Mom and Julie flew back to South Carolina, and we got busy rehabilitating Drew. The insurance company paid for a physical therapist to come three days a week. She had Drew pushing the walker back and forth, between the kitchen and the living room, again and again.

But that wasn't enough. Drew needed six days of aggressive therapy, and someone who would believe that he could wean off the oxygen machine. I had a gut feeling Nicole, his therapist from Restore, was that person. I hired her to come work with Drew three days a week.

I asked her straight up, "Do you think we can get him off the oxygen?"

Nicole hesitated. "Maybe," she said, not making any promises. But I caught a flash in her eyes, and I knew she was already scheming a way to make it happen. She believed it was possible—and that was all we needed.

Nicole was short, like me, but strong and muscular, with light brown hair always tied in a high ponytail that swished as she moved. Drew nicknamed her "the little bulldog" because she was a combination of brutal tyrant and loving nurse. She pushed him hard, then carefully checked his SpO_2 levels and his heart rate. I trusted her with his life.

Nicole moved fast. It wasn't long before she had Drew ditch the walker for a cane. With her hand under the gait belt at his back, she spotted him as he shuffled up and down the driveway. "Turn left. Turn right," she commanded, training his body to find its balance again.

She would wheel Drew into the backyard and have him do sit-to-stand exercises in the wheelchair over and over again as he groaned in pain. "Squeeze your butt, squeeze your butt. One more now," she would yell, like a drill sergeant. Then, in a softer tone, "Catch your breath, catch your breath. Good, Drew, good."

Drew came to love Nicole, even when she bossed him around. Because it meant she believed in him.

Nicole

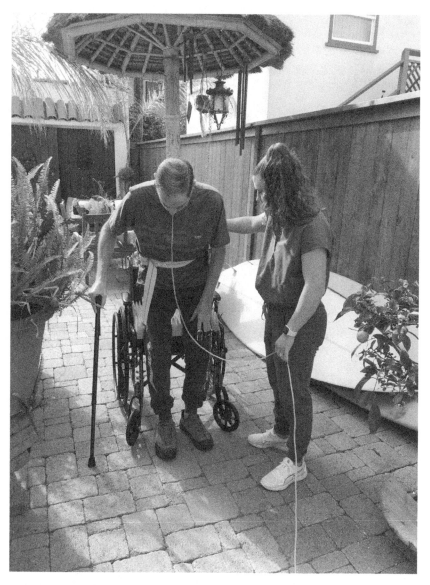

Nicole guiding Drew's "sit to stand" moves

97

WEEK 2

I thought I'd be a lot happier when Drew came home—but I wasn't. Taking care of him around the clock was brutal. I'm not a natural caregiver; I don't have the stomach for it. I worried constantly about him and couldn't focus on anything else.

I spent my days obsessively researching alternative treatments, desperate to find a magic cure. At night, I'd wake up every hour to make sure he was breathing—like we did when Dylan was a baby. Drew's chest violently heaved in and out with each breath, in the most unnatural way, and it frightened me. *Will it always be like this?* I wondered.

A lack of sleep, being a full-time caretaker, trying to run a business, and ignoring my own health—it all wore me down. I was running on adrenaline and coffee, the only things that kept my body moving so I could do the million things that needed to be done each day.

But strangely, my love for Drew grew stronger. Watching him work so hard to rebuild his body gave me a whole new level of respect for him. He was in so much pain, and I did everything I could to make his terrible life a little more joyful. I made sure that I only smiled and joked in his presence. His life was in my hands and I was his protector.

I never really knew what love was until I met Drew. I was not raised with it; my mother was distant and my father violent. Drew taught me what true love is by being the example: forgiving and generous—and he was that way with everyone.

The more he depended on me, the deeper my devotion grew, expanding beyond the intimate love between a husband and wife. It was a level of selfless love I had never known before. I surprised myself, loving him so fiercely even when he had nothing to give. That's when I realized: real love isn't just a feeling. It's a choice—especially when things get hard.

Drew had his first appointment with Dr. K, a twenty-minute drive North. We rented a portable oxygen unit, fashioned as a backpack on wheels. It was battery-operated and had a two-hour limit. We packed the cord to the battery and planned to recharge it at the doctor's office.

I was nervous about our first outing and glad that Dylan went with us. It took both of us to get Drew in the front seat. At the last second, I threw an extra oxygen tank in the trunk, just in case we got stuck in traffic or there was an accident on the freeway.

We parked in the handicapped spot and Dylan playfully pushed Drew erratically in the wheelchair up the ramp to the front door. Inside, Dr. K pulled up Drew's last lung scan.

"Drew, you have one of the most impacted, restricted lungs I've ever seen," he said.

My heart sank. *The worst he's ever seen? My God, how will he ever come back from this?*

Dr. K told us that he hadn't seen a patient as critical as Drew get off the oxygen. But, then a flicker of hope: "I've seen Covid Fibrosis clear up on some. Your lungs could improve."

Week 2

I held onto this statement as evidence that Drew's lungs would heal one day.

Before we even left the office, the portable oxygen unit stopped working. It had only been ninety minutes. I plugged it into the wall, but it wouldn't charge. I felt a flutter of panic.

Dylan ran out to the car and grabbed the extra tank for the drive home. Thank God we brought it. My biggest fear these days was that Drew would lose access to the oxygen he needed to live. I hated being dependent on it.

That night, the three of us watched a cowboy movie that took place in 1896. Dylan and I sat on the couch while Drew sat in his recliner. I tried to pretend things were normal, but the sound of the big blue monster ruined it, *Whooosh. Wheeee.*

The movie ended with the main character's daughter dying in his arms. I caught a tear in Dylan's eye. There was a sad feeling in the room. We were all thinking the same thing: how close we'd come to losing Drew. The truth was, Drew's health was so compromised that we could still lose him, and we all knew it.

The next morning, Dylan said, "Mom, I had a nightmare that Dad's doctor told us he has terminal cancer."

He looked so sad. I felt a wave of grief rise up from my belly for everything we had been through. And I had to remind myself: things were getting better. Slowly. Day by day.

98

ROUTINE

We fell into a routine. Every morning, I'd roll out of bed, walk to Drew's side, and grab the three pee jugs hanging from the headboard. He'd grin and say, "It was a three jug night," and I would laugh, empty them into the toilet, wash them out, and hang them back up.

Then I'd shadow Drew as he pushed the walker to the bathroom, my hand under the strap on his back for support. After that, we'd make our way to his recliner in the living room, carefully maneuvering his oxygen cord so it didn't get caught on any corners. I'd bring him a cup of lemon balm tea and hit "play" on an audiobook for him. This week's read was *BREATH* by James Nestor.

We exercised together: Drew in his wheelchair using resistance bands in front of the kitchen mirror, and me doing yoga on the carpet nearby. Then, I'd cook a breakfast of eggs and fruit, and we would sit at the kitchen table and eat.

The rest of the day was a revolving door of healers, physical therapists, occupational therapists, and Kim. During physical therapy, he would push himself well beyond his limits, despite the pain. I would obsessively check his pulse oximeter, heart rate, and his blood pressure all day.

He wrote a new set of goals and taped them to the kitchen mirror:

Breathe easier

Be independent

Walk alone with the walker

The rehab was brutal for Drew. And for me, this was harder than I could have imagined. There was absolutely no time to rest because I was the boss, the planner, the caretaker. I managed the meds, coordinated the medical team, kept the house running, made sure Drew got to the bathroom without falling. It was too much. To survive each day, I would tell myself, *This is temporary. It will get better.*

To help Drew reach his goal of walking on his own, we had to keep him moving. Every hour, I'd make him scoot from the living room to the kitchen and back again. "Time to move!" I'd say in a booming voice, obnoxiously clapping my hands. "If you want to walk again, let's gooo!"

To track his milestones, I recorded every little thing on the big calendar taped to the mirror in the kitchen:

March 11 - Drew sat in the backyard. No hot flashes. Skipped Trazodone and didn't sleep.

March 12 - Walked 200 feet. Exhausted.

March 14 - Practiced going in and out of the front door. Watered the lawn from the wheelchair. Hot flashes gone for good!

March 15 - High heart rate all day. Fever of 102.

Drew barely used the phone because it was too hard on his numb fingers. But one morning he called a friend. "I'm alive," he said. He

Routine

had the phone on speaker and I heard his friend tell him, "When I heard you were put on the ventilator, I pulled my car over to the side of the road and cried."

Hearing that took me right back to that terrifying day. I had buried my grief so deep I forgot it was still there. My shoulders started to hurt. The weight of being the one who figures it all out suddenly felt unbearable. I had an overwhelming urge to get out of the house—to run away, to do something, anything, to release these pent-up feelings.

"Dylan, will you stay here with Dad? I need air," I asked.

I walked quickly down the street to the beach. My chest started to heave, and I couldn't breathe. A feeling of being utterly helpless washed over me. Grief rose up from my stomach, like steam escaping a pot, about to boil over. I felt trapped with no way out.

I desperately needed to talk to the only person who would understand. I called Andrea from the beach trail, and she answered on the first ring. As the words flew out of me, I felt a tinge of guilt. "I don't know how I'm going to do this. I've lost my husband. He's not the man I married," I said, breathless.

"He's not the man I married," I repeated. And then I became hysterical. The tears came fast, and this time, I didn't stop them. A guttural cry released from my throat, a sound I had never heard myself make before. A tall man walking two tiny dogs stared at me as I hunched over, phone in one hand, face in the other. Andrea listened with patience as I sobbed. She talked me off the ledge.

"You're doing a great job, Maria. Everything will be okay. You can do this," she said softly.

I stood there, staring at the ocean for a long time. It felt like I had released a few demons I'd been carrying since the ICU. I watched the waves and tried to convince myself that we would be okay.

I walked back up the hill, breathing deeply. My mind began to quiet. A strange peace washed over me. Halfway home, I heard Spirit whisper in my ear: *Write the book. Write the book.*

"I'm not ready," I said out loud to the sky. "The story is still unfolding."

99

A MIRACLE IS NOT ENOUGH

It was the Spring Equinox, March 20—a time of rebirth and regrowth—and Drew was entering a new phase of recovery. He had finally reached his goal of walking on his own with the walker, and now his focus was on building enough muscle strength to do normal things, like opening jars and lifting a cooking pot. He had gained a healthy amount of weight. Today, the scale read 138 pounds.

"We will get you off of this thing," I said, pointing at the big blue monster.

He nodded and wrote down a new audacious goal: Be surfing by September.

"Yes, you will," I said, trying hard to believe it. But, I had no idea how we'd get from walker to surfboard in just six months.

I researched "How to safely wean off oxygen" and lowered his flow from 3 to 2.5 liters. Dylan and I hovered over him like hawks, checking for signs of weakness. Every hour, we would clip the pulse oximeter onto his finger—it usually read between 92 and 93. I figured we'd give it another week or two before dropping it again.

On the evening of the full moon, Raz and I hosted a women's circle at the gallery. Our theme this month was "Planting your seeds of intention." We had a big group–fifteen women. We hugged each one as they arrived and we created a welcoming, safe space that encouraged them to share their feelings.

I guided the women through a visualization to imagine something new they wanted to create in their lives. Many came to heal from their own traumas, and the support of the group was enough to help them feel better even if just for a night.

After the event, I walked home under the moon's glow, my heart filled with joy. Being with those women reminded me of how lucky I was to be able to do the things I loved, even in the midst of the hardest time of my life. A renewed sense of peace washed over me as I reached my driveway and stepped back into my new reality—the one that waited for me in the recliner chair of the living room.

That night, I reflected on how I had been mourning the loss of the life I used to have. I wrote in the Dear Drew Journal, "The seeds we water are the plants that we grow."

Then I asked myself, "What seeds do I want to water now?" The answer came clearly, "I want ease." So instead of saying, "This is hard," I decided to say, "This is such a rich experience."

I had been handed the most raw, awful, yet extraordinary experience of my life. And it was up to me to create an empowering story around it.

I ended the entry with, "Drew, you and I are writing the story as we create it."

It felt strange to write to him while he lay sleeping beside me. I hadn't shared these journals with him yet. There was too much sorrow on these pages, and I didn't think he was ready for it. Not yet. He still had more healing to do. It would be another year before I let him read them.

> need you to know, that as a nurse , I really appreciate how involved you were in his care and seeing all the updates (I didn't get to care for him at Mission) ..You advocated, as you should have and I personally am always grateful for loving wives, moms , sisters , brothers , all family members like yourself who push and advocate, that's what it takes , and I truly believe you saved his life by being there daily doing all those things and did not let anything or anyone get in your way. I witnessed many many covid patients die over the last two years

100

REASON TO LIVE

We'd failed, and I felt defeated. Lowering Drew's oxygen to two and a half liters didn't work. It made him dizzy and sick, and after a couple of days, we had to bump it back up to three. Dr. Kamatow's smug voice rang in my head: *"He will never get off the oxygen."*

I wanted so badly for her to be wrong. I fantasized about writing her a letter that said, "Well, Drew is breathing on his own again. You underestimated him."

Maybe we were delusional. According to every doctor I spoke to, Drew was the only patient they knew who had even survived what he'd been through. They didn't know how to fix his body. There was no roadmap, no case to compare him to.

To wean Drew off the oxygen, he had to strengthen his heart and lungs. The only way to do that was through exercise. But after just a minute, he'd be winded, gasping for air, and needing a break. It was a maddening paradox: *The lungs won't heal unless you exercise—but you can't exercise until the lungs heal.* The only way was to push through the pain.

Despite our failed oxygen attempt, Nicole now had Drew walking without a walker in the backyard. Drew walked circles as I trailed behind, holding the long oxygen hose that stretched from the back door of the kitchen. The ground was lumpy, making it hard to balance, and I hovered like a helicopter mom, terrified he'd trip.

Community support was still pouring in. One day, a little girl from down the street came to the door with an envelope stuffed with twenties, singles, and quarters. "This is for Drew," she said shyly. "It's from my Girl Scout cookie sales."

I stood there about to say, "No thank you, keep your hard-earned money," but I saw the pride on her face. I hugged her and told her what a beautiful gesture it was. As I closed the door, a wave of guilt and gratitude washed over me.

I kept wondering, *Why are so many people giving?* The generosity was overwhelming, on a scale most people never get to see. Maybe they just wanted to be a part of the miracle. Maybe Drew's story touched them in some way. Maybe this thing didn't just happen to us–it happened to them, too.

And I was grateful. Because the love and support took the edge off the depression we were both sinking into.

One night, Drew and I got into bed and I snuggled up next to him. He felt so skinny, all bones. The brutality of his pain was getting to him.

"I'm depressed," he confided. "This is so hard. Sometimes I wish I hadn't come back."

His words crushed me. I wanted so badly to take away his suffering. I wanted him to be glad to be alive. I hugged him and started to rub his chest. And then, as I ran my hands on his body, I felt his erection. He was surprised when I took off my clothes and climbed on top of him.

Reason to Live

I reached over, clipped the pulse oximeter to his finger, and watched his heart rate climb, making sure he didn't have a heart attack as I brought him to a climax.

"There. Now you have a reason to live," I said.

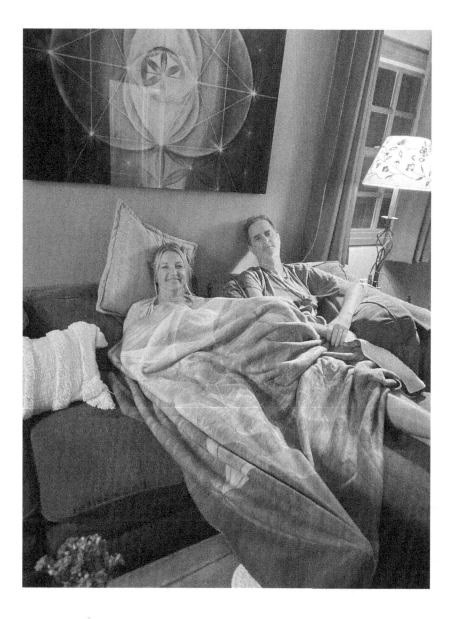

101

GOOD SIGN

By week four, Drew could stand up to pee, and I could get him in and out of the shower by myself. These little milestones felt huge. He now weighed 140 pounds, and we celebrated that. His next goal was 150.

Then, for the first time since coming home, Drew asked to go to the gallery. He hadn't been to work in six months. Dylan charged the portable oxygen backpack, and we drove him the two blocks from home to the Brophy Art Gallery.

"I can't wait for you to see your new office!" I said as we pulled into the parking lot.

Raz had cleaned and made the gallery look nice for him. His office had been completely redone: a new brown leather couch, a comfortable rolling chair, and a pretty blue-and-gold rug. Sliding glass doors opened to a small patio out back, where we had added two potted palms, an outdoor rug, and a long wooden planter overflowing with red ginger.

When Drew walked in, Raz ran to hug him. "I'm so happy you're back," she said, letting out a loud cry. I envied her ability to let her tears flow so freely. I just stood there, legs strong like a tree trunk, and watched as she expressed what I secretly felt. She cried for the loss of the Drew we once knew—the man who protected us, who was our rock. She cried for all the days she and I had prayed for him to come home, and for this moment—him here, now. And she cried for our new reality: that shaky, unknown future that lay before us.

Drew admired his new office, but he was too weak to be excited. The last time he'd sat at that desk, he had weighed 220 pounds and felt invincible. Now, he was frail, with oxygen in his nose, hunched over his walker like an old man.

He pointed to the acoustic guitar hanging on the wall. "Hand me that, please," he said.

I passed it to him, but he could barely hold it as he tried to strum a song. His numb fingers hurt, and the effort frustrated him. He handed the guitar back to me.

"I don't know if I'll ever be able to play again," he said, suddenly very sad. "I'm ready to go home now."

Dylan and I packed him, the walker, and the oxygen backpack into the car and took a quick detour to drive along the coast. I thought the ocean might lift his spirits. He didn't even look at the waves.

When we got home, I swapped out the backpack oxygen cannulas from Drew's nose for the cannulas to the big blue monster, and Drew sat down in his recliner.

A few minutes later, Drew said weakly, "I feel really, really sick."

"Well, you did just get a ton of exercise getting out of the car," I said, but then I noticed his face was white as a ghost. He was about to pass out.

Panic struck my heart, a familiar feeling of helplessness and terror. But I didn't let it show. I clipped the pulse oximeter onto his finger. Oxygen: 88. Heart rate: 130.

Good Sign

Oh no. This was bad. Very bad.

My mind spiraled—*Do we take him back to the hospital? Please, no. Not again.* I grabbed my phone, about to search for answers.

And just then, Dylan pointed to the big blue monster, "Mom, the oxygen is off!"

We had forgotten to turn the big blue monster back on. A rookie mistake. The house had seemed unusually quiet—but none of us had noticed.

Dylan rushed over and flipped the switch. *Whoooosh. Wheeeee.* The sound filled the room.

Within minutes, Drew's heart and lungs stabilized.

He had gone seven whole minutes without oxygen—and didn't die. I saw this as a very good sign.

Drew's first day back to his office

102

DRUGS

I hated all the pharmaceuticals Drew was taking. The old Drew wouldn't even touch an aspirin. Now, he was on a cocktail of drugs: Phenobarbital, Protonix, Metoprolol, and the most dangerous offenders, Trazodone and Temazepam. Skin lesions had started popping up across his neck, back, and arms, and I was convinced it was from toxic overload.

I made a vow to wean him off the drugs. I added a mix of natural supplements, following a protocol developed by doctors for healing Long Haul Covid. There were too many pills to keep track of, so I came up with a system. Every Sunday, I lined up twenty-one jars for the week: seven for breakfast, seven for lunch, and seven for dinner. I filled each one and labeled it.

Drew's addiction to his nighttime drugs worried me the most. Temazepam can cause memory loss, labored breathing, and blurred vision, and it's not safe to take long-term. Drew had been taking it for months. Withdrawal could cause tremors and heart problems, and I researched the safest way to wean off it.

Part of his addiction was psychological. Every day, I'd suggest he cut back, and Drew would say, "Not yet. I need to sleep tonight." He was still haunted by the ICU—by the screams he'd heard in the dark from other patients. That trauma had turned into a deep fear of not being able to fall asleep. Every night, he begged for his pills.

I realized the only way to get him off them might be to trick him. Fortunately, Temazepam came in capsules. The first night, I secretly pulled apart the capsule, emptied a third of it into the sink, and then put it back together. He didn't know he was getting less. And he slept the same as always.

The next week, I emptied half of two capsules. Technically, he was down one whole pill—but he didn't know it, since he was still swallowing four capsules. That night, he had trouble sleeping. I felt guilty and questioned whether I should keep going with this plan. *Doing the right thing is hard,* I reminded myself.

By the third night of being down one Temazepam, he was sleeping again. I waited a week, then started cutting a third capsule. And so on.

After three weeks, I convinced him to agree to drop one capsule entirely. A week later, another one. Once we had Temazepam behind us, we started on the Trazodone.

Six weeks later, he was off all of the nighttime drugs.

103

BACK TO ER

In early April, Nicole had Drew walking a block up and down the sidewalk with just a cane, dragging his oxygen backpack on wheels as neighbors peeked through their windows, stunned. His recovery was progressing day after day—and they got to witness it.

Over Spring Break, Andrea and Jackie came to visit with their three kids and Drew's mom. Andrea rented the same apartment around the corner that Mom and Julie had stayed in last month. I ordered a lasagna dinner from Guicho's Eatery on the day they arrived, and we all crammed into our tiny kitchen and told funny stories and laughed all night.

The next morning, I went to empty Drew's pee jugs and was shocked to find them filled with dark, bloody urine. I took a sample to Urgent Care, and an hour later, the doctor called. "Drew needs to go to the ER right away," he said.

A terrifying flashback hit me—dropping Drew off at the ER and never seeing him again. "What if we wait a day and see if it clears up?" I asked, my voice shaking.

The doctor was on speakerphone. Drew, Andrea, and Mom all listened. "It could be fatal," he warned.

Drew's eyes locked with mine. We were thinking the same thing: There was no way we could do this again.

"I can't go back to that hospital," Drew said, and we both started to cry. It was rare for Drew to show fear, and my feeling of horror amplified as another nightmare was about to unfold. I felt faint. There was no way out of this. We had to face it head-on.

"Let's go to the Laguna Hills Hospital," I said. It was a place that held no bad memories for us.

Andrea drove, Mom sat up front, and Drew and I held hands in the back seat. It was dinnertime, and the ER was quiet. They took him for a scan: kidney stones. Big ones. Drew needed surgery asap. But this hospital couldn't do it. Tonight, he'd be transferred back to the house of horrors: Hospital One.

We had no choice but to accept it. "It's going to be okay," I told Drew, faking bravery as I surrendered to another bad chapter in our story.

I held his hand in the hospital room and stayed until they kicked me out. Andrea and Mom had been waiting in the car the whole time. On the drive home, Andrea tried to reassure me. "This is easy to fix. Drew's going to be okay." I wanted to believe her, but my imagination went wild. What if he wasn't strong enough for surgery? What if it killed him? Wouldn't that just be a kick in the ass. I could already see the headlines: *"Miracle man who survived ventilator and collapsed lung dies from kidney stones."*

Drew was transported to Hospital One by ambulance. I tossed and turned all night. I had a nightmare–there was a massive earthquake, and Drew and I were separated in the rubble.

The next morning, I woke up anxious. I made Drew a mango, pineapple, and coconut cream smoothie, then drove the familiar route to Hospital One, memories from months earlier flooding back.

Back to ER

When I arrived, Drew was out of surgery and recovering. This part of the hospital was quiet and peaceful, far from the Covid unit. His room on the surgical floor was huge and beautiful—pretty curtains, mahogany furniture, and a window with a mountain view. A very friendly nurse escorted me in, pointed to a comfortable pull-out lounge, and said, "You're welcome to stay the night if you'd like, Mrs. Brophy."

The urologist, Dr. P., came in with a warm smile and sat at the end of Drew's bed. He was unhurried and took his time explaining the surgeries.

Dr. P. told us that Drew's kidney stones were caused by being immobile during the coma—his bones had been leaching into his kidneys. They placed stents on both sides to prevent a blockage, and in two weeks, he'd have the second of three surgeries. They'd do a lithotripsy on one side first, then wait a few weeks before doing the other. Lithotripsy sends ultrasonic sound waves to break the kidney stones into smaller pieces that can pass. The stents would come out once the stones had cleared.

"Any questions?" Dr. P. asked.

I looked at Drew, hoping he'd ask the one we were both thinking. He didn't. So I shyly spoke up, "Um, yes. Can he have sex with those stents in?"

Dr. P. pulled down his glasses, gave me a serious look, and said, "Yes. Just not with you." Then he cracked a smile, and we all burst out laughing.

I felt safe with Dr. P. He listened, he explained things, and he was funny.

The Universe was showing us the brighter side of a hospital experience. The yin to the yang. That there was a good side to every bad, and that even just one floor up, you can have a completely different experience.

104

INOGEN

Drew was discharged from Hospital One for the second time. Just a few months earlier, he'd left this place on a stretcher, paralyzed and barely hanging on. But this time, he proudly walked out on his own two feet.

Andrea stayed a few more days before she and the family flew back to Atlanta. Then it was just the three of us again: Drew, Dylan, and me.

The kidney stents considerably slowed down Drew's recovery. They were so extremely painful that sometimes he would cry out, "Why does God hate me?!" It was heartbreaking for me to watch. But even through the suffering, he showed up for therapy with Nicole every day. He refused to go backward.

Dylan and I agreed—we had to do something to lift his spirits. We took him to Antoine's, his favorite breakfast spot, and Raz met us there. It was his first outing in public since everything had happened. For a moment, it felt like old times—until his portable oxygen backpack malfunctioned, and we had to rush him home to the big blue monster.

That was it for me. I decided to make sure we never had to stress over the oxygen again. The insurance company wouldn't cover a reliable portable unit, so I used the GoFundMe money to buy the best one I could find: the Inogen. It cost $4,000, and it was a life-changer. It weighed only five pounds and had a battery that lasted eight hours. It fit in a small pouch with a strap, so Drew could wear it over his shoulder like a bag.

The Inogen gave Drew his freedom back. I could now take him to the beach, and that put him one step closer to getting his old life back. Dylan would drop us off at the pier, and I'd set up Drew's red folding beach chair and a butt pillow so he could watch the waves from the sand.

Drew knows just about everyone in town, and I was surprised at how comfortable he was with letting people see him like this—frail, oxygen over his shoulder, no longer the big, strong athlete everyone remembered. He had let go of his ego, and I was proud of him for that. He'd accepted who he was now and surrendered with grace. He'd sit in his red chair, watching his friends surf, holding onto the dream that one day, he'd be in the water with them again.

105

BOARD RIDERS

Drew's first surgery to break up the stones in his left kidney went well. Dr. P. scheduled the second one, the same procedure on the other side, for a couple of weeks later. With one stent gone, he was in less pain, making therapy easier. I knew that as soon as that second stent came out, he'd accelerate his recovery.

The very next day, the San Clemente Board Riders Club held a fundraiser at the gallery. The Club is a group of surfers who help other surfers in need - and this time, they chose Drew. They hired a reggae band to jam in the parking lot and brought in a taco cart and beer. Dylan and I went to the event, so I had my friend Tish stay with Drew at home.

Our parking lot was packed with surfers, families, kids eating tacos, and locals bidding on silent auction items. Cory and Raz were busy running credit cards as people bought up Drew's art. There were tables covered in silent auction donations from local businesses, and a fun buzz of community filled the air.

People lined up to hug me, teary-eyed, expressing how happy they were that Drew had survived. One by one, they told me how they had been praying for him. One woman told me her family had lit a candle for Drew every night at dinner. I felt embraced in love.

Then I saw something I didn't expect—Tish pulling my Subaru up at the bottom of the parking lot. Drew was in the passenger seat. He climbed out of the car, slow and feeble, with the Inogen strapped on his shoulder. He wore a black mask over his nose and mouth, and his legs were wobbly.

Everyone was surprised to see him, especially me.

"I want to say some words," he said, breathless from the five steps he took from the car to the asphalt.

Some of the people started to walk up to hug him, but I waved them off. We couldn't risk him catching anything. The crowd parted like the Red Sea, giving him space as I escorted him to the band's microphone.

The crowd hushed as Drew picked up the mic. "I got through this because I could feel all of your love and prayers," he said. It was just like Drew to give everyone else credit for his achievements.

He spoke slowly, from the heart, thanking everyone and sharing what it took for him to have the will to live. You could have heard a pin drop; even the children were quiet as they listened to Drew's inspiring words.

He ended with, "We are all dealing with different things. Give people a chance and have compassion for them when they are at their worst. Tell someone you love them today."

The crowd erupted in cheers and applause, many wiping tears from their eyes. His short talk was both emotional and uplifting. But he suddenly looked very tired, and I walked him to the car so Tish could take him home.

The Board Riders Club raised a lot of money for us that day. Until then, I hadn't realized just how much Drew and I meant to this community—or how deeply generous people could be.

That night, I wrote out thank-you cards, letting people know that without their kindness, we would have had to close our business and that Drew wouldn't have had access to all the therapies needed for him to heal. But more than that, I wanted everyone to know that it was their love that gave us the strength to keep going.

With each card I wrote, one truth became clearer: love is the ultimate healer.

106

SHIMMER THE WEB

I was working at the gallery one afternoon when Jack, a longtime friend, walked in to buy a print of Drew's *Life Well Lived* painting. As he turned to leave, he paused.

"Can I tell you something?"

"Sure, what?"

His voice got quiet, "Last year, I was miserable. I honestly thought the world would be better off without me. I made a plan to end my life."

This was a shocker. I've known Jack for years, and he always seemed happy. But then he told me how he had planned to drive up to the mountains, hike the highest peak, and jump off a cliff. He had written a goodbye note to his family, ready to follow through. Just before pulling his truck out of the driveway, he picked up his phone to post a final message on Facebook.

He started to cry. "That's when I saw your post about Drew being on a ventilator. I couldn't believe it. Drew Brophy, fighting to stay alive—and here I was, choosing to die. I started yelling at myself, "What the hell are you doing with your life?"

He said something changed in him instantly. Right then and there, he made a decision to live. His eyes opened to the gift of being alive. He told me he felt happier than he ever had before. He had let go of the fear, the pain, the old way of seeing things. He had truly transformed.

We hugged before he drove off. For the rest of the day, I couldn't shake Jack's story out of my mind.

That evening, I sat under the plum tree in my backyard, asking myself over and over, *Why did Drew's experience have such a deep effect on so many people?*

Maybe it was because Drew was always the strong one, the last person you'd expect to see fighting for his life. His illness forced people to look at their own vulnerability. And seeing him fight so hard to live inspired people. His miracle gave everyone hope.

And suddenly, I had a vision. In my mind's eye, I saw a vast web of silver cords connecting Drew, me, and everyone else. The web shimmered with light, energy flowing back and forth between all of us. We were all inextricably connected.

I began to understand. There was a divine purpose to the suffering that Drew and I were experiencing. It wasn't just about us. It was about transformation—his, mine, and everyone's.

It had to happen to show Jack that his life was worth living. It had to happen so the doctors and nurses could witness the impossible. Dr. Q became a better doctor, aware of new ways to save Covid patients. Nurse Danielle learned she could move a ventilated patient into a chair. Alicia proved that you can get a patient off a ventilator, even after 70 days.

It had to happen to show our entire community that miracles are real, and to teach me how to open my heart to more love than I ever imagined.

As for Drew, he was rebuilding a brand-new body from scratch. He had seen that beautiful place you go to when you die. He learned what it was like to lose everything and come back from it.

Our suffering was the only way to deliver the gift of more profound wisdom—an understanding of just how powerful our intentions truly are. Every prayer, every hopeful thought, sent energy to the collective web, and that is what helped to create a miracle.

107

OCEAN MEDICINE

One sunny afternoon, I took Drew to the beach and set him up in his red chair, the Inogen slung over his shoulder. He watched the waves, wishing he were in them. But he was too weak to go in the water alone, and the surf was too rough for me to take him out there safely by myself.

Micah, a longtime surfer friend of Drew's, walked over to say hello.

"I'm dying to get in," Drew said, nodding toward the water.

"I'll take you in," Micah offered.

We removed Drew's oxygen, and I watched as Micah walked him into the waves, holding onto him as Drew floated on his back. The moment the salt water touched his skin, Drew's face lit up. He was back in the ocean he loved so deeply, for the first time since the ICU.

After a few minutes, Drew was out of breath. Micah helped him back to his chair, and I quickly slipped the cannulas into his nose and turned on the Inogen. He sat with a smile, happier than I'd seen him in a long time. For Drew, getting in the ocean was like reclaiming a part of himself that had been lost. This was the medicine he needed.

The next day, Nurse Ally came to visit us at the gallery, and she bought a painting for her boyfriend. Drew was sitting at his desk when I walked her to his office. He didn't recognize her, but he remembered her voice. She sat down on his couch and started to cry. "Drew, I can't believe you're here right now."

I was surprised at how emotional she was, and I asked her, "What made you so sure he wasn't going to make it?"

She answered, "Because every single Covid patient who was as sick as Drew...died. He was the only one who left the hospital alive."

I realized at that moment just how much I had denied reality back then. How I pretended that he would make it, not facing the truth of just how dire it was. Now I needed to understand why Drew lived when everyone else did not.

"Why do you think he survived?" I asked, expecting her to say it was his will to live. But her answer surprised me.

"It was the two rounds of high-dose Vitamin C," she said with confidence. Ally explained that during her doctoral training, she learned how it knocks down inflammation in infections; she said it was like "throwing water on a fire."

I thought back to all the stress I had endured, battling the hospital to get it approved—how exhausting it had been and how close I had come to giving up. I remembered the messages from Kayla, the woman who told me that Vitamin C had saved her brother, and how she kept urging me not to quit. We had never even met, yet she texted me daily and refused to let me stop fighting.

Looking back now, I saw it clearly: she was a divine answer to my prayers, the ones where I had begged God to send me answers on how to save Drew.

I couldn't wait to tell Andrea. I texted her: "You won't believe this. Nurse Ally said it was the high-dose Vitamin C that saved Drew!"

A week later, Drew had his third kidney stone surgery. Dr. P removed one of the stents, which cut Drew's pain in half. Physical therapy was still brutal, but with less agony, he could do more. Only two more weeks until the last stent would be removed.

Dr. Tyler, a local chiropractor, started dropping by a few times a week to alleviate Drew's back pain. One day, I asked for the bill, and he shook his head in response. "Oh no, this is a gift."

I couldn't understand why he would make house calls and not charge us—he didn't even know us that well. "Why would you do it for free?" I asked.

"Because for the last twenty years, every time I've heard Drew Brophy's name, it was someone telling a story about how he helped them. Now I want to pay it back. That's the kind of community I want to live in."

I hugged him, overwhelmed with gratitude. We were being shown, over and over again, just how compassionate and generous people could be.

And then came the day that Drew and I both had been dreading. It was early morning when we drove Dylan to the airport. It was time for him to return to his life in North Carolina.

My heart broke as Dylan waved goodbye—it felt like another part of me was being ripped away. I tried to shake the feeling and refocused my attention on the road as I drove us home. Drew kept repeating sadly, over and over, "I can't believe our boy is gone. I can't believe he's gone."

The house felt depressing when we got home. It was quiet and dull, Dylan's computers gone from the kitchen table, and empty space all around us.

Now, it was just the two of us, a new, empty feeling. We were on our own.

108

JUNE

By June, we were seeing glimmers of proof that Drew would breathe on his own again. We had lowered his oxygen down to 1.5 liters, and he was doing okay with that. We even turned it off completely for a few hours a day. Little by little, he was getting stronger.

One night, Drew and I lay in bed holding hands and meditating together. We accidentally fell asleep without turning his oxygen back on. He went all night without it, and we didn't realize it until morning. It didn't make him feel sick at all, and that was a good sign that his lungs would heal.

He was also finished with his kidney surgeries. Now that the stents were out, he could push harder in therapy. He was finally strong enough to stay home alone, which meant I could return to work full-time at the gallery. We celebrated our twenty-second wedding anniversary with dinner at a local Mexican restaurant.

Dr. K got Drew approved for Pulmonary Therapy, and I drove him there three times a week. On top of that, he was still doing physical therapy at home five days a week. I wondered if we were pushing him too hard, but Drew was determined to do everything he could to get his body working again.

Nicole had become like family. Her visits were more than just physical therapy; they were Drew's social hour. He would tell her funny stories about our adventures in life, and she would listen and laugh with him. She spent so much time with us that she had come to know all of our quirks, our dreams, and our weaknesses.

She pushed him hard—squatting, walking up and down the steps on the back porch, throwing a ball over his head. He had finally gained enough strength to lift his arms, something he couldn't do just two weeks before. "Throw it over your head. Good, Drew!" she'd shout in her drill-sergeant voice.

Nicole wanted to get Drew back in the water just as much as we did. She turned off his oxygen during exercise and closely monitored his SpO_2 levels. Now she had him walking partway down the hill to the beach—the same path he'd eventually take with his surfboard. They'd stop at the halfway point, turn around, and face the steep climb back. Drew would stop and catch his breath every two minutes, his body heaving in pain. It was so strenuous that he often didn't know how he was going to take another step. Nicole would gently pat his shoulder and say, "I know it's hard, Drew. But this is the only way." Then her voice would change, and she would yell, "One more step. You can do this! Now another..."

One day, I decided it was time for Drew to meet Dr. Gibbons. After all, he was one of Drew's angels. I introduced them on FaceTime, so they could see each other. "Drew, this is one of the doctors who helped you beat this."

Dr. Gibbons was very happy to hear from us. "Drew, you're a walking miracle," he said. They talked for an hour, and I knew Dr. Gibbons felt good knowing he played a part in Drew's survival.

Before we hung up, I said, "I'll never forget your kindness. Thank you."

June

Dr. Gibbons replied with conviction, "Maria, you're a hero for fighting the bullies."

His words hit me. I thought back to all the battles I fought against doctors who were far more educated than I. How I worried I was being annoying, or worse, wrong. How exhausted I was. But I fought anyway. Now, I knew it was worth it.

The truth is, they didn't believe that Drew would live. And who could blame them? No one else in his condition ever did. So they wrote him off and didn't take action to save him. Even now, they didn't believe that he could wean off the meds or oxygen, and they discouraged us from trying.

The people who actually saved Drew were those who tried, even in the face of a grim reality. They were the ones who took action, believing it was possible. The medical professionals, our friends and family, and Drew himself, with his sheer badass will. And it was me, too. I was the one who fought like hell on the frontlines of the battlefield, every single day.

I had been afraid to say these things out loud, worried about backlash from people who hadn't been there and had no idea what we lived through. But I was starting to learn that the truth needs to be spoken, out loud and with strength, because it might help someone else. And every day, I was getting a little braver about speaking it.

109

JULY

With July came bigger milestones: Drew caught his first wave on a boogie board. He held his breath underwater and went a full twenty-four hours without oxygen. He was going into the ocean a few days a week now, and it was accelerating his healing.

Nicole's therapy sessions had shifted to focus on getting Drew back on a surfboard. She placed his ten-foot paddleboard on pillows in the grass to mimic the unstable surface of the ocean. He would stand on the paddleboard, with a paddle in hand, and go through the paddling motion, working on his balance and core.

Next, she had him practice pop-ups. He would lie face down on the board and move his arms as if paddling for a wave. Nicole would count to twenty, then say, "Rest." Once he caught his breath, she'd command, "Now, pop up to your feet!"

His muscles weren't strong enough to spring up quickly. He'd struggle to get to his knees, then slowly stand and mimic riding a wave. He would be so winded from this simple movement that he would have to take a break before doing it again. But day after day, he got a little stronger. A little faster. A little better.

We had also weaned him off Metoprolol, the last drug he was on. We cut the pills in half, then quarters, and then stopped altogether. Drew was getting a variety of alternative treatments: Chinese acupuncture, hyperbaric chamber, and red light therapy. He tracked his steps on a FitBit. One day, he hit 10,000 steps—and that became his new daily goal.

An attorney had contacted us to join a class action lawsuit against hospitals that had administered Remdesivir to Covid patients. According to the lawsuit, Remdesivir caused kidney and liver failure, a contributing factor in the deaths of many Covid patients. Drew would be one of the few plaintiffs who had been given Remdesivir and survived.

The attorney explained that Remdesivir had gained such a bad reputation that hospitals began calling it by its brand name, "Veklury," instead, just so people would agree to take it.

Then he dropped a bomb: "Only unvaccinated patients were being prescribed Remdesivir."

I held the phone in my hand and started to shake. Was Drew given a deadly drug because he was unvaccinated?

Chills ran down my spine. This was too horrific to believe. I wanted to reject it from my mind. But that night, I lay in bed tossing and turning, wondering if there was any truth to it. And if there was, would the world ever know?

Drew and I considered joining the lawsuit but decided against it. We didn't want to be consumed by the darkness of that accusation. Besides, we were not the kind of people to sue. If we were going to create change in the world, we wanted to do it by inspiring people in a positive way.

My emotions swayed between gratitude for Drew's recovery and waves of depression over what we had witnessed through this ordeal.

July

My obsession with "fixing" Drew took over my thoughts every minute of every day.

One morning, I sat in the backyard with my journal. I took in a few deep breaths and went into meditation. I asked Spirit, "What do I need to know right now?"

The words came quickly: "You already have it all. The good and the bad. The love and the laughter. You are the wind and the chimes. You are all of it. It is in you, and it *is* you."

I felt the peace that came from this wisdom. But I had one more question, and I desperately sought an otherworldly, magical answer.

"How can I help Drew heal his pain?"

The answer became clear as my pen moved on the page, guided by something greater than myself: "This is his path. You do not need to do anything but flow with joy."

Okay then, I will try to be joyful.

Training to surf

110

SURFING

August had ushered in a new energy of hope. We donated Drew's walker and cane to Goodwill. I tossed the pee jugs and shower chair into the recycling bin, then held up those hideous yellow hospital socks with the grippy bottoms and gleefully said, *"Buh-bye,"* before chucking them in the trash. Finally, we shed the last reminder of Drew's paralysis when our friend Dave Talbot came and dismantled the wheelchair ramp, hauling it away for us.

Drew was back to work, part-time, doing easy tasks like signing art prints. He couldn't paint yet—his fingers were still numb from neuropathy—but he was off the oxygen during the day, needing it only at night. We were easing back into our lives. It wasn't "normal," but we were getting there.

On the morning of August 8th, exactly five months after he came home, Drew sat up in his recliner, coffee in hand. He looked up and announced, "I'm ready to surf."

My heart jumped because I knew how risky it was. I wasn't ready for it. But Drew knew himself well, and I had to trust that.

All of his surfboards were too heavy for him to lift, so that night we went to Costco and bought an eight-foot soft-top surfboard, usually ridden by beginners. In a way, Drew was a beginner again.

The next day, we walked to the beach, Drew struggling to carry the new foam surfboard under his skinny arm. Even though Drew wore his big wave safety vest, I worried that he would have a coughing fit out in the ocean and drown or that he would fall off the board and not be strong enough to get back on it.

Like a mother about to send her child out to surf for the first time, I nervously walked Drew to the water's edge. Usually, the waves were strong here, but today, they were soft little peelers, as if the Universe conspired for us to win.

Drew said, "I'll just catch waves on my stomach. I don't think I'll be able to stand up on the board yet." He paddled out into the surf, feeling instantly at home.

A few surfers in the water didn't know him. One shouted, "What's up with this kook wearing a float vest in small waves?"

A local turned and yelled back, "Don't you know, this guy's a fucking miracle. He just came back from the dead."

A wave came, and Drew turned to catch it. I pulled out my phone and hit record, butterflies in my belly. *Please don't let him wipe out.* He paddled smoothly into the wave, his board gliding along the face of it. Then, in one quick motion, he popped up to his feet and rode it—standing—all the way in. I couldn't believe my eyes! He was like a fish that had just been returned to the water. His body remembered exactly what to do.

Drew caught a total of eight waves before he paddled back to shore, and I met him as he came out of the water. He was exhausted, struggling to hold onto the surfboard in the shore break, but there was a huge smile on his face. He stood at the water's edge, gasping for breath, and then he started to cry with joy. The emotion we both felt was overwhelming. Being able to surf again meant everything to Drew.

One week later, a storm hit off the coast, bringing bigger waves. Drew wanted to surf again, ready to test himself in more challenging conditions. I didn't think he was ready for the kind of beating waves like that could deliver. But he insisted. He put on his safety vest, and I helped him get the foam surfboard to the beach. We had friends out in the surf, and I felt better knowing they'd be there to keep him safe. I watched as a huge wave rolled in. Drew turned, caught it, and rode it all the way to the sand. He was happy—it was the best day he'd had in a long time.

The next day, we had a checkup with Dr. K. This time, Drew walked in without a wheelchair or a walker, and we left the Inogen at home. Dr. K was surprised to see Drew without his oxygen. "You're looking good, Drew," he said.

"How's the medical study on Drew going, Doctor?" I asked.

Dr. K answered, "They canceled the study."

I knew this was going to happen.

"But why?" I asked.

"They said it would only be anecdotal evidence," he said.

Drew frowned. But he shouldn't have been surprised. Of course, the hospital would not want it on record that what worked was what they had fought against.

I told Dr. K we'd been weaning Drew off the Metoprolol, and he gave us the green light to stop it completely. He flipped through the file folder in his hands and then suggested Gabapentin for the neuropathy. But Drew had already looked up the side effects—and he didn't want to risk it.

"We want to avoid pharmaceuticals if we can, doc," I said, hoping he had a better solution.

Dr. K closed the file with a loud slap and said, "Well, Drew, you don't need me anymore."

Maybe he was right. Drew was getting results from alternative treatments and getting back into life. It made sense to keep doing what was working.

The next week, Drew's resting heart rate improved, now hovering around 70. One day, he got 15,000 steps on the Fitbit. Surfing, physical therapy, and sunshine—this was the medicine that worked.

Now that his energy was back, Drew made a video thanking the angels who helped him—doctors, therapists, friends, and family. I posted it on his social media channels. There were not enough words to show how much love we felt for everyone, but this was a start.

One day, as I was locking up the gallery, Dr. Stan stopped by with his wife, a pretty woman with a warm smile. I expressed how much his support meant during the darkest hours when Drew was on his deathbed. We talked about how incredible it was that Drew was surfing again.

Dr. Stan said, "It truly is a miracle." And then he looked me straight in the eyes and added, "You saved his life, you know."

A wave of raw emotion hit as I flashed back to those brutal days at Hospital One. How I fought the doctors and how Dr. Stan had been caught in the middle of it. I remembered the times I nearly gave up, how draining it was to go to war with an entire system, completely alone.

And now, to hear Dr. Stan say I saved Drew's life? It meant my relentless fight had been worth it. I wasn't crazy. I had been divinely guided the whole time by a force bigger than all of us.

111

BYE BLUE MONSTER

September brought my favorite time of year in San Clemente—sunny skies and no more tourists. Drew no longer needed the oxygen at all. I packed the Inogen away in a closet and called the rental company to pick up the big blue monster. That machine had been a constant reminder of the hell we'd been through, and I was happy to see it go. We watched with joy as the driver loaded it into his van and hauled it away.

It had been six months since Drew came home in a wheelchair. Now, he was walking home from the pier without stopping to catch his breath. He could drive again. He was back to painting. His first big painting was on an eight-foot surfboard—a vivid scene of what he saw during his near-death experience. He named it *Have No Fear*.

Best of all, he was surfing nearly every day. No one could believe it. It seemed impossible how he beat death, the ventilator, the oxygen machine, and the paralysis. People started coming to us for advice, those who suffered their own challenges like strokes, heart attacks, and injuries.

Drew's advice to them was always the same: "Never give up, trust your mind and body, and surround yourself with people who believe in you."

Our friend Rich called to invite us once again to his private music and art retreat in Costa Rica. He wanted to gift us with a very special plant medicine journey—a rare psychedelic experience that only a small number of people ever get to do.

"It could help you heal from the trauma you both went through," he said.

He was right. We were traumatized by the horrors in the ICU, the fear of losing Drew, the helplessness, the battles. I carried the trauma in my tissues. It showed up daily as teeth grinding, stomach aches, and body pain.

Still, I wasn't sure if I wanted to do the psychedelic journey. I was leery of putting anything into my body that I didn't fully understand. But I was excited about the rest of the retreat. We accepted Rich's invitation and booked our flights. It gave us something fun to look forward to.

Drew and I took our first road trip since he got sick. We drove seven hours to Phoenix to hand deliver paintings to an art collector. Along the way, we talked about Rich's offer. Neither of us had ever done plant medicine, and we thought maybe it would help Drew with his physical pain. He was willing to try anything.

The next day, we drove to Sedona and hiked to a waterfall called Grasshopper Point. It was only one mile long, which was perfect for Drew's first hike. When we reached the waterfall, he waded into the freezing cold water while I sat on a rock and meditated.

On the way home, Drew did all the driving, just like old times. Life was starting to feel a little normal again.

112

OCTOBER

October arrived with harsh, dry winds that blasted like a hair dryer on my face. Some Californians call these seasonal events "Santana winds," while others argue that they're called "Santa Ana winds." Either way, it felt like summer in New York, and I was still wearing shorts and flip-flops.

One morning, Drew woke up early and said, "Let's visit Santa Ana." He hadn't forgotten the promise he made back in February that he'd return one day when he recovered. We planned for a day when Alicia, the respiratory therapist, would be at work. We packed up the Subaru with gifts for the staff: a box full of Drew's art prints and stickers.

The last time we were at Santa Ana, Drew had been wheeled out the front doors on a gurney. This time, he proudly walked in on his own two feet. Alicia and a dozen others gathered to greet us in the reception area. Most of them hugged us, some with tears in their eyes. Drew was the first patient who had ever come back to say thank you. They got a rare glimpse into how their work had made a positive difference in one person's life.

The following week, we threw a "Paint Party with Drew" event at the gallery. Drew lit a fire pit in the parking lot for ambiance, and Raz set up tables and art supplies. I invited Dr. Gibbons and was surprised when he showed up. It was our first time meeting in person. He was a tall, healthy man in his seventies with light hair and a gentle presence. He and Drew painted side by side, and Dr. Gibbons impressed us with his artistic talent. By the end of the night, he had painted a beautiful ocean-and-sky landscape.

Dr. Gibbons became emotional when we talked about Drew's recovery. Still searching for answers, I asked, "What do you think would've happened if Drew had been approved for the lung transplant?"

"He wouldn't have survived it," he said in a somber voice. He confirmed what I already knew in my heart, and I was grateful for the divine intervention that stopped the transplant from happening.

Drew kept pushing his limits. The next day, he gave himself the ultimate test: surfing at Lowers, his favorite local spot. Lowers is a world-class surf break and is hard to get to, especially with compromised lungs. It's a long hike in, and you have to navigate hills and rocks. Catching a wave is a whole other challenge. There was a rough crowd out there, and even seasoned surfers had a difficult time getting waves at Lowers.

We hiked in, and Drew was already breathless by the time we hit the sand. He put on his float vest and carried his board in the water, as I watched nervously from shore. The local crowd was shocked to see him, and they all clapped when he paddled out. This made me feel better because I knew they'd keep an eye on him. Drew caught two perfect waves, another test passed.

That night, we had a Zoom call with Rich to plan our trip to Costa Rica. He asked Drew if he'd be willing to do a live painting during the musical performances, alongside a few visionary artists from Peru.

Drew said yes. He'd decide what to paint after our plant medicine journey.

October

On October 25th, we celebrated twenty-six years together—the anniversary of the day we met. Over dinner and a bottle of red wine, we reflected on all the wild adventures we'd had. Despite the hell we had just gone through, I felt incredibly lucky.

Drew looked at me and asked, "Would you change what happened if you could?"

I went silent and thought long and hard. "No," I finally said. "I wouldn't change a thing. It showed me everything I needed to learn."

It showed me the magnitude of Drew's spirit—a light so bright, nothing could dim it. I discovered new things about myself, too. That I was capable of true love and devotion, even to a man whose body had been broken.

I learned to trust my intuition, and most of all, that I'm capable of winning an impossible battle using sheer will and determination.

Drew nodded. "I wouldn't change anything, either. There's a gift that comes with suffering."

And he was right. We were both handed a profound transformation—one that couldn't have come packaged in any other way.

113

COSTA RICA

It was November, and we were coming up on the one-year mark since Drew got sick. So much had changed, and even bigger changes were ahead. Nicole was pregnant and moving to Texas with her husband. When she came for her last physical therapy session with Drew, we were both feeling sad. She had become a part of Drew's miracle, and we loved her like family. If it weren't for Nicole, he might still be hooked up to that oxygen machine.

Nicole's goodbye was a symbol that we were entering yet another new phase of our journey. We got ready for Costa Rica. I was thrilled to be traveling again. I packed my favorite clothes—shorts, bathing suits, and little summer dresses. Drew packed his paint supplies and a surfboard. This time, I remembered to bring the Covid kit.

But I still had a big decision to make. *Should I do the plant medicine journey?*

There are many types of psychedelic journeys that people do—Ayahuasca, Psilocybin, and others. The one that we were offered was referred to as a "clarigenic experience," one that would introduce me to my soul, a higher part of myself that held deep wisdom. It promised the potential to heal the PTSD we'd carried from the past year.

Drew was all in. He was excited to see if it would help him understand what had happened in his near-death experience. For me, I had fear around psychedelics. But I was tired of letting fear run my life. I did a meditation, asking Spirit if I should do the journey. The answer came quickly and clearly: yes.

Our flight was out of LAX on the morning of November 4th. I worried that being around so many people on a plane might make him sick, but Drew wasn't going to let that stop us.

Still very frail, Drew didn't have the strength to carry bags and surfboards or do all the walking you have to do in a big airport. But he refused to ask for help. By the time we got on the plane, his feet were throbbing, and he was exhausted.

When we landed at the airport in Costa Rica, Rich had a driver waiting for us. It was a long, bumpy two-hour drive on dirt roads through the jungle. The driver took us straight to Rich's house, at the end of a crooked path leading to a cliff that overlooked the tropical forest and the ocean.

Rich's house was alive with people talking and playing music. There was a buffet of grass-fed beef, organic salads, and roasted vegetables. We ate at long tables surrounded by world-class musicians, artists, and healers. Rich was on a mission to bring talented people together to make positive change in the world, and I felt lucky to be a small part of it.

We were introduced to the couple who would be guiding our psychedelic journey: a pretty blonde woman with a sweet smile and a tall, fit man in his fifties with a serious demeanor. The woman pulled us aside and whispered, "Your journey starts at 4 a.m." She handed us a small container of capsules. "You'll each take four, go back to sleep, and we will come to your door at 7 a.m. to get started." I felt a flutter of excitement in my stomach.

It was midnight when our driver dropped us off at our hotel in the jungle. Our suite was large, with a living room, a huge deck, and two big windows on the second floor of a small hotel. Howler monkeys called from the trees outside. It was the tail end of the rainy season, and a soft rain began to fall.

At 4 a.m., my alarm went off. We sat up, swallowed our pills, and crawled back into bed. I wrote in my journal, "I surrender. I allow this to take me where it wants to go. Let the trip begin."

That was the start of our 10-hour journey.

114

THE JOURNEY

There was a *tap, tap, tap* on the door at 7 a.m. Even with the big windows in the room, it was dark. A storm had swept in, and thick clouds and rain hid the sun.

Drew opened the door, and my heart jumped. Now that it was really happening, my body tensed for a moment, remembering how leery I had been about taking any foreign substance. But I reminded myself that this could help me heal. Besides, the "medicine" I'd swallowed at 4 a.m. had already calmed me just enough to push my worry aside.

The four of us sat in the living room and talked as more medicine was administered. The woman handed each of us a small wooden bowl filled with a variety of pills. She set a timer, and every fifteen minutes, she instructed us to swallow a different color. My mind stayed clear as my body relaxed into the medicine.

"When you drop in, we'll take you to your room, and the journey will begin," she said.

"How will I know when I've dropped in?" I asked.

"Oh, you'll know." She smiled.

The man explained that this journey would train new neural pathways in the brain. "It strips away all the bullshit and leaves only truth."

"It gives your soul a voice," the woman added, pointing to the bowl and letting us take two more.

They told us that we would be put in different rooms for the deepest part of the journey. We would lie down on the bed, put on an eye mask, and listen to music through headphones. The woman would watch over me, and the man would watch over Drew. Each room had recording devices so that anything we said could be listened to later. After the heaviest part, they would bring Drew into my room with me, and we'd spend the rest of the journey together.

I was incredibly relaxed now. My heart was softening, and the tension I'd carried in my jaw for the last year had melted away. The timer went off again, and she pointed to the bowl. "Now, the green ones."

There were still pills left in my bowl when I slid all the way down in my chair, smiling—more relaxed than I had ever been in my life.

"She just dropped in. It's time," the woman said.

They helped me to my room, and suddenly I saw black-and-white geometric patterns everywhere. "This is so cool," I said, laughing. My mind was still very aware, but I had broken through the veil just enough to catch a glimpse of the matrix.

115

TRIPPY TRIP

It felt like I had been gone forever. My consciousness had left and floated to another realm, one that was euphoric and beautiful. I came back into my body slowly, wiggling my fingers and toes. I was in bed, wearing an eye mask and headphones, with music guiding me along the journey. Words began to flow from me in a voice that didn't sound like mine.

"My Drew, you're all that's ever mattered since the beginning of time. You represent all that is perfect in the world. You are my life and my soul, Drew."

I kept repeating—out loud—the messages I was receiving from my own soul. I was told that if I could learn to love myself the way Drew loved me, I would heal from all my ailments. I was shown that Drew was one half of a heart, and I was the other. Together, we were inextricably connected to everyone else.

Then came words from Spirit that I'll never forget. They put my entire life with Drew into perspective and explained why I had taken on the role of managing his art so many years ago. The message was loud and clear:

"Drew gives the world hope, and it's your job to deliver it."

I slowly sat up, dazed. I kept my eyes closed and said, "That was the trippiest trip I ever tripped. How long have I been out?"

"Nearly two hours," the woman whispered. "We're going to bring Drew in now."

The man and the woman helped Drew in and sat him facing me on the bed. Rain thundered on the rooftop. They pulled off our eye masks. I opened my eyes and blinked, staring at Drew's face. He looked strong—almost warrior-like. He wasn't the same frail Drew I'd seen just a few hours earlier.

After getting us settled, the man and woman left so we could be alone. Drew and I sat on the bed for hours, sharing our insights. A device recorded our conversation so we could transcribe it later.

"How did it feel not to have a body?" Drew asked, his voice deeper than I remembered.

I reached for words, struggling to describe the indescribable. I had become the music, the river, the drops of rain—I was part of everything that existed. It was the most beautiful thing I had ever felt.

There was a surprising, otherworldly wisdom flowing from Drew. Fascinated, I asked him question after question, and he answered each one with clarity, like a wise mystic who held all the answers to the Universe.

Drew had received massive downloads of information during his journey. He was shown that there is no death, that our energy simply returns to where it came from, and that we are here to love, to experience, to laugh, and to feel. We are the ever-expanding light.

"You are the energy bursting through the mind, animating this body. The energy never ends," he explained.

I asked, "But who am I?"

He responded, "You are the Universe, creating from multiple tips of perspective. You are everything and everyone."

At that moment, it all made sense. We are like a drop of ocean water, one small part of the whole ocean. That's what it means to be one with all.

I looked into Drew's eyes and felt love burst through my heart. He was alive, and I knew how lucky we were. I felt so incredibly grateful. I remembered how, on the day we met, it was as though I already knew him.

"Have we lived many lives together?" I asked.

"We've been together since the beginning of time," he answered. "We've never been apart."

116

TRANSFORMATION

The next day, I was a new Maria. The world looked brighter, even through the Costa Rican rainfall. I felt lighter, as if the weight of the world had fallen from my shoulders. I finally remembered who I really was and where I came from. And I wondered, *How did I ever forget?*

That evening, Drew painted on a large canvas during the retreat's musical performances. People gathered to watch as he freehanded a wild scene: an exploding sun, an all-seeing eye at its center, and twelve embryos of life about to burst forth in a sea of energy. It was bright, colorful, and psychedelic. He named it *The Circle of Twelve*. It embodied the wisdom he had gleaned from his near-death experience, deepened by the clarigenic journey we had shared.

He described the painting like this: "Somewhere in the Universe beats an internal vibration which is our soul, or consciousness. It is an awareness, it is an everlasting energy, and it never dies. It is all-that-is."

One night, we joined sixty of the retreat guests for dinner and live music in a courtyard in the jungle. The opening act was a woman from the Appalachian Mountains, who played harmonium and sang about the healing power of medicine women.

Rich approached our table and asked Drew, "We've got ten minutes between artists. Want to talk about your near-death experience?"

Drew hesitated. He hadn't talked about it publicly—not yet. He was still trying to find the words to describe all that he experienced through his NDE. He had only a few minutes to decide, so he said yes: 'I'll just wing it.'"

When he took the stage, I hit "play" on the recorder on my iPhone. I worried about how he'd manage, giving a speech without preparation on a topic that he himself did not yet fully understand.

Then, I watched as the perfect words flowed through him. He described what it was like to leave his body in death. "I instantly knew that I was not this body. It was seamless; your consciousness does not stop."

His voice shook with emotion. "In that instant, I felt a part of everything and everyone like I lived every one of your lives and everybody else's at the same moment. I instantly had compassion for all the people." The courtyard went silent as everyone wiped tears from their eyes.

Drew spoke of seeing the intentions of everyone who prayed for him. "You are all more powerful than you know," he emphasized. Then he raised his arms and said, "I saw that I was light." At that instant, lightning flashed in the sky behind him, as if the Universe were collaborating with him. He ended with, "You are everything. You are the Universe. You're all-powerful."

It was the most incredible, inspiring talk. Drew was humble and authentic, and his words flowed as if they were coming from a higher source. I uploaded the video to YouTube, and it went viral overnight. People are hungry to know that their lives have meaning.

Transformation

On our last day in Costa Rica, we went to Playa Guiones. I borrowed Drew's surfboard and paddled into the warm, green-blue water. Sunlight danced like sparkles on the surface, and I felt at one with the ocean, the earth, and the sky.

A wave came. I turned around and caught it, gliding on the energy of the ocean. I rode it all the way in and felt an inner peace I hadn't known before. I could feel love radiating from Drew as he sat on the beach, waiting for me. I felt deeply connected—to the Earth, to the sand beneath my feet, and to the friendship and generosity of Rich and so many others. I felt the rawness of suffering and the intensity of love all at the same time. And it was beautiful.

I brought the board to Drew. "Good job, Spunk," he said. It always made him happy to see me surf. Then he took his turn. I watched him paddle out to bigger waves—testing his lungs, but this time I wasn't worried.

Drew caught a big wave, jumped to his feet, and rode it gracefully to shore. Then he paddled back out for another. The sun was glowing, dipping lower and lower on the horizon. I felt different. I no longer feared death. It was so freeing.

He caught one last wave, then joined me on the sand.

"You did good out there, honey," I said. He nodded, catching his breath.

It was exactly one year to the day that I'd dropped him off at Hospital One, where he was whisked away from me. I looked at him and said, "It's crazy, all we've been through. It's hard to believe it really happened."

He smiled and reminded me of his new favorite saying: "You know, Maria, there's a gift in the suffering."

He was right. The gift was the experience and how it transformed us. Seeing people around the globe pray for us altered my belief about how everything worked. I saw how much love there was in the world.

Drew's gift was the knowledge that we are not our bodies. We are the energy flowing through them.

But the gift was not just ours. It was for others, and probably more so. Our story was impacting people in a profound way. It gave them hope.

We watched the sun go down, and I reflected on how much I had grown this past year:

I learned what true faith is.

I came to believe in miracles.

I now understand how our thoughts and intentions create reality.

And most of all, I learned that love is not finite. It expands so much that your heart cannot contain it all.

Now, what should I do with all this newfound wisdom?

The answer was clear. Drew gives the world hope, and my job is to deliver it. And that's exactly what I'm going to do.

The End.

AFTERWORD
YOU ARE THE LOVE STORY

For months, while Drew hovered between life and death, I knew losing him was a probability. But then, one day, the energy shifted. He went from dying to living, and a miracle occurred.

I owe my deepest gratitude to all who helped us. It wouldn't have happened without you.

Thank you to Drew's healers, who fought for his recovery despite the reality.

Thank you to those who brought food, donated money, offered friendship, and lifted my spirits, giving me the energy to keep fighting for him.

Thank you for taking the time to visualize Drew surfing, painting, and living again.

To the families who gathered in prayer and to those who sent him healing energy: thank you for sending a powerful message to the Universe to bring him back, not only to life but to his surfboard, his easel, and back to living vibrantly.

Afterword

Your intentions are powerful. Every single prayer, visualization and wish made a difference.

By activating your desire for Drew to recover and aligning it with the collective intention of so many others, you co-created a force field of energy so potent that the Universe had no choice but to deliver the miracle.

When I say we couldn't have done this without you, I mean it with all my heart. We made a miracle happen together.

Can you see how powerful you truly are?

You are the love story.

And I am forever grateful.

Drew Brophy, painting this book cover art.

BIOGRAPHY

Maria Brophy is a global speaker, art business consultant, and author of eight nonfiction books, including the Amazon bestseller *Art Money Success* and *Empowered Women's Circles*. The owner of a Southern California art gallery, she has spent over two decades merging entrepreneurship with adventure, traveling the world surfing, hiking, and paddleboarding with her family.

Photo Credit: Vdon Farias

Overcoming a challenging childhood, Maria built the life she once dreamed of and is passionate about helping others do the same. Through her Artist's Mastermind group, women's circles, and energy healing sessions, she empowers people to transform hardships into joyful, purpose-driven lives.

Since 2001, Maria has been the art agent for her soulmate, Drew. Together, they raised a family, grew a thriving art business, and cultivated a life of creativity. Now, they embrace a new chapter—sharing their journey through speaking engagements around the world and inspiring others to create their own miracles.

Drew & Maria Brophy 2024 Photo Credit: Vdon Farias

Connect with Maria online:
www.MariaBrophy.com

YouTube:
https://www.youtube.com/@mariabrophy1

Instagram:
https://www.instagram.com/mariabrophy/

RESOURCES

Watch Drew Brophy's Near-Death Experience (NDE) Talk on his channel: https://www.youtube.com/@drewbrophy

Books:

- *Every Deep-Drawn Breath: A Critical Care Doctor on Healing, Recovery, and Transforming Medicine in the ICU*
  - by Dr. Wes Ely
- *Coma and Near-Death Experience: The Beautiful, Disturbing, and Dangerous World of the Unconscious*
  - by Alan Pearce, Beverley Pearce, and Dr. E. Wesley Ely
- In Shock: My Journey from Death to Recovery and the Redemptive Power of Hope
  - By Rana Awdish, MD, FCCP

Health & Recovery Resources:

- **Walking Home from the ICU Podcast**
  - Hosted by Kali Dayton, Critical Care Nurse Practitioner: https://daytonicuconsulting.com

RESOURCES

- **FLCCC Alliance Protocols**
  - Treatment guidelines for Long COVID and vaccine-related injuries: https://covid19criticalcare.com/treatment-protocols/
- **ZYESAMI/Aviptadil Medical Study**
  - PR Newswire release on breakthrough therapy: https://www.prnewswire.com/news-releases/nrx-pharmaceuticals-files-breakthrough-therapy-designation-request-for-zyesami-aviptadil-in-patients-at-immediate-risk-of-death-from-covid-19-despite-treatment-with-remdesivir-and-other-approved-therapies-301451392.html
- **VAERS**
  - CDC and FDA's Vaccine Adverse Event Reporting System: vaers.hhs.gov

BOOKS BY MARIA BROPHY

Art, Money, Success
Empowered Women's Circle
Painting Surfboards, Chasing Waves
How to Start Your Spiritual Business Today
How to Draw with Drew Brophy
How to Make Money Painting Live
How to Understand Art Licensing Contracts
Living the Dream - Break Free From the Status Quo and Create Your Dream Life

Connect with Maria and Drew:
Maria: www.MariaBrophy.com | Instagram: @mariabrophy
Drew: www.DrewBrophyArt.com | Instagram: @drewbrophy

Made in the USA
Las Vegas, NV
26 September 2025